CURTAIN CALLS

CURTAIN CALLS

Travels in Albania, Romania and Bulgaria

LESLIE GARDINER

READERS UNION
Group of Book Clubs
Newton Abbot 1977

Brief extracts from one or two chapters have appeared in
The Times, the *Guardian* and the *Scotsman*. Parts of
chapters 4, 9, 11, 13, 15, 16 and 19 have appeared as
complete stories in *Blackwood's Magazine*.

First published by Gerald Duckworth & Co. Ltd

This edition was produced in 1977 for sale to its members
only by the proprietors, Readers Union Limited,
PO Box 6, Newton Abbot, Devon, TQ12 2DW.
Full details of membership will gladly be sent on request

Reproduced and printed in Great Britain
by A. Wheaton & Co Exeter
for Readers Union

Contents

Preface   7

Albania

1. Thoughts of Chairman Misto – I   9
2. Thoughts of Chairman Misto – II   17
3. Palace of Varieties   24
4. Confessions of a Marxist Mum   31
5. Greek Roots, Albanian Flowers   39
6. Heroine Madonnas   44
7. Military Intelligence   55
8. Reds Under The Seabed   63

Romania

9. Pillar of Heaven   70
10. The Iron Crown   83
11. Time and Tide at Constanza   98
12. Venice on the Danube   111
13. Scandal at the Quiet Nest   117
14. Disbanding the Monarchy   129

Bulgaria

15. Moonlight and Roses   135
16. The Tears of Radka Boboshevna   146
17. Beside the Seaside   162
18. Looking Back   170
19. Scrap Iron Curtain   181
20. The Oracle Speaks   195
    Index   201

To Carmen Vairo

Preface

These pages contain an account, as honest as he can make it, of what one tourist – who is not a great reader of spy fiction or political columns, who takes a rose-tinted view of life, who cannot get the idea out of his head that human beings the world over are pretty much alike when you get to know them – has been seeing and doing in the communist lands over the past fifteen years. They cover Albania, Romania and Bulgaria and a second volume will deal with Yugoslavia, Hungary and Czechoslovakia.

Each of these lands, for me, is lit with brightness, movement and romance. None is 'sad'. Each has its mystery and conflict, though not of the Kremlinological or Orient Express kind. Every man to his own experiences, and I must confess before I start that I shall not be shadowed by secret police or have my rooms bugged or be invited to an orgy (worse luck) for blackmail purposes. I shall collect communist friends, some in positions of influence, but none will offer me a place in an espionage ring. I shall wander round city centres and back streets and farmyards, but the opportunity to sell a jacket or a pair of shoes will not arise.

I shall talk to people. Already I know that not everyone in the east is seeking desperately to escape to the west, that nearly everyone has an old-fashioned pride in his nation, a love of country which transcends the claims of Islam or Byzantium or the Politburo or whatever the controlling edifice may be.

I find people who pity us for the ignoble lives we lead in the west, as we pity them for the intolerable time they are having in the east. I meet men who are dissatisfied with their wives, wives who worry about what keeps their daughters out so late, daughters who suspect their boy-friends care more for a do-it-yourself car kit than for them, boys who . . . in short, people battling with the splendours and miseries of everyday life, not much concerned with what happens in the palaces of power. Just like us.

Gifford, Scotland. January 1976.   L.G.

I

Thoughts of Chairman Misto - I

The telephone rang. The voice announced itself as that of the Albanian ambassador. I was not aware that we had one in the United Kingdom. We had not. He spoke from Paris, in French. My French is not very good, but I gathered that he was inviting me to visit Albania. He was. My passport was in the post within the hour, and was back in my hands within the week, stamped with a spectacular visa.

Thus swiftly and painlessly, after close on two years of appeals from me and no response at all from her, Albania opened her gates to one innocent non-aligned British traveller. I am not sure what turned the key. It may have been that in a letter I had touched a soft spot with a reference to Skanderberg, the national hero. The five-hundredth anniversary of his death was coming up. Certainly my host, when I reached Albania, had it fixed in his mind that I had come to write a new biography of Skanderbeg. They had been making a film at the Tirana studios about that old-time freedom fighter, and a preview was arranged for the evening of my arrival. Starting the way I meant to go on, I said if it was all the same to my host I would rather see the cup final at the Qemal Stafa stadium. (Qemal Stafa was an athlete, shot by the Italians in 1942 while acting as political secretary of the communist youth movement.)

He agreed. 'Skanderbeg will always be with us, but 17 Nëndori Tirana may never appear in the cup final again.'

'If you do manage to get into Albania,' said someone whose advice I had asked for, someone who had known the country in the old days, 'you will find it a most beautiful land, and the people absolutely charming.'

He did not exaggerate. My experience confirmed all that. You do have uneasy moments – or you did then – while piercing the case-hardened curtain-within-a-curtain which seals off the deep-red land of Marxist mystery from her neighbours, from all Europe, virtually from all the world except Mao's China. The rather tatty turbo-prop from Bari in Italy bumps down on a runway marked out with haycocks and lined with soldiers who bring their rifles to the 'Present' as you taxi in. Security police board the aircraft, lock the doors behind them and take your passport off you. It is several days before you see it again.

When they let you out, you stand in hot sunshine on red terrazzo paving over which the bitumen — a commodity the Popular Republic is not short of — generously flows, and you face what looks like a wayside railway station, banked up with sunflowers and hollyhocks. The flower-bed slogan, picked out in red and white dahlias, reads : WE DEMAND PEACE FOR VIETNAM. WE SHALL FIGHT, NOT BEG FOR IT. (That was the prize slogan of the year, selected from thousands in a competition. When I flew into Tirana more recently the Albanians were off the bellicose tack — the war was over — and the dahlia slogan said : LET US MARCH FORWARD RELYING MAINLY ON OUR OWN EFFORTS.)

But the natives are all smiles and handclaps, and the passengers clap their hands also as they walk off the apron, tucking brief-cases under their arms to do so. Young Pioneers in white shirts or blouses, blue trousers or skirts, and red kerchiefs, hardly visible behind wreaths of roses and gladioli, come to greet you personally and hang the wreaths . . . well, not actually round your neck, but round the necks of the sad-eyed party of plump little men who travelled with you from Italy. 'It's our trade delegation, they're coming back from Indonesia,' your own reception committee says. He has sad eyes also and a mouthful of silver teeth. The scuffed sandals, shabby brown jacket and trousers and rose-coloured open-necked shirt suggest an impoverished farm worker, but Ramadan is a senior civil servant and this is his best suit.

Things seem pretty cordial on the whole . . . and at that moment scuffles break out, cries are heard, an airline official comes running, policemen's hands go to their holsters. It is nothing, only someone's suitcase stuck in the bitumen.

Ramadan, hangdog, resigned, deferential, was a harsh symbol of the cause, a monument to the Pyrrhic victory of the proletariat. His boss, Misto Treska, looked bourgeois by comparison : short, portly, dignified, in a grey cotton suit. He did not quite aspire to a tie, but at least he had his shirt-collar buttoned. He had a touch — just a touch — of that polish which cabinet ministers the world over seem to take on with their portfolios – the silver hair at the temples, the clean smooth handshake, the unsurprised eyes; in Treska's case, eyes of disenchantment, reflecting bitter memories. Ramadan once told me that Albanian eyes registered what Balkan peoples call *sevdaf*, a yearning for happy days which have passed and cannot come again.

Silver-wrapped chocolates, currant cake, the green brandy of Përmeti (a village of the southern mountains) covered a low table in the Chairman's drawing-room, in the hall of the Foreign Relations Committee. We sat side by side, in the positions dignitaries and signers of protocols usually take up. It rules out eyeball-to-eyeball confrontation, and it helps the press photographer. No pressmen, however, intruded on this audience.

Chairman Misto's French was the kind I could handle, the schoolboy kind, and conversation never flagged. He thanked me for making the journey; I thanked him for his hospitality. He said hospitality was something of an obsession with Albanians, I would have heard tales of the extraordinary lengths to which they went to satisfy their guests. I said that naturally Albanian hospitality was proverbial in my country, but no specific tale . . .

'Even lately. Even during the patriotic struggle of 1943. A mountaineer suspected of sabotage was captured by the Italians and brought to this town to be hanged. The commander of the execution party was astonished at his calm bearing. With the rope round his neck, he showed no sadness. The commander shouted : "Old man, you are about to die. Do you understand? Be wretched, this is the most wretched moment of your life." The shepherd replied : "You are wrong, sir. The moment most wretched in my life was some years ago, when a stranger came to my house and I had no bread to set before him." '

The house we sat in, Misto said, formerly belonged to General Giacometti, viceroy of Albania during the four-year period after 1939, when the country was a new jewel in Italy's imperial crown. 'This room was his chapel.' He got up to trace the outline of the altar behind a plastered wall. 'That villa next door, the one painted yellow, belonged to Zog's sister.' Zog, a tribal chieftain, climbed to power in the feudal wars of the nineteen-twenties, proclaimed himself king, made Tirana his capital and was driven out by the Italians at the Easter invasion of 1939. Zog is dead but his son Iskender, born two days before the royal family fled the country, is alive and resident on the French riviera.

'Zog had multitudes of sisters, dozens of them,' Ramadan chimed in. (He had six.) 'All with expensive tastes. He, and the Hungarian woman he married, and these droves of sisters – they used the national treasury of Albania as their private bank account. The people starved, and up in the hills even the hens ate pebbles.'

This was the Chairman's cue for an oration on the dismal condition of the old Albania, the spirit and promise of the new. Industrial expansion, a new look for agriculture, vital statistics, health statistics, education statistics . . . one hears the recitation more than once in the course of a few weeks in the Popular Republic. One tries to look suitably impressed . . . one would like to, for the figures are impressive and genuine. But Albania spoils the argument with repetition.

'Why, then,' he went on, 'do the nations condemn us for our aims? Is it a crime to build up new industry? Banish disease? Teach children to read? Plough up waste land and irrigate marshes?

'Some speak of our warlike ambitions. They say we have a large army. That is true, but we have large enemies, a long frontier to defend. Yugoslavia wants to swallow us. With Greece we are technically still at war. We have no friends in Europe. Yes, we have an air force – of small fighter planes which can scarcely fly beyond our borders. Our navy – we'll show it to you, it's lying at Shkodër – consists of coastal craft which can scarcely sail out of sight of land. Defence, defence. Not attack. Whom should we attack? We are so small, it would be foolish.

'We ask only to be left alone. We have adopted, democratically, a certain political system. It is not the system of Britain or America, it is a system which suits us best. You have made your own choice of system, we do not interfere. In Russia the same. Why, then, should the nations interfere with us? Why should foreign peoples tell us what is best for us?

'No, we were never allies of the Soviet Union. We proved that by giving her the *rebuffade* when she tried to impose troops on us and manipulate our economy. It was to our disadvantage – the Tirana culture palace, have you seen it? The Russians started it as part of an agreement and when we broke with them they walked off the site. They even took the plans away.

'Neither are we allies of the Chinese People's Republic. It happens that China operates a political system like our own. Therefore we are companions on the same road. That is all. We trade with China, we welcome the Chinese among us, but if China should try to interfere . . .'

Misto took a handkerchief from his breast-pocket and waved it, saying : '*Lamtumirë, lamtumirë*' ("Farewell").

I had brought him a gift, a bottle of malt whisky. The bottle, the label, the paper it was wrapped in . . . the products of a more sophisticated technology looked so rich and ostentatious that I felt ashamed. It was like turning out for village cricket in immaculate flannels and blazer, when everyone else wore braces. Misto inspected the label and smiled.

'Twenty-one years old. Nineteen forty-six. The Albanians were fighting to build socialism, and the Scots were making whisky.' He unlocked a drawer and laid the bottle inside. 'I shall keep this for those who will appreciate it. If a member of the Politburo comes to my house, it must remain hidden.'

We talked about books. He gave me a reading list on Skanderbeg, a big bibliography, mostly in Latin and French. Terrorist or patriot? It depended which way you looked at him. He mentioned the English-language classics on Albania : Edward Lear's *Travels of a Landscape Painter*, Miss Edith Durham's *High Albania*. Nothing has been published in English for about a century, no Baedeker or Blue Guide, not even a grammar of the language. Misto said he was filling in time translating *Les Misérables* into Albanian. The State publishing house is slowly working its way through the land-marks of nineteenth-century literature. *Oliveri Tvisti* was in the bookshops, and on a subsequent visit I saw *Aventurat e Tom Sojërit* and *Aventurat e Hekëlbër Finit*.

Like many of his colleagues, Misto had taught himself French as a young communist. He learned Italian while a prisoner of the fascists. He was studying English, but at that time lacked the con-fidence to speak it. 'But I'm reading the journals of Lord Byron, who travelled in this country. We shall show you the plaque we raised to him at Tepëlenë, where he visited Ali Pasha.'

We walked round the garden, over lawns and through the pur-lieus of the ministries. Misto's car, a close-curtained grey Varshava saloon with white-walled tyres (the V.I.P. symbol) followed at a crawl. This was central Tirana, a city of 150,000 people, like several little clumps of city planted out in a forest of poplar, acacia and mimosa. I forget how many trees per head of population there were – Ramadan did tell us. The new public buildings, which one is expected to admire, are grey, solid, functional and depressing,

the new culture palace a scandal of neo-Empire ferro-concrete. The
nicest buildings, which one must despise, are those left behind by
the Italians – the primrose-coloured, arcaded University and the
villas on the principal boulevard, which are now Party secretariats
and part of the Chinese embassy complex, and the smaller mustard
and terracotta houses with deep pantiled roofs on the minor boule-
vards, which house the embassies and consulates of lesser nations –
only a handful, for Albania is choosy about whom she maintains
diplomatic relations with.

Beyond Skanderbeg Square, where the lonely traffic cop sleeps
on his feet and jumps to attention to greet a car like an old friend if
it happens to pass by twice in the same day, you are in Old Tirana.
Not much is left undeveloped, the gypsy quarter has been swept
away to the last flea, but you get an impression of the dark winding
suq, the dirt streets, the tiny shops at the doors of which shoe-
makers, lantern-makers and candlemakers would sit working, there
being no light and hardly any room inside. There you know you
are in the Orient, but it will not be there much longer. Even in Zog's
time the authorities were sensitive about the slummy heart of the
capital city, and sketching and photography were forbidden. The
present régime is sensitive too.

'We invited an Italian writer here,' Misto said. 'He took a picture
of a cabin in the bazaar and a black horse-drawn cab, and in his
newspaper he called it "A View of the Capital". It was typical of
his articles. He dealt in falsehoods. He spoke of a way of life which
is found nowadays only in our museums. We replied, of course,
through the press agency.'

I sympathised with the Italian writer. Humble ways, primitive
trades, vanishing traces of communities built for people and not for
motor-cars have an appeal for me also. I could hardly explain that
to the Chairman.

I took no guide on my journeys, only a driver. He was attentive,
more of a nursemaid than a guard, and he commanded respect. I
would not have known how to behave without him, for Chairman
Misto's tales and old travellers' yarns of the mountaineers' ferocious
hospitality were not repudiated by anything we experienced. 'Have
you eaten?' – 'Have you slept?' – 'Have you smoked?' – '*U pini
duhani?*' (literally, "Have you drunk tobacco?") – these were the
ordinary salutations of highland folk casually met, and they would
not take yes for an answer.

We made lightning tours of the statutory sights : factories, State farms, martyrs' monuments and war-of-liberation museums. Then we slowed down and enjoyed the country, the ruggedest in Europe, much of it above 5000 feet, scattered with sharp peaks, swordcuts of ravines, karst plateaux, alpine pastures and snow-water lakes, a pocket compendium of European geography, a microcosm of Mediterranean botany.

Albania is about the size of Wales but, rolled out flat, it would probably cover the British Isles. On an average day's journey you pass from banana groves to Himalayan wastes, from steaming coastal swamp to highland torrent. You drive through citrus orchards, cotton fields, rice and tobacco plantations. You view Great Lakes, pine-fringed and smothered in lilies, unfished since time began, and you descend on columns of red rock edged with ribbons of sand which glisten like trails of rock-salt . . . sands which cry out for tourism, which tourism in our lifetime will probably not know.

Enver Hoxha the Party secretary has said : 'Why should we turn our country into an inn with doors flung open to pigs and sows, to people with pants on or no pants at all, to the hirsute and long-haired hippies to supplant with their wild orgies the graceful dances of our people?'

Periodically you return to Tirana to top up with petrol. There are fuel depots in several towns, but one way and another it is best to go back to Tirana, where they know you.

Whenever I reappeared in the capital, Chairman Misto, no doubt bored with the languid days of the summer recess, came in for a drink or a meal.

'And what are your impressions of our country so far?' (Everyone asked this question; everyone seemed anxious to know.)

'It's a revelation. But when are you going to let the foreigners in? In the west, you know, when we have a good thing we like to share it around.'

'Albania is glad to see foreigners. She has nothing to hide. But for some years she will not be able to accept large numbers. She cannot take the responsibility. The welfare of her own people must come first, we have to supply the needs of the population. Something has been achieved : that chair you sit on, the wine you drink, the glass and the bottle, those chocolates . . . the suit I'm wearing, my shoes, my glasses, everything but the buttons on my jacket is made in Albania.

'We still have obstacles to overcome in the education of the people. There are some areas of backward people, quite unsuitable for foreigners to travel in. But give us time. Your United Kingdom has had two hundred years in which to modernise herself, we have had only twenty-two.'

2

Thoughts of Chairman Misto - II

Misto arrived at Durrës, the seaport and holiday resort. I believe he came chiefly to show off his new transistor radio, an object the size of a portable typewriter in a black imitation-leather case. It was a gift, he said, from the Chinese chargé d'affaires. He set it up on the terrace of the Adriatik hotel, pointed the aerial towards Brindisi a hundred miles across the sea and listened to an Italian news bulletin, nodding wisely at each item as though the western world's day had turned out no better and no worse than he expected. 'There is to be a *putsch* in Greece,' he said, and two weeks later there was.

His theme was Democracy. In the west, he said, they do not have it. It meant people's power, rule by the masses. 'No, you do not have it.' He instanced the U.S.A., where vice-presidents, through scandals or assassinations, find themselves elevated to the presidency. 'Who votes them into office? They are chosen by one man, like a favourite at a medieval court. The most powerful ruler in the world, the sultan of the land of liberty, and no one voted for him.'

Albania's elections had taken place the previous year. Of 929,975 registered voters, forty had spoiled their papers and three had voted for unsuccessful candidates. The remaining 929,932 had cast their votes for candidates of the Democratic Front, who were duly elected or re-elected.

'Isn't that farcical?'

'No. Many liberal people assume that democracy is served only when elections are conducted between two or more parties. But a State is always the ruling mechanism of a dominant class – in your case, the class of the large capitalists. In your country there is no fundamental difference between parties, they all stand for the preservation of a capitalistic society.

'Now, as to the candidates. Whom do you vote for, may I ask? Is he known to you personally, do you consider him the best person among all your acquaintances to represent you in parliament?'

'No, I've never set eyes on him.'

'Nor has the majority of the electorate in your country. He is
unknown to them. They have not chosen him, a party machine has
chosen him. Is that democracy?'

Misto switched off the radio and leaned forward, stroking his
chin. 'In Albania, on the other hand, the most important parts of
our elections begin months before polling day when the urban and
village organisations nominate their provisional candidates. At wider
and wider meetings their merits and demerits are debated. Those
who receive the greater support go forward to the next stage.
Eventually, when all but one have been eliminated, he or she becomes the candidate for the constituency. Polling day, therefore,
is a confirmation rather than an election. It sees the formal ratifi-
cation of the electoral processes which have preceded it. It is a
holiday in Albania and a demonstration of true democracy.'

'And all your successful candidates are communists?'

'By no means. Many of those finally selected are members of the
Party of Labour, which you call communists. But others are not.
All, however, whether of the Party or not, form a bloc called the
Democratic Front. That is the political force of the people in the
State machinery.'

'So, from the local level, even a monarchist or a capitalist – if he
were well supported – could enter parliament . . .?'

'No. Having taken away power from the capitalists of former
days, how could the working people permit capitalists to organise
again? To restore private enterprise, exploitation, a monarchy? It
would hardly be logical.'

'Mr Chairman, last year a million people voted for the deputies
now in parliament, and only three voted against them. Human
nature being what it is, can you believe that there are only three
people in Albania who disapprove of the popular choice?'

He smiled. 'If you are asking my private opinion, I would say
that Albania contains more than three. I believe that some people
are afraid to express their wishes at the ballot box. The ballot is
secret, but we have not yet persuaded everyone that it *is* secret.
Human nature being what it is.'

He twiddled the knob of the transistor radio, picking up a defiant
harangue (Radio Tirana hurls invective at Yugoslavia most evenings) and a marching tune which I had heard sung by teenaged
volunteers in the Qukës highlands as they marched with a red
banner along the uncompleted Road of Youth. 'They work hard,
those boys and girls,' I said.

'The young must work. They have not suffered. You and I, at their age, were fighting and suffering. They *must* work, they have a debt to repay.'

Misto as a schoolboy had been one of the Two Hundred, the hard-core communists of the nineteen-thirties. 'My school was a centre of revolutionary activity. At thirteen, every pupil was a rebel. By the time I was eighteen I had spent two years in prison.'

He came out in time to join the partisan battalions and ended up commissar of the Fifth Brigade, the group which bore the weight of the last German offensive. As commissar, he had to handle human problems.

'When men and women lay down side by side at night, sharing the same blanket . . . We couldn't afford pregnancies, we couldn't afford to put a weapon in our enemies' hands. We ordered that no man should fraternise with his female comrade. Our forces obeyed that ruling, all but a few. Human nature being what it is. In their case I adopted severe measures. *Des mesures draconiques.*' He raised an imaginary rifle to his shoulder. 'The moment liberation came, every soldier in my brigade was instantly in love. The young men married the young girls who had shared their campaigns. I, too. I married my despatch-rider.'

He rarely mentioned his wife. I doubt whether she or the children had ever sat, as I sometimes did, on the plush seats of the curtained Varshava. The married woman's routine in New Albania is not far removed from that imposed on them under Turkish rule : housework, dressmaking, gossip within four walls.

I hinted that we might have Madame Treska to dinner one evening. He said no, but he would take her the empty tin from which we had just smoked the last of fifty cigarettes. '*Les femmes aiment toujours la nouveauté.*'

To our next meeting, our last, he brought cigars. Dinner at Tirana's Dajti hotel – a cosmopolitan scene, the capital city was entertaining some kind of a congress for which numbers of brilliantly-swathed delegates of African states had flown in – emphasised for once the gulf between minister and populace. We sat in a curtained recess, with white linen, crystal glassware, flowers, a lot of *raki* and a bowl of cherries in cracked ice. The head waiter assisted. After serving each course he retreated out of earshot but remained on guard with his arms folded under a napkin. Misto produced his cigars. 'A present from the Cuban ambassador.' Between puffs he announced : 'Tonight I am Tsourtsill.' He hardly needed the cigar for the impersonation. The resemblance struck me for the first time : chubby cheeks, a range of expression which veered from benign to tyrannical, a stubborn line in argument, a persuasive oratory . . . almost a twinkle in the sad dark eyes.

'What was your opinion of Churchill?' (Far from finding my questions embarrassing, he seemed amused by them. Probably he had never met anyone so naïve.)

'You ask my opinion. I will give it. It is a personal opinion only. Churchill for me personified the capitalist society and therefore he was my implacable enemy. Churchill for Great Britain was a formidable champion. He assembled the resources of imperialism, that cannot be denied. One must say the same of Hitler for the Nazis and Mussolini for the Fascists.'

I said that we remembered Churchill as a great parliamentarian, but history showed that in some instances the other war leaders had outmanoeuvred him.

'That is true. Stalin for one. In February 1944, when the Allied armies were in difficulties in the west, it was agreed that Russia should relieve the pressure by launching an attack in the east. The date was fixed for the seventeenth of the month. Churchill allowed details of this plan to reach the Germans. It was his ruse, to put the Russian head into the German mouth. The time had come, he decided, to destroy the Russian army. Marshal Stalin, however, discovered this *complot*.'

'And did not attack?'

'He attacked. He attacked nine days earlier, on the eighth. He forestalled the *complot*.'

'Mr Chairman, forgive me asking, but is there historical evidence for this?'

'It is contained in Marshal Stalin's memoirs, you can read them for yourself. I have also heard Comrade Hoxha refer to it.'

The personality cult is not strong in Albania, not as strong as it was in the nineteen-thirties, when King Zog ordered every shopkeeper to display his portrait. But in Skanderbeg, Stalin and Enver Hoxha the nation has a trinity of more or less deathless gods. In anecdote and myth, folklore and fable, they are curiously interchangeable.

This man Hoxha : his features are familiar from news pictures and the public posters, but is he real? Where does he live?

Just round the corner, the Chairman says. There are a couple of policemen at the end of the street, as it might be in Downing Street.

No pomp about the two-storied colour-washed villa. No secrecy.

And Stalin, whose bronze uniform cap, moustache and greatcoat lean over Skanderbeg Square, and whose plinth is littered with fresh roses? The "little father" of the nation, which does not appear to be aware that he told Tito he could engorge Albania whenever he liked? Stalin is fourteen years in his grave and the Chairman never knew him. When Hoxha travelled to Moscow, he wanted to take Misto with him, but some quite trivial domestic matter intervened. *'Devo dir sospirando, "Io non v'ero"*,' he quotes – the eternal regret of the man who missed the grand battle : 'I must say, with a sigh, "I wasn't there".'

He knew Khrushchev. Khrushchev came to Tirana in the days of promise, 1954 or thereabouts, and all was amity and good cheer. The sacred traditions of hospitality dictated the treatment : Skanderbeg himself succoured his enemies when they called as fugitives, and gave them an hour's start before going out to slaughter them. Mr Khrushchev stood on Misto's balcony and looked at the roses and the dahlias in the gardens, and sniffed the perfume of the mimosa, and said : 'We shall make Albania the flowering orchard of the socialist lands.'

Two years later he was advising the Albanian leader : 'You have poured a bucket of filth over me, Comrade Hoxha, and you are going to have to wash it off.'

'Unfortunately,' Misto said, 'it was beyond the power of our Party secretary to wash the filth off Khrushchev. He was too steeped in it. He did enormous harm to the Soviet state and to international communism. His predecessor Stalin was honourable and open, he did everything *en clair*. In Stalin's time, no man was judged without an open trial. Khrushchev by contrast was devious. He intrigued continually, held secret trials and ruled by the *putsch*. He was *putschiste* supreme.

'His successors are the same. They rule with informers and secret police. Kosygin and Brezhnev must go the way of Khrushchev. They have failed the people. Living standards over there are falling, not rising. We sympathise with the heroic Russian people, but we do not admire their leaders.

'Albania hoped for a new era after the fall of Khrushchev. We were the last of the socialist countries to announce his removal, or to comment on it. But at length we realised that the system had not changed. Khrushchev was sacrificed in order that *le krushchev-isme* might continue.'

Did it never seem odd to Misto that, on the march to socialism he spoke of, all the nations but Albania were out of step? He replied at some length. I did not comprehend it all, but understood that some socialist states did not have the courage of their convictions, they trimmed their sails to the economic wind, they compromised, they flirted with the west. Albania alone stuck to her ideological guns. She did not want to go it alone, her people were co-operative by nature. Albania was ready, and had said so, to rejoin the Warsaw Pact when a few trifling conditions had been met : a condemnation by the eastern bloc of Russia's hostile acts against her, the return of military property seized by Russia, the payment of compensation by Russia for broken contracts, the minute-books of all the Warsaw Pact meetings submitted for her inspection, the partial test-ban treaty of 1963 revoked . . . It wasn't a lot to ask.

Lights flickered in the restaurant beyond the curtain. The guests in their dark suits and striped robes sauntered off, casting inquisitive looks as they passed. Only the head waiter remained in the shadows.

We got up to go. I paid another compliment to Albanian hospitality. Misto told a story of one of his ancestors, a Koplik tribesman who received, as a homeless wanderer, the murderer of his eldest son. The women brought bread, cheese and wine and lit the chiboukis for host and guest. The old man entertained his visitor with song and story, as custom prescribed, and put him to sleep in his own bed. Next door lay the son's corpse. In the morning the tribesman roused his guest, provided water for his journey and accompanied him an hour on the road. Then he returned home, gathered his clansmen and oiled his rifle. The *besa*, the law of hospitality, had been fulfilled and the vendetta could begin.

It was quite late. Apart from the moths which fluttered round the sodium lamps, there was no life on the boulevard. Misto flapped a hand, the grey Varshava slid to his elbow.

I was thinking about that story – that fable, allegory, whatever it was. I liked Misto, we were parting on good terms, it was a melancholy thought to me that anything I wrote was bound to offend him. An article about Albania had to be kaleidoscopically coloured, but for Misto there were only two colours, black and white. If it was not positive, it had to be negative. If not north, south. If not top, bottom. All else was compromise, cant and hypocrisy. 'We don't want anyone writing propaganda for us,' he had said, when I tried to hint that I would have to write about Albania as I, rightly or wrongly, saw it. 'We're capable of doing that for ourselves. All we ask is that you write the truth.'

'You mean the factual truth?'

'Of course. What other truth is there?'

'Well . . .'

It was too difficult to express it in French, as it had been to follow much of what he told me about Albania and politics and people. And now he was in the car, ready to move off. 'I christen you Thomas *douteux*.'

'Thomas?'

'*Douteux.* He had to see the imprint of the nails before he would be satisfied. Well, you have seen it. Like Thomas *douteux*, the worst of the disciples.'

The car rolled forward and the Chairman put his head out of the window.

'*Le plus réaliste, pourtant*,' he called out.

3

Palace of Varieties

Durrës, formerly Durazzo, anciently Dyrrachium. Sunday on the beach. Hot-smelling buses thunder down poplar avenues, squashing tortoises. Slogans float between the trees: GLORY TO MARX-ISM – LENINISM. Soft pale sand, a shallow sea, two merchant ships on the horizon, anchored, awaiting permission to enter the commercial harbour. They have been there for five days to my knowledge.

On the beach a square concrete candy store, frescoed with something unusual for Albania: an advertisement. DRINK PARTISAN PEPPERMINT CORDIAL. I do so and it is like diluted mouth-wash.

Thick-bodied Chinese factory technicians from Tirana dip their toes in the sea. Venturing deeper, they giggle like little girls. Fifty yards out they are still paddling. They wear swimming trunks like cut-down boiler suits and they carry their big black transistor radios into the water. A beautiful slant-eyed girl wades by, holding her silk dress below her knees. She declines to be photographed and when I persist several tough-looking Chinamen trot up, waving their arms.

Albanian children, mixed dark, fair and redheads, some Mediterranean-looking, others with a touch of the Turk, but most of them indistinguishable from British children, scuffle, splash and shout like children on any beach. Some distance off-shore, in four feet of water, the bright red and white motor-boats of the Policia Popullorë are patrolling. On the pink and grey terracing of the Adriatik hotel, some Chinese guests take refuge behind palmettoes, aspidistras and basket-chairs from a party of Austrian tourists in transit – identifiable by the photographic equipment they are festooned with.

Mob-capped waitresses serve drinks at tables which bear the sign in several languages, including English: CONSUMPTION IS OBLIGATORY FOR ALL PERSONS THAT STAYES ON THE PREMISES OF ADRIATIK.

A walk along the foreshore. Abrupt '*Një-dy-tre . . . katër-pesë-gjashtë*' of Young Pioneers' keep-fit class. Behind a chain-link fence stand the parents who have come down from the city to watch them. A mile of desolate sand. Frogs snore in an irrigation ditch. Notice-board on the dunes : BEWARE OF UNEXPLODED MINES. Twenty-five years after liberation, New Albania remains reluctant to get rid of its mementoes.

Rock rose and sea holly decorate the promontory. MILITARY PROPERTY – KEEP OUT. A bronzed youth in footballer's shorts has just finished building himself a pinewood beach hut and is adding the motto of the house : SOCIALIST ALBANIA WILL ENDURE FOR EVER. A strand of barbed wire runs from tidemark to shrubbery, in which a more elaborate seaside bungalow is planted. When I step over it a soldier puts down his parasol, takes up a rifle and hisses a warning. I walk towards him, making ingratiating noises. He takes an equivalent number of paces to the rear, but raises his rifle and clicks the bolt. I step back over the wire.

In another town, while circulating with members of the administration, I had had some talk with a boyish schoolmaster named Poxi. He spoke excellent English. He followed us round, a few steps behind the mayor. He had, he said, an hour to spare. At the end of the day he had told me that he might have a day to spare, and could come travelling with me if I liked. In the end it turned out that he had a week to spare. He came almost everywhere, and if I journeyed alone I would find him waiting at the other end.

Poxi came into the Adriatik's sun lounge, apologising for being late. He had been getting himself a room for his summer holiday.

'As a matter of interest, what will it cost?'

'A hundred *lekë* for the room. (Thirty-five pence.) Meals are too expensive, fifty pence or seventy pence a day. I have studied the prices, butter is tenpence each piece, for bread also they make some charge. I shall not have my meals here. Why should I?'

Durrës, at one period the capital of Albania, has a stormy history and a rich classical past which no one suspected the existence of until the bombs of the Second World War uncovered it.

'This man,' said Poxi, introducing Vangjel Toci, the city archaeological director, 'has cost the State ten million *lekë*.' Whenever they went down under Durrës to excavate for the foundations of new apartment buildings, Toci discovered Byzantine mosaics and Roman baths, and the State had to find a new site for the tower blocks.

He brought bronze and terracotta figurines, gold rings and Illyrian blue-glass jewellery, wrapped in a handkerchief, to show us. Many treasures of the nation – including statuary and columns which proved the cultural integrity of the Albanian people in the face of historical theories that they were only a heterogeneous bunch of refugees – were removed by foreign archaeologists to the museums of Rome, Vienna and Paris. The antiquities which Toci finds in Durrës are therefore politically important. I would not be surprised if they allowed him bit by bit to pull down modern Durrës and rebuild old Dyrrachium in its place.

'In the soil, in the streets, under the houses, we are bringing the pre-classical city to life again,' he said. 'Fragments of Illyria are scattered in private houses, and the owners know nothing of their value. Tablets in the Illyrian language. We are still catching citizens who cart rubble away from the building sites and use ancient statues to prop up roofs and make fireplaces.'

'How do you catch them?'

'He has an espionage system,' Poxi said. 'He has his own *sigurimi* (secret police). His friends inform on their neighbours.'

Groping with a torch in the catacombs of Durrës you stumble into a concrete ramp with a gun emplacement on top of it. The Germans put it there in 1943, and the Albanians have kept the rack and turntable in place to work the revolving stage of the theatre in the culture palace.

Stair by dark stair, from the bottom up, you approach foyer and auditorium by way of stagehands' cubby-holes, caverns of ropes and pulleys, studios, workshops and lecture rooms for the off-duty dockers and housewives of a city of 50,000 people.

The façade is a sheet of pink and white granite sprinkled with electric lights. The theatre manager demonstrates the system, bawling his orders to someone out of sight under the roof : lights full on during the performance and before it, a rapid flickering and two-minute black-out to denote that it is beginning and ending. All Durrës, even those merchant ships far out in the bay, get the message.

Bills announce forthcoming attractions : children's variety show with clown costumes, balloons, magic lanterns, tumbling acts and a bear "trained in the Circus of Peking". A serious play to follow, *Le Roi Lyr, pièce de Shekspir.*

Tonight is opera night and streams of patrons converge on the culture palace from the four corners of the market square, which is about the size of an airfield. The ancient bazaar quarter, no doubt. Men wear sleeveless silk shirts, the girls are like flowers in their cotton skirts and blouses.

"In *La Bohême*," the programme says, "Puccini is ill at ease about the plight of the heroes of the proletariat in a bourgeois society. He writes with sympathy about their pangs and their worries, their quest for happiness under a régime which can offer them only misery."

I am ill at ease too. For one thing, we are at the back of the pillarless Great Hall and I cannot make out what is keeping up the ceiling. The seats are steeply banked, thinly cushioned and disconcertingly self-adjusting. Secondly, I have perpetrated a gaffe by asking who was that twelve-foot statue in front of the palace, where we came in. Poxi clutched his hair. Not to know was bad enough, not to know in the presence of the manager and the archaeological director let both of us down. 'I told you, you should remember it. Aleksander Moisu. The grand tragic actor of Albania. All London knows about him, even in America they have heard his name. Why should they not?'

Vangjel Toci says kindly: 'He was the Lorenz Oliveri of our nation.'

Thirdly, all the lights have gone out. All Durrës is in darkness, a late arrival reports – as much as to say, 'It was raining when I came in.' No one minds. An occasional return to the black night of the Zogist-clique era reminds citizens of what they have to be thankful for.

'Mishaps do occur,' the manager says, lighting a cigarette. 'You have them in your country too. We're making progress. When I was a boy, Durrës was a city of oil lamps. Already we have two power stations and the next Plan provides for five, and that will abundantly supply the whole of Albania.' (Albania established her national grid in 1972.)

In the dark a government minister joins us. He bounces about in his seat and when the lights go up I see that he rather resembles a rubber ball with his rotund, tightly packed body, seamed brown skin and perfectly bald head. (Pictures of Albanian warriors show their long hair falling in ringlets. Shoulder-length hair, heavy beards and moustachioes used to be the sign of virility and wisdom in young and old, but Hoxha has spoken. The badge of New Albania's males is a bald or close-cropped head. Diehards says this is merely making a virtue of necessity, the nation has lost its hair because it has abandoned the skull-cap and white fez.)

Our friend is Education Minister. This opera house, he confides, was designed by his wife, probably I noticed her portrait in the corridor. She won the open competition and supervised the construction. Perfect acoustics, identical seating and viewing from all parts . . . Again the lights go out, but this time it is official.

Footlights. Music, a twelve-piece orchestra. Rudolf's garret, stark and surrealistic. The four heroes of the proletariat wear natty drape suits, one purple, one orange, two clerical grey. In the garret and at the café they keep their grey top hats on. Benoit the rapacious landlord and Alcindoro the sugar-daddy are garbed in morning coats and pin-striped trousers, like western heads of state in eastern cartoons. Mimi is a stunning redhead, dolled up for Ascot.

When you get used to them the sets are rather clever. Between acts it takes a lot of hammering and a long time to ring the changes – as though they have to build up the scenery from the floor. No doubt the revolving stage gets in the way. At the first curtain – one call for the whole company, one burst of restrained applause – there is time to look down on the house and see what is what. A patient attentive audience for such a hot night. Multicoloured shirts, pastel blouses, a few headscarves, predominantly red and white. We seem to be perched on the rim of an overflowing basket of flowers. Conversation across the hall is cheerfully uninhibited. Durrës is a small town, the minister says, everyone knows everyone else.

No one leaves his seat. To us, seated in the totalitarian equivalent of the royal box, come trays of *raki* and dishes of peaches in ice. I look down again and have the feeling that the opera company has become the victim of a cultural take-over. A young man in white tunic and baggy trousers delivers a monologue from the stage. Who is this intruder?

Entracte, Toci says. An amateur. An employee of the local tobacco factory. The monologue is an old favourite entitled *How Khrushchev Unfurled the Banner of Discord and Betrayal*.

I can make nothing of the sketch which follows Act Two of *Bohême*, except that it involves 'the new American ambassador in Cambodia' and his native mistresses and tommy-guns and a suitcase full of dollar bills. At the end an explosion under his desk blows his trousers off. The audience falls about laughing. Poxi's eyes stream with mirth, the faces of minister and archaeologist are

lit with happy grins. By the time the applause has died down we
are back at the gates of Paris.

Not a speck of snow on the set, but a composition wonderfully
evocative of a midwinter dawn in a cold climate. Shaban Hays's
laconic decor, as the programme calls it, is for me the high point
of the evening, well worth the price of admission in itself. (Durrës
opera costs seven pence, first come best seated, war veterans and
pregnant women half price, work brigade medallists free.)

Work brigades are the theme of the next entracte. Marching men
with pick and rifle blend in silhouette on a backcloth and a vivacious soubrette sings about them. The audience, knowing these
catchy tunes, joins in. I know one myself, at least I know two lines
of the refrain, which go :

> *Prane buldozërit,*
> *Prane buldozërit . . .*

– a haunting ballad of unrequited love. The lady bricklayer would
like to attract the attention of the bulldozer driver on her site, but
he is intent on his work and all her ruses are in vain.

Back to the garret. On, while candles burn low, to the death of
Mimi and Rudolf's anguished cry. One candle remains alight. It
symbolises a hope for a better future, the dignity of man un-
quenched beneath the smothering blanket of bourgeois-capitalist
apathy. That, anyhow, is what it says here on the programme.

One curtain call. No flowers for Mimi, but a tailpiece for us all.
The tobacco factory's drama group perform a playlet about a clerk
who helps himself to the office stationery. We hiss this villain in
the manner of an audience at a Victorian melodrama. Indeed, from
the way people are getting steamed up about it, I suspect the plot
is drawn from life. Conscience pricks him at the last, he tears off
an eloquent strip of self-criticism and makes full restitution as the
curtain falls . . . to line up with the rest of the company, displaying
one of the letters in their sandwich-board slogan : LET US MARCH
FORWARD RELYING MAINLY ON OUR OWN EFFORTS.
They turn about and the slogan reads : LET US PLANT MORE
TOBACCO.

Tumultuous acclaim. An orderly exit into the sticky Durrës
night. No buses, no traffic on the boulevard, the main square is
serene under the stars. Everyone marches home, relying mainly on
his own efforts.

Backstage we meet the players. Their dressing-rooms are a show-piece of furnishing, with smart flimsy chairs, strip lights and loud-speakers which dispense with call-boys. The embassy Chinese are there, crowded into the star dressing-room, their eyes slanting wide as Mimi takes off her make-up. Has the national opera not yet had a shot at *Turandot*? Not only has it not had a shot, it has never heard of *Turandot*. *Così Fan Tutte*? (There are Albanians in that one.) No. It did *Carmen* for Cuban Friendship Week and it does *Mrika* quite often.

Mrika, the first full-length Albanian folk opera, written about 1963, was composed for the opening of the Shkodër culture palace.

Bohême completed the national opera company's repertoire. Off stage, Rudolf and Mimi, Marcel and Musetta are more bohemian than that dapper quartet they portrayed for the audience. They lounge about, half undressed, undisturbed by the ministerial aura, indifferent to the polite questions of the Chinese second secretary. Out of their make-up they are raffish and impudent, like urchins. Mimi bites her finger-nails. Marcel smokes cheap Partisani cigar-ettes. To Rudolf, the roly-poly tenor whose voice alone raised the performance to something like provincial British standards, I con-fide my shame at not knowing about Moisu. 'Why should you?' he says. 'Who ever heard of him, outside Albania?'

They chatter among themselves, exchanging a theatrical jargon incomprehensible to the rest of us. Every society, the minister says, half apologetically, needs its non-conformists. They are the bohem-ians of the régime, these artists of the State Opera. They speak their minds, pursue their arts, cold-shoulder the Chinese and look for happiness under a system which does not offer it to all. To the palace, the heart of organised culture, they have brought a little Latin Quarter, and the palace is letting them get away with it.

4

Confessions of a Marxist Mum

I wanted to see how the other two-thirds lived, far from the *villes musées* and *villes héroiques* of the seaboard. Poxi recommended the mountain trail to the copper-mining country. He knew those parts, he had taught in schools in that region. Several times he disputed the route with our driver the Bear. ('Why do you call him Bear?' – 'Because he is like a bear. In Albania, if one is powerful and rough and doesn't speak much, we call him Bear. Why should we not?') Poxi was generally wrong. Occasionally the Bear went wrong. Then we had to seek directions from a native.

'Brothers, you may go this way,' a walnut-faced shepherd cried. At night, in his *kulla*,[1] he would swagger a little at having spoken with motorists. The common salutation was *'Tungjatjeta'* – 'May your lives be preserved' – but we also heard 'May good things attend you' and (a forlorn hope on those rugged boulder-strewn mountain passes) 'May your path be ever smooth'.

In the foothills old habits of life persisted. Donkeys outnumbered the racketing rock-loaded trucks. Men, women and children trudged down the middle of the road, their heads and shoulders bowed down with cargoes. One woman carried a wooden ploughshare which must have weighed a hundred pounds. Female field-workers – cotton, rice, mulberries – wore baggy pantaloons and were muffled to the eyebrows in veiling. They straightened their backs to watch the car pass by. Men had abandoned the red cloaks, green waist-coats and silver chains loaded with trinkets such as their grand-fathers had worn, but they still sported the white fez or *pileus*, and some of the women of the Mirdita district were gorgeously dressed in *xhubleti* (voluminous red woollen garments), jackets and cum-merbunds, bell-shaped skirts with showy silk sporrans and white trousers underneath, tucked into moccasins . . . all this for a working outfit in temperatures of ninety or so. We tried to persuade a few

[1] Highland cottage, square and windowless, like a small fortress.

to be photographed, but all declined; some on religious grounds, some because their menfolk would beat them, some because they had 'better clothes at home'.

Poxi expressed astonishment that we had not so far been asked for our identity cards or 'written papers'. Every river bridge and main-road junction had its sentry-box, with a member of the highway gendarmerie posted – dozing – inside it. It was a mystery, he said, that not one of them hailed us. He thought it a retrograde act of the British government, to abolish identity cards after the war. 'By giving false names, criminals escape. How should they not?'

Poxi was growing argumentative. Like many a republican, he had kings on the brain and wanted to know more about the royal family than I could tell him. Why did a modern industrial nation tolerate a monarchy, much less respect it?

'Perhaps it's traditional with us. Our kings and queens go back a few centuries, you know.'

'You needn't tell me that. King Harold of Hastings. King Henry of Tudor. What right had they to call themselves king? Many I think couldn't write their own names.'

'I believe they could. Alfred, they say, was a celebrated scholar.'

'I know of him. King Alfred the Great. Also King Henry called Beauclerk for his learning and wisdom. I have read about them all. Albanians don't like kings, they prefer freedom. They sent their king away. Why should they not? What use was he?'

Trucks loaded with calcium rock came bouncing off the heights and pounded the top dressing of a narrow gravelled carriageway, thrusting the donkey-trains to the cliff edge. Not so many pedestrians these days on the old highland routes, the Bear said. He remembered when people went on foot to Lurë or Peshkopi and came back two weeks later with a sack of grain on their backs. He stopped to lend a hand to a truck-driver mending a puncture – mutual aid on the road seemed to be the rule, and as often as not the driver was an old friend of the Bear's. It is a quiet land for traffic : drivers get to know each other.

Poxi and I walked on, stretching our legs. 'Yours is a curious name,' he said. 'All the English have funny names. Heath, Wilson, Rolls-Royce.'

Where Poxi passes without comment, I suppose they do sound strange. The foreigner accepts Zog ('bird') and Hoxha ('teacher, holy man') without a smile, but you can hardly say the same for an army general named Ded Gjo and a chief of staff called Jello, especially when their names are preceded by *Shoka* ('Comrade'). Years ago the leading light of the regency council was Bishop Bumci and Zog had a minister called Coco Cota. As to the Albanian language, one cannot make up one's mind whether to take it seriously or not. Most of the time it sounds like a private language made up by schoolchildren. 'I am' is *jam*, 'I have' is *kam*. 'No' is *jo* and 'yes' is *po*. The polite Albanian, eagerly agreeing with everything you say, goes like a two-stroke engine, *po-po-po-po*, briskly shaking his head the while.

The grammar is impenetrable. Verbs in common use are monosyllabic barks and grunts : *ha*, 'eat'; *pi*, 'drink'; *flë*, 'sleep'. For such a courteous race, expressions of greeting and politeness are naturally made the most of. 'Thanks' is rendered *u falem nderit shumë*; 'so long', *mirë u pafshim*; and 'good-bye' is a lilting, sorrowful *lamtumirë*.

To my delight the car broke down and Poxi and I had to catch a bus, a scarlet Italian-built sixty-seater, with the blinds drawn over its plexiglass roof. Poxi found a seat beside a patriarchal mountaineer, I sat with a French-speaking schoolmistress. We climbed so slowly to Rubik that the clouds of white dust we raised caught up with us. We paused in that former 'town without houses', now a flourishing settlement on the edge of the copper belt, and climbed on more slowly to an identical place.

The bus stopped for ten minutes. Some passengers got out and drank water at the fountain in the square. The old man beside Poxi shaded his eyes and looked to right and left.

'Where are we?'

'This is Rreshen, my uncle. Town of the copper miners.'

'Is this Rreshen? Why, where's the old town gone? I knew it well. Before you were born. We used to pass with the caravan. We always spent the night at a *khan* up there on the hill.'

He started to get out, but at the sound of an engine starting up he sank back into his seat. 'Are we off again already?'

'No, no. It's the miners' bus.'

From the grey vehicle which had pulled up opposite, the miners descended, carrying their lamps. A similar group, in khaki rubber suits, took their places. Some of the home-going miners came aboard us and two or three young women got up to give them seats. I got up too. Poxi stayed put and stared at the tired men with all the disdain of the intelligentsia for the proletariat. 'They're the best-paid men in Albania,' he said afterwards. 'They earn half as much again as I do, and they have social privileges. I don't give up my place to a miner. Why should I?'

We arrived in the dark at Kurbnesh, terminus of the road. The street-lamps were few and dim. On weekdays the orange glare from the furnaces lights up the town, but next day was a holiday and the smelters were shut down. The mountains crowded in. Darkness restored this town to its age-old solitude. Not long ago, Poxi said, a Kurbnesh family which possessed candles could give itself airs. The district was known as the land of ragged coats, illiteracy ran at ninety-eight per cent of the population. Now they had five schools and a technical college and the youngsters who might once have herded goats were tending sophisticated machines at the copper plant.

We sat in the long, low public room of the Kurbnesh inn. One moment it was crowded with customers, chiefly truck-drivers, drinking *raki* and shouting at each other. The next it was empty. Where did everyone go to? What did visitors and populace do with themselves at night in a place like Kurbnesh, if they did not patronise the hotel?

Across the square a neon sign KINEKLUB brightened the sterile face of an apartment block. A few doors away a light blinked as someone passed into a hall. 'The *Teknikum*,' Poxi said. After a wash and brush up, most of the miners would be making for it, to attend their evening classes. 'We can go there,' he said. 'It's Sunday evening, it will interest you.'

The meeting is scheduled for eight. In the library section a neat young woman in western-style jumper and tartan skirt – the librarian, presumably – welcomes us. A child in Pioneer costume shows us to a couple of seats.

Children of the sub-teenage group are arranging desks and a centre table with a lectern beside it. Older children take their seats at the table. The rest occupy cane chairs like ours. Parents and teachers – Poxi waves and smiles at a few – stand round the walls, pressing against bookshelves which seem to be filled with the golden treasury of Marx and Engels and very little else. The children look composed and serious, as though to defend the solemnity of the occasion against any mistimed adult levity.

A stocky maiden rises, rings a bell, achieves silence with a glance round the room. She begins reading rapidly from a roll of notes.

Secretary of the high school youth committee, Poxi whispers. They are going through the minutes of the last meeting. Nothing arises. My friend borrows a copy of the agenda and translates the first of its two items for me.

' "To denounce [here follow a dozen names] without mercy and take steps to eliminate their defects ".'

The denouncers, three older girls, revel in their task; you don't need to speak the language to see that.

'What is she saying.'

'She discusses his faults.'

The victim, a big, shambling, sleepy-looking boy, stands at the lectern, smoothing a written statement with the palm of his hand, awaiting his turn to speak. He appears less than contrite, whatever his crime. I imagine he has a complete answer to the charges. The chairman, another plump little highland lass, gives him a nod and he starts reading.

'What is he saying?'

'He discusses his faults.'

The boy finishes, sniffs, tucks the paper inside his shirt and steps down. Catching the eye of a friend in the audience, he winks. Various committee members take up the tale.

'What are they saying?'

'They discuss his faults.'

This is routine stuff. Several delinquents are dealt with in this manner and then our acquaintance in the tartan skirt is called to the lectern. She is not the librarian, she is one of the teachers. A very young girl, a flaxen-haired little beauty, stands at the other end of the table and makes a statement. I do not grasp who is denouncing whom, until Poxi explains that the teacher is under fire for having left her class too much to themselves and for dodging a physical training session. Her speech ends : 'I recognise my errors and shall take care to avoid them in future. I shall devote special care to new pupils and the very young.'

The admission gets a round of applause. No hard feelings : she and her flaxen-haired accuser shake hands.

I feel sorry for the girl who follows the teacher to the stand. Bespectacled, lank-haired, pale, she looks fragile and defenceless. In that crowded room she stands alone, without a friend.

A committee member reads out a statement and her colleagues discuss it in low tones, looking grave. We of the west are brought up in the belief that police-state children shop their parents, but

Poxi says this frightened child, for a change, has been denounced by her father. She begins to defend herself, speaking without notes.

My sympathy is entirely misplaced. Though fragile, the child is resilient and articulate, with lots of spirit. Her eyes flash and she goes on for a good five minutes. Poxi can give me the gist of only the end of it :

'I admire my father, I admire him sincerely and respect him in some ways, but I can't agree with many of his outdated concepts. I don't blame him, it's the way he was brought up. But when I saw how old-fashioned his ideas were, and how deep-rooted his prejudices, then I assumed an attitude of indifference towards him.

'This was wrong. It was an inexcusable mistake on my part and I regret it. I have truly realised my error and I intend in future to fight with patience and persistence to convince my father of his faults.'

This child will probably go far. She has given her father a slap in the face without malice, without bitterness, without deviating from the approved formulae of self-critical analysis. We the adults applaud. The children smile at each other. The committee will not cross-examine such a mistress of dialectic.

A red-haired boy named Bardhok is coaxed to the lectern. He is under-sized for his twelve years, but tough. He embarrasses everyone by standing dumb and going fiery red. It is hardly playing the game. (Girls, clearly, are much better at this than boys.) The chairman tells him to stand down. Apparently it is only a question of fighting and truancy.

The boy retires a short distance and remains standing. A big shapeless woman takes his place at the lectern. Poxi says we have arrived at the last item on the agenda, and that it will be worth staying for. I shall have a running commentary.

She is a brawny creature, this woman. She wears a rubber suit, like the miners, and carries a helmet with a red star on it. She takes off a sweatband and a cascade of chestnut hair falls to her shoulders. Her strong features are streaked with dirt. I see where Bardhok gets his hair and his obstinacy from : the woman is his mother. It is she, not he, who is to cry *peccavi*, and she has come up from the mine to do so.

Poxi used to teach at the school. He knows the background, and will give me the story, but first we shall hear what Bardhok's mother has to say.

'My young heroes,' her voice booms out. 'I want to know something. How is Bardhok getting on at school?'

'He's doing well, fairly well,' his classmates shout.

'Good. I'm pleased to hear it. And what about the rest of you? Eh? Is everybody doing well?'

She glares at them, a row at a time. Some giggle, some nod doubtfully, some shake their heads and some look at the floor.

'Not everybody? That's no good. That's no way to build socialism. Can we build socialism if we're not all doing our best? Eh? If some of us misbehave?'

The children, enjoying the drama of it, shout : 'No.'

I cannot get the hang of this confrontation, do not see where it is leading. Poxi, I believe, has nailed the wrong suspect. But later he explains it, and the position is this :

Bardhok is the high school's black sheep, the despair of the youth committee. His behaviour grew so anti-social that the committee deputed its chairman, little Marijka Koleka, to have a word with his mother : a procedure rarely resorted to.

Mum was born a coarse shepherd-girl and pitchforked into the mines. She works shifts and doesn't see much of her son. Her husband lost his life in a shot-firing accident some years ago. To her, then, comes fourteen-year-old Marijka with a rebuke from ₜthe youth committee : Bardhok is disgracing the school, he is out of control, his mother is neglecting her parental duties. 'I'll neglect him,' I can imagine her muttering, as she receives the admonition. 'Wait till I get my hands on him.'

She thrashed him with the leg of a chair. Somehow the news got about, though Bardhok made out that he got the bruises from falling off a bicycle. The youth committee decided that it was a case for a flash poster – the latest word in denunciation techniques, imported from China with the cultural revolution.

Watchdog organisations put up flash posters, addressed to groups or individuals, on house fronts, public buildings, school halls and factory notice-boards. They are word-and-picture bulletins and sometimes they run in series like a strip cartoon, a fresh instalment every day. Children of Kurbnesh paint them in the art class and juvenile despatch-riders post them round the town. They are used sparingly, and are no laughing matter.

Bardhok's mother found the flash poster on the bulletin-board at the mine-shaft. It depicted a mother with uplifted cudgel and a cowering child and underneath was written : 'We beg to enquire, comrade, whether you consider children are beasts to be treated like this? We beg to ask, which in your opinion does the Party consider more important, copper or children?'

She grinned and bore it. Next day another poster appeared and the following day a third . . . the leader of her work brigade advised her to answer the children. 'Otherwise there'll be no end to these flash posters.'

So she has come to face the music.

'No,' she booms. 'If some of us misbehave, socialism cannot be built.' She pauses and looks sternly over our heads. This woman could give points to the actresses of the State Theatre. She lowers her voice.

'Not only do children misbehave. Parents misbehave too. Here is one, for example. Myself. I used a stick on my son. Before that I neglected him. Let him run wild. Play truant. Get into fights.

'Why, young comrades? Because I am busy. Eight hours a day in the mine, sometimes more. And the Party tells us that copper is important, it's almost as important as bread. But which are more valuable to our nation, copper or children?'

One small boy, as confused as I am, shouts : 'Copper' – but it is drowned in cries of 'Children . . . human beings.'

'My young heroes, you are right. Very well, then. And so . . .'

And so on and so forth and so to bed. Mrs Bardhok's confession is the climax of the meeting. Several people are waiting to shake her hand as she leaves the hall. Tomorrow the mine manager will congratulate her. It is possible that a photographer from Tirana will visit Kurbnesh and that her picture and her speech will be in *Zëri i Popullit*, the *People's Daily*. There will be no difficulty there, Poxi tells me. The speech is on paper, and Mrs Bardhok learned it by heart. The youth committee composed it for her.

5

Greek Roots, Albanian Flowers

Squadrons of eagles, the black birds of Zeus and Skanderbeg, whirled down and sailed over the gorges. When Pyrrhus was a subaltern, in these debatable lands of the Epirus from which he took his name, he called his company the Sons of the Eagle. Strictly speaking they were Greeks, but Albania has borrowed the name. The whole country is sometimes known as the Land of the Eagles, and some say it is the literal translation of Shqipëria, the Albanian word for Albania. That is not so. Shqipëria more likely means that Land of Those Who Can Make Themselves Understood, from an old verb *shqip*. (Compare Russian *németz*: 'German, foreigner, dumb man, one who cannot be understood'.)

But the Gramos gorges are a land of eagles. And of hares, partridges, foxes, of a good deal of wild life. Our driver the Bear, in his good-natured way, said the only Englishman he knew, before myself, was a naval officer from Corfu who came for the shooting. The Bear was a small boy at the time, and he went to beat game for this stranger and was rewarded with a packet of chocolate. Then his father beat *him*, for neglecting his sheep.

All the southern mountains are an encyclopaedia of myth and legend. Tales of demigods and heroes dot the landscape like thousand-year oaks. Here is Shpiragrit and there Tomorrit : two mountains, one ribbed with chasms, the other pitted with craters. They were giants who went to war over a Berati maiden. The one hurled boulders, the other slashed with a sword. They slew each other and the girl drowned herself in her tears, which became the river of Berat. So the topography determines the character of the legends, and the legends influence the character of the people, and in Albania everything ends violently.

Beyond the ridge, at 8000 feet, fringed with midsummer snow, Qukapec ('Peci's Peak') rears up. Peci was a shepherd who undertook to spend the winter there – he knew of a snow-free depression and built himself a cabin in it. He spent the winter all right.

First arrivals in April found his frozen corpse.

A curiosity to match those natural features stood at a T-junction below the summit of the road : a signpost, the first we had seen in Albania. Sarandë 35 km. – Gjirokastër 30 km. 'Where does the third road go to?' – 'Only to Greece.'

We followed a grey bus, the mountain mail-carrier, with a short wheelbase and a big overhang at the back. We drew up at a fountain, where its passengers, half stifled with dust and heat, were tumbling out to refresh themselves.

'Imagine finding a bus on a road like this.'

'It's nothing,' Poxi said. 'In summer the driver thinks nothing, it is pleasure for him. In winter, a different story.'

Poxi, humble and diffident in Tirana, treated the southern provincials with patronising condescension. He was anxious to be rude to some Greeks and at the fountain he had words with a pathetic old peasant woman half his height and three times his age.

'That devil-creature,' he said, climbing into the car again. 'She spoke to me in Greek. I said, "Dear lady, this bus is not going to Athens, it's going to Gjirokastër, please to speak Albanian and then I shall understand you". The other passengers, they laughed so much.'

The road falls over a precipice and lands in the Dropull valley. You expect poverty and oppression – I thought the whole region would have been forbidden to travellers – because this is where the minority lives, a people of Hellenic traditions over whom the Greek monarch, when Greece has one, claims sovereignty. Enclosed within Albania's borders, yet isolated from the rest of Albania, they have attracted the strident sympathy of right-wing romantics who have evidently not seen how they live.

The gaudy wraps and mufflers of Moslem folk are missing from this land. The people are Orthodox in their religion and outside the village tavern you see the priest in a black gown, his hair gathered in a knot at the nape of his neck, comfortably seated and laying down the law to his parishioners. 'The Vicar of Wakefield,' Poxi sneered. 'Yes, I have read the book. Very comical. I laughed too much.'

The Dropull is fruitful and well-populated by Albanian standards – a restful scene, a valley exempt from provocative slogans, which bears on the arches of its pack-donkey bridges nothing more disturbing than the painted exhortation UNITY! PRODUCTION! EDUCATION! As evening approaches, the harvest workers come home from the meadows, clean good-looking peasants, the men in woollen waistcoats and tight white knee-breeches, white cloth caps and rosy stockings with tassels at the knees; the women unveiled, with coloured kerchiefs and embroidered bodices, loose white trousers and green cloaks – no two dressed alike, a pageant of Balkan costume through the ages.

Healthy young girls, plump as pigeons, perch side-saddle on donkeys. They card wool as they ride home, the stick of yarn trailing behind them in the dust, and they glance at you with soft unashamed eyes. Poxi drew in his breath with horror. He had not expected this. In his part of the country, a woman dared not ride. 'They would stone her if she tried it.'

The villages are swallows' nests of grey stone and blue slate, tucked in pockets of the hills. You turn off the main road at right angles to reach them. No track connects one with another. To visit a neighbour you come down to the main road and take another turning off it. The Greeks value their privacy. This, then, is the submerged tenth of the population? The downtrodden minority, of which many fanciful atrocity tales are told?

'No, they are not submerged,' Poxi said. 'They have their own life, their customs, their newspaper, even their own radio programme. They are rich. They won't return to Greece, why should they? They have better land here than they would find in Greece.'

I was brushing up my Greek, thinking we might have roamed about and chatted with the natives and sipped ouzo under the plane trees. But the Bear was consulting his map and asking people the way : it was plain that we were bound for some particular village.

A rustic dignitary awaited us. Poxi was barely civil to him. We did the guided tour : a put-up job. Cobbled streets, a medieval room with a red-curtained stage and some library books, described as the culture hall . . . a woman guiltily rose from the floor, caught in the act of scrubbing it. We had arrived ahead of time. Steam rose from the damp floor. We hung about for a while and then the charwoman's shock-headed daughter, in red blouse with hammer-and-sickle emblem, rushed breathlessly up and presented a posy of stocks and asters.

Our guide's house was a nice old villa with vines and a courtyard. THIS IS A CLEAN HOUSE said a notice on the gate, and a green rosette was pinned to the lintel. First prize, he said, in the summer hygiene competition. His wife, shy and pretty in coloured silks, the

Greek equivalent of a tea-gown, showed us her embroideries and the contents of her marriage chest. I studied a cartoon on the wall, cut from a magazine. In the first picture a cow munched corn in a field marked "Co-operative Plot", and the farm-worker stood idly by; in the second, the cow turned her attention to the "Private Plot", and the farm-worker took swift action.

'The land belongs to everyone, as you know,' our host said. 'But a small plot is reserved to each household for private use. It's an old joke that we'd all be rich if everyone put the same effort into the co-operative fields as he does into his personal patch.'

Would that be regarded as a slightly risqué joke in another part of the country? 'No, it's the same everywhere.'

Most Dropull villages operated as a collective. They started twelve years earlier with eighteen families and now they had more than a thousand. They grew wheat, barley, tobacco and rice and they raised plough oxen. Eighty per cent was mechanised – everything but the tobacco. 'Those field workers, they've been gathering the tobacco crop. The machinery for it hasn't yet been devised.'

Our host offered Turkish delight and peppermint cordial, a delicious drink, having nothing in common but the name with the insipid stuff we drank at Durrës. Poxi knocked off three tumblers full and said : 'I do not like this drink.'

As director of the co-operative, the Greek said, he earned ten per cent more than his labourers; the maximum allowable. (Managerial rates in industry are up to forty per cent more than those of the lowest-paid workers.) In cash, what did that work out at?

'It varies. It depends on what we earn as a group. This scheme has been relatively profitable. We borrowed two million *lekë* from the State and we're paying it back over twenty years. But already we have savings, we have about nine million (£20,000).'

'Does that include your . . .' (I was going to say "capital") '. . . the value of your machinery?'

'We don't own machinery. We hire it from the Tractor and Machine Depot, you passed the place coming down the Gjirokastër road.' (We did, and I wondered if those gaunt threshers of antique Middle European lineage were part of an industrial archaeological museum.)

'How about the private farmers, then?'

'They hire it too. There's no discrimination. To each according to his need. Sometimes the private farmer makes better profits, because we have to sell at fixed prices. But against that we have a guaranteed market. My wife prefers it too. She no longer has to waste a day standing in the bazaar to strike a bargain over a few eggs or a sack of rice.'

Our host had statistics at his finger-tips. At the lạst count, 1972, Albania had forty-four State farms and sixteen hundred co-operatives . . . and forty thousand private farms. But the co-operatives owned five-sixths of the agricultural land and when land is taken for industry it is often the private sector which yields it up.

There was a stir and a rustle and a girl glided in. I was expecting her : every stranger in the Dropull has this experience, the tête-à-tête fashion parade. She wore bridal dress, white silk, with labyrinths of gold thread. The red velvet bodice was belted with gold and her breast and forehead were covered with chains of golden medallions. When the definitive work on Balkan peasant dress is published, this girl will be on the jacket of it.

She was pale and stately in her red, white and gold, and her long-lashed eyes proclaimed both the inviolability of the virgin and the chaste expectancy of the bride. Had she been asleep, or a statue, I could have studied her for a while. But she had a role to act, and when she took my arm to walk among the villagers I was reminded of the phoney marriage ceremony people are subjected to when they come off the coach at Gretna Green.

We said good-bye to this pageant. '*Chaire . . . eucharisto*' – the Greeks had no idea what I was talking about. The population closed in and grouped themselves photogenically, the bride knelt and kissed my hand and pressed it to her forehead in the fashion of her country. I was tempted to *ad lib* my way out of the ritual by taking the charming creature in my arms and kissing her in the fashion of *my* country . . . but I suppressed that urge, and kissed the charwoman's shock-headed daughter instead.

6

Heroine Madonnas

There is always something new out of Albania. In bygone days her tormented mountains, disappearing lakes, rivers which changed their courses, inspired a mass of myth and legend. In modern times, the difficulty of getting news out has prompted frustrated journalists to create a mythology all their own.

The big news from a British Sunday newspaper's special correspondent – a man noted for his vivid imagination – was that the Red Guards were on the rampage. In the famous Franciscan cathedral of Shkodër and the house of the White Friars nearby they have jostled worshippers, shot priests, looted the silverware and set chapels on fire. This silverware has been looted several times since 1945, and the White Friars have been exterminated more than once. By western newspapermen, that is.

I visited the Shkodër cathedral and the monastery a few weeks after the 'purge'. Five members of the historic company, the White Friars of Scutari, were on duty, shabby but undaunted. The cathedral's main door was a bulletin board for town council notices, but a printed card was prominent among them : THIS IS THE HOUSE OF GOD. PLEASE TREAT IT WITH RESPECT. The banns of a marriage had been posted. Inside, in the stone-flagged nave which might have seated a thousand, I counted fourteen worshippers and no signs of damage . . . it was a Tuesday morning, and Father Gabriel said we would see a better turnout, including children, on a Sunday. (Since 1972 the Shkodër Christians have dwindled, and the cathedral is a youth centre.)

Albania was never a great church-going nation. Old writers christened it the Land Without a Creed, from its pagan preoccupations with feuding and fighting. Nominally it supported three faiths : Roman Catholic in the north and midlands, Greek Orthodox in the south, Moslem (the greatest number) more or less all over. Among officials, one detects a touch of hostility towards the Catholics :

they have a reputation for involving themselves in politics. The other religions are regarded by the masses with no special favour or antipathy, with a little respect or a little amusement perhaps, rather as the Close Brethren or the Salvation Army might be regarded in the west.

Between them, harmonious co-existence has long been the rule. It was the only way to live, though it took Albanians some centuries to learn the lesson. In Shkodër, for instance, Catholics and Moslems joined in each other's feast days, with the result that the city used to proclaim two hundred and four holidays every year, not counting Sundays.

From the minaret of the Great Mosque of Shkodër no *muezzin* calls the faithful to prayer, but I found in the bedroom in my old-fashioned hotel two reminders of the days when he did : a pair of felt slippers   a notice asking residents not to go out in their night clothes to answer the dawn call. The Great Mosque is a splendid building which gleams from afar (you can see it from Yugoslavia across Lake Shkodër) now they have regilded the dome. We found it open. The decorators were in, touching up the arabesques. Where does the money come from for such costly restoration work? The State declares the building a national monument, and puts up the money itself. All the fine old ecclesiastical buildings of Albania have been saved in that way.

Others, too far gone, remain among the sights of the country-side, but theirs is the picturesqueness of dilapidation : unroofed chapels with pink and yellow pantiles heaped against a wall; plaster walls of churches in thickets of cypress, fig and pomegranate, their frescoes fading in sunlight; churches transformed into village halls, private houses, stables, cowsheds and beer shops.

You see many a well-kept mosque. The Moslem jewel of Albania, for me, is the so-called Leaden Mosque in the marshes of the Drin river near Shkodër, sixteen toy domes on Moorish arches. But they are for show. Snakes are coiled in the dry fountain basin, where men would of old have washed their feet. 'It is Friday,' the caretaker says. (Or Monday, or Tuesday as the case may be.) 'The mosque is closed today.'

Our driver the Bear had no religion. His father had none, nor his father before him. Poxi's grandfather, still alive, was passion-ately Moslem. 'He washes himself all over five times a day.' Poxi's father entered the mosque on special occasions. Poxi never went near the place. 'It is for old people. I laugh at it too much. The old people in my village pray for rain, but everyone knows that it is meteorology, not God, which brings the rain. We laugh at these old people, but we don't harm them. They have been left behind, no one worries about them any more.'

A most beautiful little church stands on a rocky outcrop in the marshland of Pojan, south of Durrës. Enclosed within a wall among a wilderness of fluted columns and broken statues (Pojan is classical Apollonia), the deep-crimson and sky-blue Byzantine pile of Saint Mary the Virgin has flourished intact, squat and sturdy, for about seven centuries. It is dark and dingy inside. Byzantine windows are few and narrow and at Pojan a huge walnut tree has thrown its umbrella over them. Icons and frescoes are suggested rather than seen. Cobwebs stretch from censer to episcopal chair, a thick grime softens the outline of the iconostasis.

Poxi struck a match on the lip of a monster behind the narthex and lit a cigarette. Unnecessary to ask the sexton if anyone worshipped there . . . I asked his age instead. Seventy-six. But then the iron gate creaked open and a worshipper came in, a tiny female in black, with a tiny pointed chin sticking out from her black veil. Lips were sunken, pressed in a blue line. She muttered as she entered, her hollow eyes sought a picture of the Virgin and Child, she made a trembling sign of the cross and kissed the wooden frame.

She tried to light a candle; but her fingers shook too much. The sexton gave her a tremendous scolding for spilling wax. Then he relented and fumbled under the bishop's chair and produced a black bun. The old lady managed to break off a piece and crumble it into her mouth before she got as far as the gate; the rest she wrapped up in a black handkerchief.

Virgin and Child? What possible interest in childbirth could this ancient creature have had? Intercession, I supposed, on behalf of a grand-daughter with modern ideas.

'Her bun, that's all she came for,' the sexton said.

Beyond the courtyard we met her again, working for the stone-masons who are giving the cloisters of old Apollonia a face-lift. Water-buckets were yoked to her skinny shoulders. Her grand-daughter was there too, a handsome girl, heavily pregnant, seated among the rubble, scrubbing a Greek head with a toothbrush. Her ensemble of white shift, purple baggy trousers and kerchief cried out for colour photography and I asked if she would mind . . . She laughed, and asked for a couple of minutes to wash her hands. But washing the hands involved slipping behind a pillar and coming out again metamorphosed, a *palais de danse* butterfly, in blouse, miniskirt and high heels. As my face fell, so grandma's brightened, and her grin disclosed two rows of diseased gums.

In Tirana we talked to a Catholic priest who described the running fight he was having with the city fathers over the new ring road : they wanted to route it through his parish church. He had not exactly won his fight, but I heard on a subsequent visit that although the church had had to come down a new one was approved for the congregation.

In the south, where the square-set, grey-bearded priests are part of the evening promenade scene, pacing alone, isolated in their reveries, too distrait to acknowledge the respectful salutes of parishioners, Poxi told me about a priest who had been elected the previous year to sit with the three hundred deputies of the Democratic Front in the Albanian parliament.

The Bear said there were two such priests.

If Albania can be said to have a holy city, it must be Berat, nicknamed "Town of a Thousand Windows". Lots of those windows are stained-glass. No fewer than fourteen churches huddle inside the château-fort, the old Christian quarter on top of an eight-hundred-foot bluff which overhangs the city : Saint Mary Vlaherne, Saint Theodore, Holy Trinity, Our Lady, another Holy Trinity, Saint Sotir . . . all dark and constricted, all musty with stale incense, the ghosts of liturgical choirs, tarnished silver vessels, icons and swinging lamps and a junk-heap of glass droplets from wrecked candelabra; all pretty much alike in the gloom. It must have been common in the Orthodox heyday for a citizen of Berat to find himself in the wrong church and maybe, with an invisible priest mumbling his office behind the iconostasis, not to discover his mistake.

At each church we put the question : 'How many in this congregation?' At each church the verger replied : 'A few.'

From the madonnas of the past to the mothers of the antiseptic present is only a step in Berat – a vertical step of several hundred feet, from citadel bluff to river bank. While we await the hospital director a blonde midwife, a keen child of New Albania, gives us biscuits and statistics. Maternal and infant mortality, 1938 and now. Number of hospital beds, 1938 and now. Position of women in society, 1938 and now.

'As soon as a woman discovers she is pregnant, she must go to

her street-clinic for tests. She's obliged to attend a certain number
of times, otherwise she forfeits the benefit. Step by step through the
ante-natal period, gynaecology accompanies her. Then she comes
to this hospital. Well, she doesn't *have* to, but she won't get her
allowances if she doesn't. Those mountaineers' children, strapped in
splints on their mothers' backs? They are a special case, it's a matter
for education programmes which are being introduced, but not too
fast. Yes, I agree, they produce beautiful children – those who
survive.

'After the birth, the mother stays here for eight days or more. It
depends on the baby, they can't be discharged until their babies
weigh two and a quarter kilos. Yes, a quick turnover, but this place
runs smoothly. Births are easy, giving birth is something our women
are very good at.'

Under the window of the maternity hospital a tableau of old
Berat is formed. A horse, wearing blinkers as big as soup-plates,
sleeps in the shafts of a four-wheeler cab recovered from the scrap-
heap. A home-going mother is arguing with the driver. She is a
Moslem girl, veiled, in red and white robes and moccasins and the
new baby, a bundle of intricate needlework, is strapped to her back.

'These are great days for working women,' the midwife goes on.
'That girl, a cotton worker I believe she is, she has received nine-
tenths of her pay while she's been here, and now she will claim fourteen hundred *lekë* for baby clothes and another fourteen hundred
for special diet. [About £7 in all.] She's amply compensated, I
think.'

For six children, she said, a mother would be awarded the
Mother's Medal; for nine, the Glory to the Mother; for twelve, the
Heroine Mother. 'We have a Heroine Mother in this hospital at
the moment, perhaps the director will let you see her.'

Pilu the director made me put on a white gown. Matron, two
sisters, a retinue of young doctors, an orderly or two . . . they
formed up and politely followed, as in the train of a renowned
consultant.

The wards compared favourably with some of the hotel bedrooms
I had slept in. Four-bedded suites with bathrooms attached, bedside lamps, adjustable reading boards and press-button breakfast
trays . . . 'I know,' Pilu said, mistaking my expression, 'I'm agitating
to do away with these rooms. Four in a ward is too many for com-
fort. Two is ideal, we find.'

I started describing our own hospitals, the rows of white cots retreating in perspective . . . He put his hands over his eyes. 'It's true, then? It wasn't a propaganda film they showed us?'

Some of the mothers were sitting up, fondling their offspring. After feeding, they could play with them for half an hour. Magnificent specimens, these women, mostly between sixteen and twenty years old, with smooth brown torsos. Young Albania tends to be sunburned and well-developed. 'Come over here, feel these strong thighs.' Once married, the girls lose no time starting a family.

Artificial feeding? He began saying something about *la maladie de la beauté* and I said : 'No, I mean feeding from a bottle. In the west, many women . . .'

'Thank you, I've understood. It's part of what we call *la maladie de la beauté*, which afflicts vain persons. They think more of their looks and their figures than of the child. In Albania, everyone nourishes her own baby. Must? Well, I would say that no woman wants to do otherwise.'

We caught one young girl in the middle of her Yoga exercises, stripped, and when she straightened up the director introduced her as a State ballerina. She had a heart-shaped little face, a mop of short-cut black hair, lovely smooth rounded shoulders and breasts. Her twins were three days old. She was waiting for her *congé*, she wanted to get back to the theatre.

Knitting patterns were spread out on her counterpane. You bought them in the hospital, one wall of the departure lounge was glass-fronted, with a display of babywear.

'But will you walk all right if I let you go?' the director asked.

'Walk? I'll dance if they'll let me.'

But is every mother so anxious to leave? What has happened to the maternal instinct? Almost at once they must return to work, handing over their babies to a *crèche*. The child's progress through kindergarten and school will leave little time for mother-love, and mother may never again be so close to her child as during that brief spell in the maternity hospital. She shops in the reception area, calls the horse-drawn cab, picks up her comic-cartoon post-natal leaflets and studies them on the way home. They refer to "the" baby, not "hers" . . . a piece of State property, it is understood, which she is privileged to hold in trust for a while.

We met Heroine Mother in a single room, a brawny comfortable-looking person, a madonna of the wild hills, with a red sash across her nightie. You see such women travelling down the caravan routes on a Sunday morning, with a shopload of goods for barter on their backs. They carry carpets and woven materials under their arms, poultry and black lambs in their hands, and they wear a quantity of clothing which is a deadweight in itself : coloured cottons, shaggy brown capotes, thick woollen trousers. You see them again in the *suq* of Elbasan, the last bazaar in Albania, elbowing a passage through a noisy mob under the stone blinds of the pantiled alleyways.

She kept her medal in a bedside cabinet, and showed it to us. I could not guess her age – forty, forty-two perhaps – but she was here for her fourteenth child. I asked about her other children, but she made a non-committal reply. (Tactless question : the eldest boy had fled the country.) And Hero Father, was he coming in to see her today? She appeared not to understand.

Doctor Pilu explained : 'We don't have visitors. The way we look at it is this : a mother comes to perform a certain task, undergo a certain ordeal. She seeks privacy – you see it in animals and primitive societies – and she concentrates better when she is secured from her family cares. Confinement, you know – we take the word literally.'

Heroine Mother nodded as though she agreed with every word. She was a placid creature.

'But tell me, now, confidentially, how do you view the whole set-up? If you had your own way, would you . . .?' – I wished I could have had a short heart-to-heart talk with this mountain woman, from whose eyes a married life of child-bearing had not driven the roguish glint. But she spoke a harsh dialect which Pilu himself had difficulty understanding.

As we left, she called one of us back. It was me she wanted. She signed for me to come closer, and the others to retire. An exclusive revelation, for my ears only . . . her little speech went something like this :

'Birth is a happy event for all society. Babies are the fragrant blossoms of our socialist State. To be a Heroine Mother like me is the ambition of many wives.'

A photographer grouped us on the steps, in the sunshine, for a news picture. The deputy director handed me a bouquet of gladioli. She was a ravaged woman, and she limped : twenty-five years earlier she had followed the partisans through the winter campaign, returning with a decoration and frost-bitten toes. Her hail-and-farewell address, while the photographer dodged back and forth, was brief and pithy. Translating, the director expanded it into a five-minute eulogy wrapped up in oriental hyperbole. Taking my cue from him, I replied with a graceful address which did not lack *floridezza*, saying among other things that, although these wonderful flowers must one day perish, the memory of my visit to the J. V. Stalin Maternity Hospital would never fade. The director rendered this as : 'He thanks us very much.'

Where many Albanian towns have flowering shrubs on their avenues and window-boxes to each apartment, Tepëlenë has only inflammatory messages for revisionists, imperialists and deviationists. What it promises to do to them would compel the admiration of Ali Pasha himself, if he could return to his fortress.

That octagonal castle on the cliff above the Vijosë river sinks under a topweight of red stars, hammers and sickles and, all round the battlements, a clarion call : PERPARA PER NDERTIMIN E PLOTE TE SHOQERISE SOCIALISTE NE VENDIN TONE. ("Forward with education for an integrated socialist society within our land.")

The mayoral lunch party, in the backroom of the supermarket café, consisted of peaches, ice-cream and some light beer. I made little headway with the mayor's French – I believe he wasn't trying, he was a bullet-headed, shifty-looking, ungracious man, much more my idea of a Party boss than anyone I had met before – and a diffident girl named Gjurata was brought in to speak English. She was not a native of the town, they had drafted her in from Himarë to run the library.

'Which do you prefer, working here or working in Himarë?'

She passed this to the mayor, who said : 'She prefers to work wherever the Party requires her to work.'

Alone, Gjurata giggled and talked a lot, through shyness. We toured the castle and admired the plaque on the gatehouse which the town council put up in 1959 to commemorate the meeting, a hundred and fifty years earlier, of the psychotic satrap Ali Pasha ("Ali the Lion") and the British poet Byron. Unlikely objects of veneration, I would have thought, a pasha celebrated for sadistic cruelty and greed and an effete pro-Greek foreign aristocrat. Gjurata explained that Ali identified himself 'with the eternal struggle of the people against complaisant chieftains and rapacious exploiters' and that Lord Byron had paid an unforgettable compliment in *Childe Harold* :

Fierce are Albania's children!
Their native fortresses not more secure
Than they in doubtful time of troublous need:
Their wrath, how deadly! But their friendship sure

– precisely the way the Popular Republic sees itself.

Byron's boat ran aground and he and Hobhouse waded ashore.
Tepëlenë was one of the first stops on their Balkan pilgrimage. Ali,
a connoisseur of masculine beauty, licked his lips over Byron's pale
features and kept stroking his knee. A snatch of conversation has
survived :

> Ali : Why have you come travelling in these realms?
> Byron : Why, to see so great a man as yourself.
> Ali : What, have they heard of me in England?
> Byron : Your name is on everyone's lips.

Neither rain nor cooling breeze had stirred the limestone dust of
Tepëlenë for some days, Gjurata said. Under the castle rock – a
thousand feet down, and it looked it, every inch – the pale-blue
South Drin dissolved in the pale-green waters of the Vijosë. A lorry
was parked on a sandbank and the tinkle of a *cifteli* (one-stringed
guitar) floated up. I saw the dotted heads of swimmers.

'Fond of swimming, Gjurata?'

'Yes. All young Albanians are fond of sports. At my home in
Himarë I swim very often in the sea. Now I will show you the
polyclinic and afterwards the library.'

Under the fortress wall the path forked, one branch to the town,
the other zig-zagging down to the meeting of waters.

'Look, they're sunbathing. Sensible, isn't it, on a hot day like this,
to be beside that cool, fresh river?'

'Vijosë is a beautiful river. In Tepëlenë they say it is an emerald
necklace clasped about the throat of the city.'

'Aren't they enjoying themselves? You can hear the shouting and
splashing from here.'

'Albanians are very gay and good-humoured people. But we
must . . .'

'Gjurata, that polyclinic can wait until the sun goes down. Right
now I'd like to test the temperature of the water.'

'No, it's not possible. I have to pick up my baby. What we can
do, I will tell you. I will take you to see my church.'

The church protruded from the cliff like half a stone beehive, roughly put together with limestone rocks and pebble-dashing – reminiscent of the votive chapels of the Greek islands, which skippers build in fulfilment of pledges made at the height of the storm. Inside, a rocky floor, an altar cut from rock and a picture of a Raphael Madonna and Child torn from a magazine. Gjurata dabbled her fingers in holy water and lit a candle. I stared round the dismal little cavern, hardly knowing what to say.

'Is there a priest for this church?'

'Yes, he comes from Himarë, my own village. He comes once a month to hear confessions and say mass. He was a friend of my father, he studied in the seminary for Albanian priests in Calabria. He's old, he won't be with us much longer. He's very good, a peaceful, earnest man. He baptised my baby.'

'You are married?'

'Divorced. At present I live *en fille*, I would like to be married again . . . My marriage was rather unhappy. I was too young, I made many mistakes, but I have recognised them and . . .' Gjurata caught herself before she slipped into the self-critical groove and giggled. 'Anyhow, I would like to marry again.'

No problem there, I suggested, for one so trim and neat and friendly. 'Is it difficult, divorce?'

'Formerly it would have been impossible. My religion forbade it, the social conditions were against it. Now it is simple. You make up your minds to part, you write a letter to the ministry in Tirana, after a time your letter is accepted and you leave each other. The State decides the baby's position. No, divorce is common in Albania today, it is recognised as an element in woman's march to equality. About one marriage in ten, I believe, ends in divorce.'

'And no stigma attaches to the woman?'

'Not any more. Rather the opposite. Nearly all divorced girls marry again. Well, there are some remote areas where it would be impossible, so high a price is set on virginity still. But as a rule even unmarried girls with one or two children are not disdained by young men.'

She set her candle under the picture, genuflected and said : 'Now we must go.' After the coolness and stillness of the chapel, Tepëlenë's streets burned through the shoe-leather and the cicadas were deafening. We stepped aside at the polyclinic door to let a pregnant girl pass. She was flushed and smiling and she talked rapidly to the small boy whose hand she held.

The grey mountain bus came in. A peasant in a white skullcap got out and the driver went round his vehicle, examining tyres. Four young men in shirt-sleeves and denim trousers lurched out of the Hunter's bar (so called from the stuffed stork which dangled from a nail over the chess-table). One of them plucked a rose from the flower-basket at the bus-stop, said good-evening and walked off, passing the flower in front of his pugilist's nose, inhaling the perfume. The bus pulled away and for a long time you could hear its growl and gear-change on the rough road to Berat. The street was empty, the banners of socialism flapped in the first breath of a breeze.

Tepëlenë, strongpoint of the southern mountains, fortified against a guerilla strategy, was dead, static and petrified, like the gorges and the precipice rocks it commanded. Gjurata shook hands.

'You need not tell the mayor where we have been,' she said.

7

Military Intelligence

'Bury me in Gjirokastër, where the clay is like honey,' recited Razu, twenty-one, the youngest town councillor in Albania. 'Gjirokastër· is a stony place, I hope I never go there,' the Bear countered.

The evening promenade was in full swing, the perambulating marriage mart and central gossip exchange of the lively old northern Epirot capital. In front, the pink stepped wynds and Prussian blue roofs reached up in an undignified scramble to be first on the acropolis. Far above, the ram-bowed battleship of the citadel had been turned to stone in the act of riding off the stormy sea of the *malessia* (mountainland) and plunging to the valley floor. Away to the left stood the birthplace of Enver Hoxha, not shown to the public. 'We are building him a new one,' Razu said. (We have, however, seen his rifle, his campaign boots, his school reports – full marks for everything – and an order for his arrest signed by one of Zog's ministers.) Immediately above us the bare twigs of a sycamore were spread, a national monument sacred to the memory of two partisan girls hanged from its branches in 1944 by – the plaque says – 'Fascist beasts and National Front traitors.' The song they sang before they died has become a regional anthem.

The land is the Mali Gjerë, which covers Albania's hinterland south of Vlorë, the last big city. Gjirokastër straggles over the edge of it. From the garden suburb in the valley to the topmost *kulla* of the town takes three hours for a man on a donkey, three and a half for a woman with a basket on her head.

By general agreement this is Albania's music metropolis. Two men from Gjirokastër make a choir. Razu said one heard the proverb illustrated when travelling to Vlorë on the bus. 'One youth at the back will start his song, making it up as he goes along. Two or three join in as the journey progresses. As passengers get in and out, the musicians converge in a group at the rear. Someone with lute or clarinet comes aboard. The song continues, *ex tempore*, for the whole trip, which takes five hours.'

'What do they sing about?'

'Formerly the epic songs of the people, their struggles against the Turk, the deeds of Ali Pasha of Tepëlenë. Nowadays they sing of the patriotic war, the battles of this region and those who fell. There are peaceful songs too, about the football teams and the contests between co-operatives to produce more wheat and tobacco.'

An unaccompanied caterwauling tenor voice died away in a burst of laughter. 'He is parodying a Greek song.'

Choral tunes, gypsy rhythms, clarinet and mandoline obbligatos . . . 'What are they singing now?'

'It's an improvised song, I can't make out . . . Yes, they are addressing the heroes of Vicu, they sing : "We keep up the work where you have left it, with courage unbent." '

The chanting went on in Gjirokastër until the street-lamps dimmed and the last promenaders vanished into dark doorways and a policeman marched down the esplanade, rapping on the shutters of houses. He rapped Razu's shoulder-blades and gave us the same good-night : 'Comrade citizens, go to your beds. Do not disturb your neighbours.'

Razu discovered he had business in Sarandë, and we took him there. 'I'm staying about three days, how about you?'

Not so long, he said. He was to attend a meeting of the League of Mothers. He was to lead the discussion on the origin of classes, with special reference to Engels's *Origins of the Family*.

'You are very young for such important work.'

'Yes. I shall also interview some people, I am one who helps decide the renewal of Democratic Front membership cards.'

'Your parents must be proud of their son.'

'They are both dead.'

'In the war? No, of course not, you're too young.'

'In the earthquake.'

I remembered that earthquake. Greece, Yugoslavia and the west promptly offered help. Albania declined it.

In the Mali Gjerë many small earthquakes must go unnoticed, the land is so desolate and so chopped and twisted in its general character. A rough passage in winter (this was February), and the journey to the coast, about fifteen miles as the eagle flies, is nearly fifty as the Varshava crawls and slithers. I remembered coming that way with Poxi in summer, arriving in overcoats of limestone dust. 'In winter, a different story.'

The Bear said he never saw Poxi these days. He was in China,

I told him, learning the language. I had his address : Flat 959, Block 1077, University of Peking, or something like that.

Sarandë marks the southern limit of Bregdeti, "the coast", the Red riviera. It is indeed *the* coast and I would nominate it for the title of most beautiful sixty miles of Mediterranean shore. That it is also the least developed goes without saying. Cruise passengers in the Adriatic see this shoreline through binoculars, but they don't see the half of it – not the frying-pan-shaped inlets, the lake-isles of Porto Palermo, the turquoise gulfs near Dhërmi and Borsh, the rivers of olives and avalanches of orange and mandarin bushes which flow down from the heights of Llogora . . . a littoral made for tourism, a littoral where hardly a tourist has ventured if you except the young Albanians who caper in the sea in the vicinity of a State holiday home.

In winter Bregdeti is mild and sunny. Up above, at 5000 feet, the *malessia* has storm-cones hoisted and the gales blow snow off the ridge. Down below, they are tying up the young shoots of the bananas. At the beginning of February the golden thistledown of mimosa drifts on the sands and two weeks later the plum and almond are in full bloom.

Sarandë is a modern town, not exciting architecturally, but every year a few more citrus groves soften its outlines. Above its shallow amphitheatre the hillside is harsh, destroyed by summer drought. The Italians acknowledged the beauty of Sarandë's situation when they occupied the bay in 1939 and re-christened it Porto Edda, after Mussolini's daughter, the countess Ciano. Its name-changes through the ages are bewildering. Originally it was Onchesmos, then Santi Quaranta – 'Forty Saints,' Razu says, 'from the forty hermits who dwelt there, each in his separate cell.'

'Not the forty Roman legionaries who suffered martyrdom, up to their necks in freezing water, for adopting Christianity?'

'No.'

Arrangements had been made for a visit to Butrinto, last stop on the north-south Albanian pilgrimage. This is ancient Buthrotum, a classical site serenely unconscious of the passage of centuries, on the fringe of a shallow lake with a tiny sea channel . . . a two-mile walk across the mountain from the Greek frontier, a two-mile swim from the Greek island of Corfu. Like Aeneas (*Aeneid* Book III, lines 293-4) we were to tilt the salt wave of the Epirus shore and go up the channel in a boat, but unlike Aeneas we had to wait for a written paper.

Endorsed by several officials, civil and military, it had gone up
to the commander of the garrison for final stamping. The boat
stood by, a piratical skipper with exuberant moustachioes at the
helm, but the sentry on Sarandë's low curving jetty refused to let
us pass. Natives with nothing better to do stood and watched us.
Their winter dress reflected that of the southern mountains : snow-
white caps, the shaggy *maquis* of a goatskin capote. A two-man
trawler clattered in, a lantern on a fishing rod hung over its stern.
Children and an unemployed naval rating drew up the net and dis-
entangled a large squid. No sign of the written paper.

The Bear kept watch and Razu and I adjourned to the once-
elegant Epirus Palace hotel, now the beer-hall Leningrad. A roving
reporter from the newspaper *Bashkimi* joined us and asked if we
would like to see a maternity hospital. I said I had seen one.

'Which one was that?'

'Hospital No 2 at Berat, called J. V. Stalin.'

'I know it. There have been some troubles there. You know the
director?'

'I've met him.'

'It started with the trades union. The nurses denounced their
organiser. He neglected his duties and showed an attitude of irres-
ponsibility. The workers' control unit of Berat was called in to
investigate. It has found the allegations true, and the trades union
organiser, along with the director and his deputy, has been dismissed.'

A workers' control unit, Razu said, was made up of union members from the industries round about. It had power to deal with
inefficient management. The proletariat gave the orders and made
the decisions. Nurses were the proletariat of the health service, as
children were the proletariat of the education system . . . At this
point the Bear appeared, waving the written paper.

Two written papers, in fact, delivered by two separate couriers
on motor-bikes. The sentry waved us through with a grin, the little
petrol-driven motor-boat got under way with a cough and its
disproportionate red flag with black eagle emblem trailed in its
wake. The soldier raced down to the jetty with his rifle held aloft
and the skipper turned back. The written papers, it seemed, were
not worth the paper they were written on.

A Russian-made jeep from the old wartime Zyl factory rolled
on to the jetty. Four more soldiers got out. Salutations all round.
'The colonel wishes to speak to you.'

The colonel was handsomely got up in a blue tunic and dark blue cavalry breeches piped with red, a red peaked cap and silver stars. His fault entirely, he said in French. Many apologies for the delay. *Bon voyage.* He stood at the salute until our boat had turned the corner of the harbour.

Our skipper, a naval reservist, told us about his voyage to China in an Albanian merchant ship. Longshoremen are still reminiscing about that historic adventure. Very occasionally you see the Albanian merchant flag in the Piraeus or at Brindisi, but it was never seen on the Yangtse until 1968.

The Navy, he declared, was run down. The Army controlled everything. The fleet, twenty-two minesweepers and patrol craft, was a force of second-hand vessels acquired from Yugoslavia and the Soviet Union in friendlier days. (I saw some of the little craft, *Semani, Drin, Vijosë* and others – they are all named for rivers – in the stream which connects Lake Shkodër with the sea. They were as good as landlocked, because Yugoslavia owns the mouth of that stream.)

No replacements were foreseen, the skipper said. It was true that Mao Tse-Tung had promised First Secretary Hoxha a yacht, but nothing had come of that. The Popular Republic herself had not the architects or engineers for ship-building. The scandal raised by the Admiral Seyko affair had brought naval morale low. (Teme Seyko, head of the Navy, was tried and shot with eleven others for their part in a conspiracy with "imperialistic Americans, monarcho-fascist Greeks and revisionist Yugoslavians". The story of the trial, *The Plot to Liquidate the Popular Republic*, was one of Albania's best-selling paperbacks in 1965, and has been translated into French.)

About once a year the skipper was called to the colours for a naval exercise. 'I joined the South Squadron. We towed targets for aircraft to shoot at, we had a mock battle and then we joined forces to repel invaders off Cape Rodonit, near Durrës.'

'Who were the enemy?'

He looked surprised. 'The American Sixth Fleet, naturally.'

Notices in the Sarandë hotel corridor forbade the introduction of caged birds and transistor radios, but a large old-fashioned radio stood under the window, and I got the B.B.C. morning news without much difficulty. It was mild even for this coast, and I pushed through the bougainvillaea below the terrace and went in for a

swim. The other early-morning swimmer was a brown fleshy man
in a bathing-cap and see-through underpants. I recognised him. He
was the major. He lived in the hotel and went away every day in
a khaki bus for manoeuvres in the hills. We had chatted about military matters and he was ready to chat again. Of Albania's new army
he had no great opinion. The war-of-liberation spirit had faded.
'And the airmen run everything nowadays.'

I had heard firing in the hills, and seen some ex-Russian Army
anti-aircraft guns, eighty-millimetre or thereabouts, similar to those
which line the hills along the Yugoslav frontier outside Shkodër.
'Who are the enemy?'

'*Les Grecques, naturellement.*'

He clambered ashore and rummaged in the bougainvillaea for his
clothes. You can identify an Albanian's rank by the smartness of his
uniform. The colonel was immaculate; this major a carbon copy,
gone shabby. The sergeant who came to call for him wore a sweat-
stained blouse and wrinkled trousers, patched behind. With the
lower ranks it seemed a point of honour to look like a battle-weary
partisan.

The People's Army, 70,000 strong (out of a population of two
millions), was born of Soviet disciplines and materials during the
patriotic armed struggle. Britain and America backed the wrong
sort of partisans, as they did in Yugoslavia, and have been abused
for it ever since. Key posts in today's army are held by the heroes
of those campaigns and Enver Hoxha still stands at their head. The
war is kept in front of the people with street banners, museums and
monuments, days of celebration and press articles. The artistic event
of 1967 was the unveiling of the painting of the year, entitled *The
First Division of the National Liberation Army of Albania on its
March to Liberate Northern Albania during the Campaign of
Winter 1944.* The fiction shelves of bookshops and libraries are
loaded with war stories : *Partisan Vision, Before Execution, Partisan
Dawn, O The Partisan Bonfire, A Song for Partisan Benko.* The
best-seller in the juvenile section is called *They Pulled Our Roof
Away* – stories of suffering children in occupied Albania.

The infantryman, holding his rifle high, figures on matchboxes,
postage stamps and banknotes. Names of the heroic dead live on in
the names of football teams, factories and State farms. In the
expanding suburbs of Tirana, streets are still being called after
battles, dates and deeds.

Albanian youth organisations, from Pioneers upward, have elementary military training, and everyone, boy or girl, has to put in a year or two years of national service, depending on the careers they have chosen. Idlers, the major said (the Popular Republic has its share), are drafted into the army and after three months they are released if they want to take a job. 'If not, they stay. That is the material our army is composed of. It's not satisfactory. Don't put that in your newspaper,' he added to the *Bashkimi* journalist who had strolled up to smoke a cigarette with us.

The journalist had done his national service. 'A good time for you?' – 'A waste of time for me.'

He had trained for one month and then gone road-building. 'I was a rifleman, but they never gave me a rifle.'

He joined the Shock Battalion which planted two thousand olive trees in a single night on the bare shoulder of Mount Dajti above Tirana – an achievement celebrated like a famous victory. He went out with the Harvest shock troops, gathering wheat and soft fruit. He helped to guard a searchlight post on Cape Rodonit and the approaches to the Karl Marx hydro-electric station in the Mati gorges. Although Albania has so many young men and women under arms, there is no shortage of work for them. They are loaned to State farms, they patrol all those road intersections and river crossings and if you happen across a small team of painters or glaziers working in an empty building you will usually find a soldier with a rifle standing by.

Military exercises, according to the major, were hampered by a shortage of ammunition – 'which can never be overcome because we are still using the weapons the Soviet Union gave us.' Communications, on the other hand, were excellent, the very latest radio and electronic equipment. Chinese?

'*Naturellement.*'

'Come and see the manoeuvres,' he offered, 'come and see how we play the war game.' Was it not forbidden? (How would Aldershot react if a mysterious Albanian were to present himself as a spectator of exercises?) The journalist was inclined to accept, I was doubtful, having a timetable of my own. The issue was settled when an emergency hit the South Battalion. The khaki trucks darted in and out of Sarandë, picking up stray soldiers, the major hardly had time to say good-bye.

I visualised the Greeks pouring across the frontier. Or was it another plot to liquidate the Republic? Neither. The Defence

Ministry had ordered the troops to inscribe XXV (for twenty-five years of People's Power) on the mountain face, in trenches five hundred metres long – the kind of activity they are well accustomed to, for carving slogans is an important part of a soldier's life.

We followed them a short distance along the Vlorë road, and it occurred to me that the reason foreign observers find it so hard to bring military intelligence out of Albania is probably tha⁺ Albania has no secrets worth knowing.

8

Reds under the Seabed

The English version of an old French motoring handbook, listing the dozen or so trickiest roads in Europe, says of the Sarandë-Vlorë corniche : "The slope is very strong and prudence is obligatory." Edward Lear passed along it in 1849 and "knew what a fly felt, crawling on the ceiling". Statistically the gradients are not impressive – an ascent of four thousand feet in seven miles is tough but not unique – but you have to take into consideration the shifting gravel of the surface, the hairpin bends too tight to swallow in one bite, the fallen boulders on the carriageway. People's Power is improving the road by inches – there are plank bridges over the torrents, you no longer need carry planks on your car roof for fording them – but of the sixty-mile *route du ciel* maybe forty miles are of Edward Lear vintage.

Villages are few and primitive, their names basic. Vuno, the hill. Himarë, the ravines. Dhërmi, the oaks. Grykë, the gorges.

> *Grykë gorges, the red gorges,*
> *Thirteen hundred peasants stand firm-footed*

– we heard the children singing it through the schoolhouse window. This was war-of-liberation country, men of Vuno performed historic deeds and now this village of perhaps a thousand people supplies two members to Albania's eleven-man Politburo.

For Himarë you descend on the Red riviera and come to rest against fishermen's bleached timber cottages on a *lungomare* of dusty palmettoes. Himarë people stem from a wandering tribe, forced on this coast by hunger. Like the Devon men of England, they set up a seafaring tradition. Two hundred years ago mariners of Himarë volunteered, or were pressed, for the Tsar's navy and some of them died at Tsushima. Not to be outdone, men of Vuno formed the amphibious wing of the Royal Macedonian Regiment of the Kings of Naples.

A doctor I met in the waterfront pub at Himarë said the régime had had trouble with sailors of that place. Thirty-four had escaped to the Greek island of Merlera, only fifteen miles away. By swimming, he said. About half of them had returned.

'What happened to them?'

'Nothing. They came back under amnesty. They're forgiven. Others refused to co-operate and they had to be reformed, but that's over too, they've taken their places in the community again. They've paid, and no one holds it against them now. Those two who went out as you came in, the two with the leather tobacco pouches, they belonged to the revolutionary junta.'

Edward Lear, I recalled, noted down Himarë as a suspicious, secret-society kind of place. So I jumped and spilled my brandy when someone tapped me on the shoulder. It was *Bashkimi*'s journalist. He turned up everywhere, and I wondered if I would find him in the next seat when I flew back to Italy.

No lunch at Dhërmi, the workers' rest-camp. The place was closed and the director said it would remain so until a coachload of city factory-hands had been dealt with for stealing fruit from neighbouring plantations.

We got a snack at Borsh, a village wiped out during the war and painstakingly rebuilt exactly as the inhabitants wanted it, with an icy torrent flowing down the main street. What must it be like in March and April, the season of melting snows? The torrent splashes against a plaque which tells us that Borsh, of all population centres of Albania, has the highest percentage qualified in the learned professions.

Down to the bananas, up to the pines, round the skirts of impenetrable massifs . . . a long descent through rhododendrons . . . and in front, still a great way off, was one of the Mediterranean's great panoramic views : the bay of Vlorë, the long nose of Karaburun, the clear line of demarcation in the sea, turquoise for the Ionian and sapphire for the Adriatic.

I constructed all the usual theories to account for the continued presence of *Bashkimi*'s man. If an *agent provocateur*, he was not all that subtle. I began to realise that in eastern Europe there are a great many bored people, and they attach themselves to foreigners to relieve the monotony of their lives. Hence, perhaps, the common complaint of holidaymakers : 'We were followed everywhere by the secret police.'

The Bear said this reporter came only for the ride, he had seen a Government car and knew it was his best bet for a trip to Tirana. But at Vlorë he teamed up with a press photographer and left us. Before doing so, he interviewed me formally and I was to be astonished, months later, to come across an English-language magazine, published in Tirana but translated and printed in Peking, with my remarks in it. They were unrecognisable.

Not having him with me, and assuming that Vlorë had only one hotel, I went to the wrong one. My host, regional Party secretary, was gracious about it. He sat waiting alone, with oriental fatalism.

He was Lazar Isaj, an ascetic, poised and quiet-spoken person – as were practically all the ministers and secretaries of the political wing whom I met in Albania. The spy-writer's photo-fit of such personalities seemed to me to be wildly wrong.

Isaj dropped his wallet and an identity card fell out. With permission, I studied it. Next to the name came an important classification : social origin. It is class distinction upside down. "Aristocrat" is a description so shameful that few are left, and they are the smart ones who saw People's Power coming and hastened to present the provisional Government with their estates, so that they have remained as managers, occupying a tiny corner of the *palazzo* they once owned and having perhaps thirty workers as lodgers.

"Bourgeois" is not much better. "Rich peasant" is acceptable. "Poor peasant" is best of all.

Isaj was "poor peasant", *fils du peuple.* 'From the very dregs of the people,' he said proudly. 'At sixteen I fought with the liberation army, then I went to train as an economist. We all went to Moscow in those days. When I returned I was appointed director of the Vlorë cement factory. My two brothers are economists, my four sisters are teachers.'

'Your family is doing its bit for New Albania.'

'I'm proud of our progressive record. My ancestors are distinguished too. My grandmother died in a concentration camp. My mother was executed here in Vlorë, by the Italians. I can show you the spot.'

The meal was typical of the cosmopolitan Albanian cuisine : garlic soup, sea trout, salami, shish qebab, apricots and ice-cream; with *raki* and the white wine of Narta, as served to Lucullus.

'I'm cement factory director, I become mayor of Vlorë, president of city council, secretary of Party. I control the city, 45,000 people, fourth city of Albania after Tirana, Durrës and Shkodër, and seventy-six small towns and villages, including the bitumen belt at Selenice.'

(Vlorë and its bay remind me of Naples, and in the burning fields of Selenice, a curiosity of Roman times, they have a little Vesuvius.)

We admired his new car, a Skoda from Czechoslovakia. Obligatory curtains, a granite chauffeur. 'Come for a ride.' Game birds flew out of thickets and hares bolted up the lane in front of the headlamps as we made for the Balcony of Vlorë, the scimitar-ridge which overlooks the bay. A full moon shone on the city, on the cement factory, on the twin humps of Sazan, which are held like two walnuts in the pincer arms of the promontories.

'Why do you call that island Red Gibraltar?'

'We don't. That was the name western reporters gave to Sazan. It was thought that the Russians would establish a submarine base there. A Russian submarine squadron was in this bay at the time of our break with Khrushchev and his clique, you know. Our ambassador left Moscow and the same day it was my duty to order the Russian admiral to take his submarines away.'

A caïque left Vlorë harbour, towing a string of fishing boats. A small tanker followed them out, from the suburb of Uji Ftotë where the pipeline from Stalin City comes down to the coast. 'The waterboat. Sazan is waterless. No, not really inhabited. A lighthousekeeper, a couple of fishermen's families. You can see the submarine pens the Italians built, the repair shops in the caverns. They're deserted now.'

Isaj's was the crucial decision in that crisis of 1956, and the events which were to keep Albania independent or send her the way of Hungary pivoted on Sazan. It was the key to the Adriatic. Franz Josef coveted the island in the last century, Mussolini in this. In the submarine era, whoever held Sazan controlled the straits of Otranto . . . but Khrushchev, like Napoleon and Hitler, was no sailor. The Soviet squadron waited twenty-four hours and then, having received no reply to a signal to the commander-in-chief in Leningrad, sailed away.

Under the Balcony the city put on a dazzling display of streetlighting and the music of Scheherazade floated up from the openair cinema. This week : *La Dernière Voyage de Sindbad*.

Vlorë is the revolutionary capital, the *ville héroique*. The People's Hero medal, gold with a black and red ribbon, posthumously awarded to the patriot Ismail Qemal, hangs in the dockyard museum. It was he who raised the flag of Skanderbeg on the window-ledge of a waterfront cottage in 1912, announcing that Albania, watchdog of the Ottoman Empire, had at last turned on its ailing master.

'Old times, another scene,' Isaj said. 'You can't imagine it. I was brought up here. It was a decaying town. One small power station gave light to the city centre, the rest was dark. In our house we were lucky, we had the electric light put in, but it failed every night and we had to keep candles handy. I'm speaking of 1938, you understand. There was no road from the town to the harbour then, only a muddy track through fields. Now we have the Avenue of Roses, a four-lane boulevard.

'At the port in those days three caïques were a crowd. Now we can take tankers of 5000 tons and they pick up oil from Stalin City through a pipe sixty miles long. Formerly the chief occupations were begging and stealing. Now we have to import labour. This is my problem : we're always short of workers, especially women. Yes, all the managers will tell you they prefer women, they work harder and need less supervision.'

As in all the bigger towns, Vlorë's hotels had their clientèle of Chinese technicians and Isaj spoke of Sino-Albanian economic relations.

Since China replaced Russia as protector, Soviet propaganda has made out that China is a grudging benefactor, that she has secured Albanian allegiance cheaply. For five years after 1956, China's aid was limited to the loan of machinery and maintenance services in the power, mining and so-called heavy industries (which are light by western standards).

The third large hydro-electric station (22,500 kw.) in the southern mountains was financed and equipped by China. So was the fourth, Bistrica No. 2 (5000 kw.), opened in September 1966, by which the national grid was extended over half of the country. The fifth and sixth, on the North Drin above Shkodër (500,000 kw.), are chiefly Albanian. Chinese radio electricians built and for a time staffed the latest radio station outside Tirana, which started transmitting in November 1966. Both short and medium wave transmitters have now been handed over to Albanians.

Few industrial areas are without a population of Chinese. They have settled down well, from my brief observations, their conduct is exemplary at work and play, but the natives are not enthused about them. 'They're not like us, they're ugly, they have disgusting habits' - such are the common criticisms. What sort of habits? 'Picking their noses, things that offend us,' you are told.

At Shkodër, in the large and successful copper-wire factory, where three thousand girls are undergoing instruction in complex Chinese machinery, the immigrant charge-hands joked with us and had to have their pictures taken.

China has had a hand in nearly all the new export industries – chrome, nickel, copper, petroleum, fruit and fish canning. Young Chinese are always to be seen on Durrës beach, and occasionally on the rudimentary ski slopes of the northern Alps. There are Chinese students learning Albanian at Tirana University, Chinese writers and artists on tour in the highlands. The modern art exhibition we saw in Elbasan was brought from the Far East and was entitled "Rent Collection Courtyard". Acrobats and dance troupes from Peking often visit Tirana and the works of Mao Ce-Dun are found in the culture halls.

Hints of Tirana's debt to Peking are seen in the flocks of Peking ducks getting acclimatised on the State farms; the silkworm eggs recently hatched out in co-operatives in the Shkodër region, where a haphazard mulberry cultivation was practised for centuries; and the appearance on hill slopes of oriental bamboos and agaves, which are to supply the raw materials for basket and string industries.

Isaj says that credits from China account for about twenty-one per cent of Albania's national income. The biggest Chinese project on Albanian soil must be the Elbasan iron works, employing eight thousand men and women. A refinery, which according to Isaj's forecast will produce a million tons of petroleum annually, was established in 1971 at Cerrik in central Albania – designed in China, equipped from China, but built by Albanians and employing only Albanian staff. This division of responsibility for major works is to be the pattern of the future.

What does China receive in return? Raffia work, slippers, writing paper, cutlery, wicker bottles and briar pipes were the first six items on the list of exports. Isaj said it was wrong to imagine that Albania was a client state, however. 'I have read,' he said, 'that China is interested in an anti-Soviet naval base here in Vlorë bay. We couldn't permit that. Those who write and speak in such terms don't grasp the nature of our free and fraternal relationship with the People's Republic of China.'

With a slow road to travel, we had to make an early start from Vlorë. I went into the dockyard – no formalities – to climb to the balcony of the villa of independence and point the camera at Sazan. If the Reds were to move under that seabed, one would think they would have to clear the channel : a sunken merchant ship blocked it. On a mast, sticking out above the water, the port authority had hoisted the Albanian flag. She was a relic of the Second World War, she dated back to the time when Sazan was Sasseno and Vlorë Valona and an Italian invasion fleet swarmed into the . . . A police officer in white, who had climbed the balcony after me, put his hand in front of the camera. 'You will get better pictures from here,' he said, indicating another spot.

At that hour, workers on foot and bicycle filled the streets. The market-place, frescoed with libellous anti-American, anti-war cartoons, was a composition in moods ancient and modern. On one side the grey buses loaded for the cement factory and the fish cannery; on the other, veiled women filled water-jugs and crop-headed boys watered their mules. Mine was the only car on the move in that bustling scene, until I turned into the Avenue of Roses and there, beside the polished Skoda, stood Lazar Isaj and a town council deputation, bearing floral tributes.

It was his practice, Isaj said, agreeable to the *kanun* of his forebears, the Moslem population, to accompany his guests for an hour on their road. Could official courtesy go farther? Yes, it could. 'It occurred to me that you might wish to drive my new car,' he said, and with an ill grace the chauffeur moved over.

On a high point above the bay, where the tarred road ended, Isaj and his adjutants said their farewells, embellishing them with Islamic formulae of which I grasped only the word *inshallah*. We stood on a plank across a ravine. Hundreds of feet down, Vlorë bay, vacuumed by the morning breeze and burnished by the sun, stretched away to the humps of Sazan, a waterlogged camel. A memorial plaque on that spot told how Vasil Laci in 1940 did not quite assassinate Vittore Emmanuele of Italy, when the King-Emperor came on a visit to Tirana. One might have made a better job of five leading communists that morning, merely by kicking away a plank.

Would the time come when Albania would raise a monument to the hero who did that? The chances, it seemed, were against it.

9

Pillar of Heaven

'From London?'

'From Albania.'

The tanker drivers at the roadhouse open their eyes a trifle. Visitors from the west are not uncommon, but a visitor from Albania does not pull up for petrol every day. Among these Romanians a little jocularity is in order at the expense of the Marxist drop-out, the disinherited child of the eastern bloc. 'Where the television announcer, when he closes down, says "Good night, Mr President" – isn't that so?' Seeing me slow to catch on, the tanker driver explains. It means that in Albania only one man has a television set.

The Romanian haulage men, dark, burly, self-assured, at least one of them wearing a U.S. Army surplus combat jacket, speak a language you feel you might understand if only they would speak more slowly and separate the words out. You are told that anyone who knows Italian, especially if he has a smattering of the Genoese dialect, can get on quite well in Romania. So far, this hasn't been my experience. So far, however, our contacts have been more than ready to have a shot at other languages, even English. The Romanians, as they themselves keep telling us, are gifted with tongues. They also have, like the Italians, a brilliant repertoire of gesticulation.

'And where are you from?'

'We are Roman,' the tanker driver says.

If you lined up random types from the nations of eastern Europe and tried to identify them, you would probably spot the Romanian first of all. He holds himself differently, he has the Mediterranean colouring, he looks a bit of a devil for the women, he is more likely to start asking you questions . . . he is Roman, he lets you know, not Balkan, not by any stretch of the imagination Slav. The grand waterway of the Danube on one side and the iron shield of the Carpathians on the other keep him intact from other breeds of European.

A very modern nation, but a very ancient country. Round Hunedoara they have uncovered finger-bones and carbon-dated them to
the infancy of mankind. It is argued by some that the Danube
marshes, not the Nile or the Yangtse basins, were the cradle of the
human race. Romanians are inclined to go along with that
theory.

Romania's rich black earth (how rich was not suspected until
the world discovered more uses for oil than lighting peasant lamps
and helping along bonfires of maize stubble) was exploited, squabbled over and settled by wandering tribes from distant ages –
Tartars and Scythian Huns, Vandals and Goths, the Magyar, Avar
and Slavonic peoples. In the physiognomy you see the features of
Dravidian shepherds and Mongol warriors reflected, and sometimes
the long nose of the Greek and the black brow of the Celt, from
the Iron Age folk who mingled with them. At an early date the
gypsies must have moved in. Although their numbers have been
reduced, Romania still has the largest Romany population of any
European country.

A strong influence was Latin. This country included Dacia, an
outpost of Rome, a redoubt in the northern wall of the Empire.
Some say that Rome forgot to bring her soldiers home when she
withdrew them from all the other colonies. Some say Rome didn't
want them, that Dacia was a garrison made up of shirkers and
troublemakers. If so, first impressions are that the lost legions did
not entirely die out.

The Latin *-iscus* is the Romanian *-escu*. Old-time travellers were
amused to hear the Romanian peasant address his oxen as Caesar,
Cassius and Brutus – and to learn that he had no idea where those
dignified names came from. (I tried this on some tractor drivers at
a depot and found one man who admitted that his pet name for his
vehicle was Hercules.) Country people used, and still use, "By
Father Trajan" for an oath. The Roman emphasis was marked in
the twentieth century when Boy Scouts were organised in cohorts,
not troops, and the Iron Guardsmen of the thirties called themselves
legionaries.

Latin town names abound: Caracal, Constanza . . . and the
place we are heading for, Turnu Severin, a port on the Danube, the
port of Severus. According to legend, Septimus Severus launched
a rescue operation there for the Dacian garrison, but the garrison
would not co-operate.

Our route is a roundabout one, part motorway from Bucharest

and part winding cross-country road, over the lower spurs of the Carpathians and through the glens of Oltul, in order to call en route at Tirgu Jiu. From behind the steering wheel, Romania looks a vast chunk of the European land-mass – as any country in Europe is bound to do, I suppose, when you have come from Albania. A continental spaciousness unknown to Britain surrounds you. The hills look capable of going on for ever, the density of the pine forest raises the question : in a land so packed with trees, where shall we find the population? Before this, it was a dismal journey. First sight of Romania, unless you have come over the mountains from Hungary, is bound to be depressing, the more so because neighbouring lands are delightful in their rustic serenity. The black Danube fens, the scent of petroleum, the plain cottages not improved by having corrugated iron roofs on them, the general air of when-it-falls-down-prop-it-up and weeding-is-a-waste-of-time . . . the first fifty miles present Romania as a land of lackadaisical living, entirely surrounded by oil wells.

Stray from the motorway, part of the projected trans-Romanian highway from the Hungarian frontier to the Black Sea, and you hit rough roads. Villages tend to be strung out along them. Rural planning, two parallel lines of cottages on a road, islanded in mud, turned out very useful for the Turkish invaders long ago. They could seal up both ends and massacre the inhabitants in their own time. King Carol I did the same during the peasants' revolts, barricading road exits and bringing up his new Krupp cannon to rake them from end to end.

"Few populations," says the French historian La Vallée,[1] "were more ill-treated, more trodden down, more tortured; their history is but one long recital of martyrdom . . . we wonder that any inhabitants, any trace of cultivated land, remain."

After Roman times the three provinces which make up the modern nation – Moldavia, Wallachia and Transylvania – continued socially on the Roman pattern, patricians and plebeians in the towns, farmers and slaves in the country. The two-hundred-year war with Turkey threw up the native warrior princes or highland freebooters, some heroic, some notorious, all mercenary. Michael the Brave, John the Terrible, Vlad the Impaler . . . they are revered today as champions of liberty. A confused exercise in modern myth-making connects Vlad the Impaler with the fictional

[1] Quoted by Mrs M. A. Walker, *Untrodden Paths in Romania* (Chapman & Hall, 1888).

Dracula, though they would have been on opposite ends, one would have thought, of the stake in the heart. The Romanians had never heard of Dracula until the BBC started investigating him.

All fought losing battles, and Turkey held Romania in an iron grip, ruling it through Phanariots – Islamic Greeks who took their name from the Phanar suburb of Constantinople. Phanariot names are still to be found in the Bucharest telephone directory, but not as many nowadays as you would find in the directories of New York and Paris. They were cordially despised by the *ancienne noblesse*, the boyars, whose medieval names such as Ghika, Bibescu, Cantacuzeni and Mavrocordati likewise survive in the international capitals. Hélène Vacarescu,[2] a lady of the nineteenth-century court, writes of the Phanariots' "deplorable defects and useless qualities . . . they boasted descent from Byzantium, even Byzantine emperors, but this has never been proved".

We are travelling through the greenwood. Apple orchards and pine trees; torrents descending in flights of steps from the Carpathians; the distant prospect of a monastery, Arnota or Hurezu, feudal piles made up of stark horizontal lines and square pyramidical bell-towers . . . but it is the countryfolk and the modest country places which take the fancy.

Both seem to grow out of the forest. Old men resemble gnarled trees, young girls put you in mind of hamadryads. One of the signs that you are leaving the hard-headed farmers behind and coming to the fey foresters is the row of white flowers round the hem of a woman's black skirt.

Many a village on the road is a little folk museum of gingerbread scrolls, flowered lintels, ribbed and leaf-patterned shutters and balustrades. A lot of this peasant art is roofed with corrugated iron.

In the glens sunshine is not so glaring, and perhaps that is why the natural colours are bolder. The landscape takes its cue from the bright foliage of the cottages and the costumes, in which greens, primroses and russets predominate. A feature most Romanians have in common is a passion for colour, and the tanker drivers tell a story of Mr Ceausescu placing a large order for harvesting machinery with a British firm, specifying only that the vehicles came in crimson, yellow or sky-blue. The British said he could have any colour he liked as long as it was grey, and the deal fell through.

[2] Hélène Vacarescu, 'Life in Romania' (*Contemporary Review*, November 1901 and April 1902).

Passing by, you connect some of these cottages with those of Derbyshire villages on well-dressing day. Stop, and you see that it is not done with flower-petals but with paint, garish and amateurish. ENTER WITH PLEASURE IF YOU ARE WELL DISPOSED, STAY OUT IF NOT seems to be the message round this arch. The sign-writing might have been done with a child's hand. If so, that child is a good age now, the date is 1810. The state of preservation is remarkable, in the forest a century is no time at all.

Through an interpreter I talk to a wood-carver, a forest giant into whose roots time has sunk a deep axe. His name is Gheorghe Borodi. He wears a cap made out of last Thursday's newspaper (the day he shaved) and with a chisel he is putting the finishing touches to a gatepost. What is the meaning of those symbols? He continues working, glancing up and down the pillar as though seeing his handiwork for the first time. After a while he speaks in a trembling, sing-song voice.

'When this oak came out of the trees he was cold and lonely. With my chisel I gave him a sun for warmth. Then I cut in a few flowers to remind him of the prime of his youth. Now I open his ribs a little, he wants to breathe . . . I would like this gatepost to have a long happy life. Give your gateposts ribs, my friend, and they will take a long time to grow old.'

When the chalet of 1810 was young, independence movements began to stir the peasants of Moldavia and Wallachia. (Transylvania had gone to Hungary, there was no such thing as Romania.) Even before they did so, the land was the slaughterhouse of Europe. Seven times the Russians came in to help get rid of the Turks, but with friends like the Russians no country had need of enemies. The liberators requisitioned unbelievable quantities of grain, flocks and herds and, having commandeered all the horses and oxen, set the peasants dragging carts for the military. While the Russians were in charge the princes – many an old family called itself princely – retired to Paris, and the customs they picked up there, and the educational arrangements they made for their children, helped give the future Bucharest the name of Paris of the East.

A three-way tug-of-war between Romania's neighbours – Russia, Turkey, Austria-Hungary – made bargaining counters of her provinces and throughout the nineteenth century Bessarabia (now part of the Soviet Union), the Bukovina (still Romanian), the Banat (claimed by Hungary and Yugoslavia) and the Dobrudja (most of it lost to Bulgaria) were often in the news.

Romania was no more than a geographical expression until after the Crimean War in 1856. Then the two provinces, Moldavia and Wallachia, demanded union but the protecting powers refused on the grounds that a combined population of twelve millions would upset the balance of power in eastern Europe. With the characteristic impudence of their race, the two assemblies got round that by electing the same man as ruling prince, and the western powers could do nothing about it. Colonel John Couza became lord of the United Principalities and Romania was born.

We have to make a detour to visit a Couza country house; it lies on one of the approach roads to the Danube. Now it is a State farm. Low, whitewashed, pink-roofed, throwing out wings and spare rooms at random, once set in orchards and now in a maize plantation, the house suggests something of the days of boyars, those haughty and benevolent noblemen with heavy beards and high turret-like caps, the patriarchal chieftains of rural districts with whom Bucharest dared not interfere.

"An hour after dawn," Miss Vacarescu wrote, "their halls and gardens would be filled with beggars, buffoons, students, tsiganes, priests and common people of all sorts, whose position in the boyar's retinue very much resembled that of the ancient Roman *clientèle*. They waited patiently, discussing their interests under the trees, helping themselves to fruit without fear of the boyar, whom they treated as lord and father; those who were more familiar with him thronging the bright corridors of the house while he washed his long silky beard and prayed before the iconostasis . . ."

The boyar heard complaints, gave advice, distributed money and finally settled down with his pipe – a signal that the audience was over. Everyone then went into the kitchens to have breakfast at his expense.

From that class Couza came. Traditionally the boyars were puritans, inexorably opposed to pleasure and relaxation, but Couza was the exception. The easy-going Romanians of the capital grew disgusted with his arrogance and immorality and when he took Marie Obrenovitch, daughter-in-law of the King of Serbia, to live with him the army decided it was time for a coup.

Half a dozen officers kicked open his bedroom door. Marie covered herself with a quilt, Couza pointed a revolver and the officers pointed theirs – at which Couza lowered his.

'What do you want?'

'We have brought Your Highness's abdication, will you sign it?'
Pause. 'I have neither pen nor ink.'
'We have thought of that,' said a colonel, producing them.
Pause. Couza got out of bed. 'There is no desk.'
'For once,' said the colonel, making a back (folklore seized on his words and gestures), 'I will offer myself.'

Couza's disgrace led the Romanian princes to formulate the principle that "the dynasty should remain apart" – the ruling prince must have no friends, entangle himself in no alliances, be a foreigner. They sought and found a Prussian volunteer. Karl-Eitel-Friedrich-Zephyrin-Ludwig von Sigmaringen-Hohenzollern, who became the first Prince of Romania, and then King Carol I, "by the Grace of God and the Will of the People." He ruled for forty-eight years.

(They were German chancellors who nudged Prussian cadets to the thrones of what are now the communist countries and overcame their reluctance with variations on a single cliché. To the Prince of Wied, prospective King of Albania : 'Go then, it will always have been an experience.' To Alexander of Battenburg, prospective King of Bulgaria : 'Accept, it will at all events be a pleasant recollection of your youth.' To Karl Hohenzollern : 'Go on, it will give you interesting memories of your youth.')

Here lies Tirgu Jiu, a garden town on a river and, like most garden towns, lacking something. A place for everything and everything in its place . . . but needing someone to breathe life into it. A few gang slogans on the blank wall of the furnitue factory would do for a start. Why do iron curtain towns appear lifeless? When we get to know them, we know they are not. We are conditioned to associate life with litter, advertisement hoardings, noisy children and traffic and without them we feel we have not yet reached civilisation.

On the road into town stands the tall epitome of all the rustic regional scrollwork : Brancusi's *Endless Column*, a ten-foot totem pole composed of rhomboid forms. It clambers skyward in imitation of a well-known peasant motif, the pillar of heaven, a design which may be said to link earthbound man to limitless space; a stanchion to support the vaults of the firmament is the way others see it. In scientific terms, according to what my guide reads out of his little red book, it is "a figure displaying a bilateral symmetry on four vertical and two horizontal planes".

Brancusi works, or copies, are scattered about the town – at the park entrance, his *Kissing Gate*; in the park, on the bank of the Jiu river, his *Table of Silence*, ten little egg-cup-shaped seats round a drum of concrete.

Tirgu Jiu was the home of archaic styles in woodworking and nearby, in 1876, Brancusi was born. (The guide pronounces him Brankoosh.) Tirgu Jiu, where he came to seek work, alone, aged nine, has his picture at the town hall. He is spare and thin-faced, with a sharp nose and wispy hair and beard; a home-rolled cigarette between his lips. Constantin Brancusi looks a typical peasant and so he was – born in a two-roomed cottage at Hobitsa, where the furnishings of every dwelling announced the folk tradition. He must have sat at a wooden drum of a table, rolled on a rug dyed blue, yellow, red or white, and stared at the stars, rosettes and animal carvings on the beam-ends, in the sort of room which is notable in that area today for its rich harmonious shapes and colours.

At seven he was a shepherd-boy, learning to carve flutes and staffs. At nine, in Tirgu Jiu, he was errand-boy, grocer's boy, ostler's boy at an inn. He took up carpentering and learned the rippling techniques of local carpenters, who could make rafters, wellheads and verandahs come alive with their chisels.

Forty years on Brancusi was a cult figure in Paris and New York, a name to be dropped around the art-and-theatre scene like those of James Joyce, Tallulah Bankhead, Nancy Cunard and Epstein. He remained a peasant. 'He is a born artisan,' Paul Morand said. 'He does everything for himself.' Strength and simplicity were his strong points. He almost always carved, rarely modelled. His *Bird*, the best-known sculpture since Rodin's *Thinker*, gave the pundits a month of field-days when Brancusi appealed against a claim for duty by the New York Customs – they classified it "piece of metal" instead of "work of art".

He died in 1957 and was buried in the Montparnasse cemetery.

What is Brancusi – draughtsman, architect, sculptor or what? Is he expressionist, surrealist, classicist, cubist or primitive? (He has been called all of them.) Is the inspiration Gothic or Far Eastern, Mediterranean or Byzantine? All of them and none of them, my guide says. Brancusi refuses to be pigeon-holed. You cannot pin him down, he represents the wayward genius of Romania, the isolation and obstinacy of its great men.

'Like Georges Enesco – musician but more than a musician. Ionesco, more than a playwright, he defies categorisation in the catalogue of the drama. Ilie Nastase, more than an athlete. With his tennis racket and his temperament he proclaims an artistry which sets him apart from other tennis players.'

My guide is named Kapitanu. He seems to me to belong to a generation which has had its fling and grown melancholy. There is a whiff of shaggy tweed and stale tobacco about him, a touch of the pedant in his speech, which I dare not interrupt. Yes, he is a pedagogue, he says. He used to lecture at the University. 'Which do you say, "world socialist economy" or "socialist world economy"?' are his opening words.

He is translating some government documents into English. His English is rusty, and he utters an abrupt *haha* while searching for a word.

'I must punish you,' he says, 'for your *haha* failure to telephone me.' (I failed because the operator had never heard of Tirgu Jiu.) 'I wish you to inspect *haha*. My first chapter. Tell me your impressions. Of the work. Do not be afraid. To *haha* criticise.' And he hauls some typewritten sheets out of a black plastic brief-case. We stroll round the park, on the river bank, in the sunshine. Mr Kapitanu delivers the Brancusi lecture and in future, whenever I see the master's reproductions, I shall associate them with the theory of the socialist economy and the proofs of decay at the heart of capitalism.

My guide is glad to have his translating job. He would rather guide western capitalists over the cultural fields of Romania, but few of them find their way to Tirgu Jiu. Luckily, since life is tough for the retired academic, he has two sons selling second-hand motor-cars on London's Great West Road, good boys both, who send money home.

His own subject was history and I am glad I resisted the temptation to bypass this town and go straight on to the Danube. Ostensibly I am in Romania to research the history of the royal family, and the State Archives and National Library have nothing on the subject . . . nothing about the estates and palaces but pamphlets on the organisation of the first communist cells, the rise of the Peasant Party and the local Ploughman's Front. In Albania they kept the monarch's memory alive in order to revile him; in Romania they pretend he did not exist.

So I am delighted to meet someone at Tirgu Jiu who knows the story of the dynasty from its beginnings; who is equally delighted to tell it to an appreciative listener. It must be hard, when you have made a career-long study of a historical period, to have the authorities ruthlessly expunge it and make that period a blank page in the records.

Having examined every stick and stone of Tirgu Jiu, we stand awkwardly in the street. My car has arrived, I am ready to leave. Mr Kapitanu would like to prolong the tour, spin it out for the rest of the day. I have an idea.

'Come with us, we'll bring you back tonight.'

His eyes accept instantly, his tongue demurs. Many calls on his time, much serious work on hand . . . at the end of a squalid lane, in a part of the town not shown to visitors, we wait outside a cottage surrounded with hencoops while Mr Kapitanu notifies his wife and exchanges his threadbare jacket for a belted raincoat.

It is fascinating to see the transformation, as he sheds his tourist-guide inhibitions, sniffs an air of controversy with the driver (a hulking Party athlete with massive shoulders – Mr Kapitanu treats him like an unruly prep-school urchin) and recognises in me an ignoramus willing to be instructed.

Before long he has impressed his authority on the expedition. He is master, we are pupils. He proposes detours and rebukes the driver for going too fast. We must get a move on, however, straight to the Danube and back. His wife, perhaps, will worry . . . He capitulates. I gather that Mr Kapitanu's little woman wears the trousers in that household.

We inspect the dam and the barrage and the unfinished motorway which is going to cut hours off the journey time between Bucharest and Belgrade, and the boiling channel of the river in these Iron Gates, roaring with anger at the latest obstacle which man has thrown in its path. Mr Kapitanu stalks round proprietorially and anyone listening as he lectures us can be forgiven for imagining that he alone conceived the scheme, designed it, built it and paid for it.

We move away, out of the noise of the waters and the spray which blows off the dam. Mr Kapitanu, on his home ground, naturally champions this civil engineering achievement against all others, but the driver, from Giurgiu, curls his lip and compares it unfavourably with the Bridge of Friendship downstream. A truly international project, he says, that bridge at Giurgiu, a monument to the fraternal interdependence of two socialist lands, Romania and Bulgaria. So is this, replies Mr Kapitanu, a joint effort between Romania and Yugoslavia. But from this barrage, the driver argues, the Soviet Union stood aside, whereas to the Bridge of Friendship the Soviet Union, and Stalin himself, gave cordial approval.

Not only did it give cordial approval, Mr Kapitanu says tartly, but it put up the money. Pure coincidence, of course, that the bridge completed the Soviet military highway and railway into the heart of her satellites.

Before something is said which both might regret, I draw Mr Kapitanu away from the present and into the past, the days of the monarchy, starting about the time the boyars threw out Couza and welcomed the first royal prince.

In April 1866, he says, a certain Herr Karl Hettingen took papers for a business journey between Switzerland and Odessa and travelled second class through Austria. He was Karl Hohenzollern, the future King Carol, in disguise. The Great Powers supported him, Romania had chosen him, but he feared a kidnap attempt by the Turks and believed that Emperor Franz Josef might betray him. No one, as it happened, took any notice of him.

Below Budapest he boarded the Danube steamer and made himself known to another passenger. This was Ion Bratianu, the dashing young Bucharest politician who had organised the whole thing. From that point on, Karl impersonated Bratianu's valet. It was a slow, chilly passage and perilous in those days, down the turbulent springtime currents of the Danube and through the Iron Gates. The railway track and the locomotives which towed boats through the rapids had not been built; travellers had to leave their craft and travel some distance overland. At Turnu Severin, Karl set foot on Romanian soil – a sagging jetty.

'Get back on board,' the steamer skipper shouted. 'It's another eight hundred kilometres to Odessa' – but Bratianu was kneeling and kissing his valet's hand, and a waiting droshky trotted up. 'My God, that must be the Prince of Hohenzollern,' they heard the skipper say.

Mr Kapitanu tells the story in intervals of acrimonious exchanges with the driver, all the way home. I have yet to see two Romanians meet for the first time without circling each other warily and starting a dogfight. A fresh row breaks out when we stop for petrol and Mr Kapitanu declines to put his pipe out, although the rubber tube of the handworked pump from which the driver is helping himself sprays out petrol as a garden sprinkler sprays water.

'What is to be done,' my guide asks, puffing at his pipe, 'with the

proletariat? With the masses? Do they not carry a *haha* burden of
guilt? For the sad state of our dear country today? History teaches
us. In every major *haha* crisis. The decision of the masses has been
wrong. Of the intellectuals, right.'

At the end of the rutted lane in Tirgu Jiu, his house is a snow-
storm of hens and his active little wife (I guess he married one of
his pupils) is clutching at whirling tail feathers. He makes his way
indoors, and we turn for Bucharest. The last I see of Tirgu Jiu is
Brancusi's *Endless Column* – or rather, the place where it should be,
for the public park is now in darkness and the régime has not
gone so far as to mount a red star on the summit of the pillar of
heaven.

The driver heaves a long sigh and lights a cigarette. That man,
he says, is typical of a class which has done harm to the State. It
has held back progress. With theorising and debate it has sabotaged
the deeds of the workers. Do I know the famous lines of Rozanov?
He cannot quote them precisely, but Rozanov describes how the
intelligentsia warmed its hands at the fires of the revolution, enjoyed
the spectacle and the excitement and then, as at the end of a
fireworks display, went to collect its fur-lined coats and return to
its comfortable homes. 'But found that the coats had been stolen,
and the homes burned down.'

We are on the motorway, approaching the suburbs of Bucharest.
From its tall buildings the illuminations glow red in the sky.
Bucharest is one of the smarter, not to say flashier, socialist capitals
and its neo-classical palaces remind one of the formidable public
works of Italian cities in the Mussolini era.

Home, to King Carol I, was never like this. In May 1866, shortly
after the events Mr Kapitanu told us of, the Prince of Hohenzollern and Romania and the national leaders he had gathered
round him journeyed on the road we are journeying now – a
muddy track, not a motorway – and arrived in the capital. They
were all crammed into one carriage, all quarrelling with each
other.

It was late at night. The carriage stopped halfway down a mean
unlit street. The Prince looked out and saw a gypsy encampment,
pigs wallowing in mud, a single-storeyed dwelling house with a sort
of sentry-box at its door.

'What building is that?' he asked politely.

'This is the palace, Your Highness,' said General Golescu with
some embarrassment.

Not hearing properly, or not believing his ears, the Prince said :
'Where is the palace?'

The general pointed to the pigs, the sentry-box and the low
building.

IO

The Iron Crown

Substantially altered by Carol and his successors, the royal palace remained squat, low and of no distinctive style until in the nineteen-thirties it was replaced by the neo-classical building of Carol II, which stands today like a rich man's town house in the middle of the rather provincial bustle of Calea Victoriei, the main street of Bucharest . . . a main street, USA, as it appears, with near-skyscrapers, drug stores and multiple traffic lanes. (The palace is now the Palace of the Republic, seat of the Council of State, with art museums in its wings.)

Prince Carol had a rough passage up to the date when he was proclaimed king. He had to create all the apparatus of government – civil service, police, army, a financial system. The native aristocracy, demoralised by war and foreign interference, contributed a network of chicanery. Carol protected himself with Prussian advisers and technicians, who built some roads and bridges and laid down the trans-Romanian railway. 'At least I shall have done something for this country – I shall have given it a railway,' he told his father. But he had to pay for the railway out of his own pocket, and for years it seemed to serve no purpose but to advance Kaiser Wilhelm II's *Drang nach Osten*. When Carol was old, it began to show a good profit and it helped him to die rich.

'Prussia rules Romania through the North German consulate in Bucharest,' they said in the 1870s. A pity, a Saxon housewife told her mother, after living there for a few weeks, that there were so many Romanians about, it would be a delightful country apart from that. Native liberals, egged on by the Tsar of Russia, made trouble for immigrants and raised the shout of 'Germans go home!' It was understood to include Prince Carol. More than once he offered the reins to his cabinet, the *lieutenance princière*, and threatened to leave; but his father, like the mother of Stephen the Great in Transylvanian legend, refused to harbour a beaten son.

Carol's story is told in two parts : before and after Plevna. That battle occurred in 1877 when the Russians, having crossed the Danube to drive the Turks out of Europe, were stopped by Osman Pasha. *"Venez à notre secours, venez sous quelles conditions que vous voulez, mais venez au plus vite,"* the Grand Duke Nicholas wrote to Carol. The Prince of Romania laid down no conditions but simply replied that he was on his way.

He was the last European sovereign to command armies in a foreign battle. Romanians had never before been seen south of the Danube and the Russians kept arresting them by mistake – which the victims considered a good joke, and cheerfully went along with. Plevna solidified into a long siege. The British war correspondent wrote : "The Russians are doing nothing, while the Romanians push forward with a pluck and perseverance worthy all praise." Carol amazed his allies and his staff. 'This is the music that pleases me,' he cried, as the first shells fell round him. And when the Tsar regrouped his armies and the great commanders Skobolev and Todleben reached Plevna, he – in the words of Victor Laferté[1] – *"s'effaça complètement en reconnaissant leur autorité suprême"* and put himself at their disposal.

I made a sortie across the Danube, into Bulgaria, to visit the so-called heights of Plevna, but saw no heights in the neighbourhood of that corn, wine and manufacturing town, unless you counted the low limestone escarpment under which a tributary of the Vit river gently rolls and statues of Russian heroes stand amid rose gardens. The chief hotel is the Rostov-on-Don, from the Russian city with which Pleven (its modern name) is twinned. The elaborate neo-Byzantine mausoleum in the town centre commemorates only Russian soldiers, and I could not identify a Romanian uniform in any of the big battle-pieces which hang round the walls. Nor is any mention made of Carol, in the mausoleum or out, although Todleben and Skobolev are well to the fore in street names. The proportion of Romanian names to Russian in the lists of the fallen, however, does suggest that the former bore the brunt of the fighting.

Romania's reward for Plevna was the loss of her Bessarabian provinces. General Ignatiev called on Carol to explain that the Tsar's honour required them. In return she was offered the Dobrudja, a tract of land on the Black Sea, south of the Danube. It was useless and desolate then, much prized later.

After Plevna the Prince of Romania received a greater personal

[1] *Alexandre II: Détails inédits sur sa vie intime et sa mort* (Paris 1882).

reward in the admiration and respect of his people. He was proclaimed king and his crown was made of iron from captured cannon.
Prince von Bülow the German diplomat, a fearless summer-up of
character, not given to paying compliments, pronounced him one
of the best and wisest of regents. Overwhelmed at first by libel and
suspicion, forced to grapple with revolutionaries, shot at by mad-
men, Carol steered Romania into calmer, though never smooth,
waters. "He never hesitated," von Bülow[2] wrote, "to get rid of the
pilot when the pilot had lost the confidence of the crew." (In 1888
Carol dismissed Ion Bratianu, the man who had brought him to
his kingdom.)

Evidently the Prussians who gave Romania a communications
system are not forgotten : the general director of roads in the
transport ministry of the Republic is a Mr Blumenfeld. He started
as a railway engineer. 'I was fifteen. Most of the men were about
that age. We rebuilt the bridges in the town of Jassy, bridges destroyed in the Second World War.'

Mr Blumenfeld says that in "the year of liberation from the
fascist yoke" Romania had four hundred miles of road, which is
about the distance from Bucharest to Tirgu Jiu and back, not
halfway across this spacious land. Now he talks about eight thousand miles of road fit for traffic, and many more miles that are not.
He is giving priority to the tourist routes to the Black Sea, widening
and tarring them and eliminating level crossings, the curse of the
motorist in the slaughterhouse of Europe.

The road to Sinaia is all roadworks. They are straightening out
bends and making a third lane for heavy traffic where it begins the
ascent into the Carpathians. In 1976, Mr Blumenfeld says, this road
will wind through the corridors of the hills as smoothly as a Brancusi
curve.

Close to Sinaia, caravan parks, minigolf circuits, chair-lifts and
tennis courts are sprouting. This is the Pearl of the Carpathians, not
yet clouded, and on any guided tour of the country it is your first
excursion. Beyond, the road climbs on to the ski resorts of Predeal
and Poiana Brasov and a switchback trail leads you to the Hungarian frontier, three hundred and twenty miles farther on.

At Sinaia you are 2000 feet above sea-level, only eighty miles
from the capital, and the peaks in front of you top 8000 feet. A

[2] Prince Bernhard von Bülow: *Memoirs*, vols 3 and 4 (Putnam, 1932).

dense sea of conifers, beeches and oaks washes green over the foot-hills. A train whistle, probably that of the Carpatsi express, Warsaw to Bucharest, echoes through the gorges and its sound conveys something of the loneliness and romance of the massif.

In Carol's golden days, architects vandalised these solitudes with a distorted enlargement of the brine baths at Droitwich Spa, a cluster of spires and turrets, woodwork and brick and stone, in which Viennese baroque and German renaissance collide with Palladian and Swiss-hotel Gothic. The place manages to look both flimsy and ponderous. Monolithic doors let you into a series of halls lined with marble and floored with Carpathian oak and wild cherry. The prevailing colour scheme was originally moss-green and gold, broken up with immense lumps of statuary and woodwork, and the roof rolled back to let the stars shine through. On a clear day people imagined they could see the Danube.

This is Peleş, pride of the stately homes of royalty when Romania was a kingdom. Carol, returning from a trip, was stormbound on that spot, and nominated it for his summer palace. The impractic-able angle of the slope cost His Majesty more in foundations and underpinning than the palace and its furnishings – which were costly enough. The stables alone outshone many a princely dwell-ing of Romania for size and magnificence. It was the first house to be electrically lit in that part of the country, and people would gather at viewpoints for miles around to see the lights come on at dusk.

Where Carol led, the court followed. Princes and politicians built themselves houses and Sinaia developed as a tourist resort, attract-ing fashionable foreigners. Some of the courtiers of Romania – a nation of shopkeepers if ever there was one – opened branches of their Bucharest emporiums and sold produce and craftwork from their estates. Sinaia has flourished to this day. You queue behind a bus party to enter the palace, now a museum of feudal arts in which the worst of *altdeutsch* excesses are displayed. 'What ludi-crous tastes, what vulgar lives they led,' you are supposed to say. 'Compare this worthless bric-à-brac with the simple cottage of Brancusi and his table of silence.'

Carol's wife, Elizabeth of Wied, commonly known as Carmen Sylva, was responsible for the grim gilded cage and stained glass of Peleş, its clutter of armour, dark panelling and medieval portraits. How the solemn king came to fall for a pantomime dame was one of the romantic mysteries of nineteenth-century court life. Rumour said she fell for him – literally, tripping over a stair-rod and landing in his arms. (At the time she was being offered, as a first choice, to the future Edward VII of England.) Then she was plump, pink-cheeked, with blonde plaits, a jolly German *Backfisch*. After marriage, and the birth and early death of her only child, she became stout and majestic, red-faced and snowy-haired, a dabbler in literature and painting and mysticism, eccentric-in-chief of a coterie of pseudo-artists. Queen Victoria adored her.

"I was delighted to see the Queen of Romania again," she wrote from Balmoral in 1890,[3] "which I had not done since '63. She has the same charming smile and bright eyes . . . but her hair is very grey and she wears it cut short . . . She is so full of cleverness and charm. She writes a great deal, poems, prose, plays and all under the name of Carmen Sylva. Her writings are immensely thought of . . . she fascinated everybody. Little Miss Hélène Vacarescu, a bright little person of twenty-four, a poetess, very Oriental-looking, also speaks English and French very well. The Queen is very fond of her . . ."

The Queen, in fact, had grown fonder of Miss Vacarescu than society liked to admit. At one stage they went to live together in Venice, where their relationship was better understood. Before that, Carmen Sylva had tried to palm off her protégée on Ferdinand, nephew of Carol and heir-presumptive of Romania. Of the crosses King Carol had to bear throughout his monarchy, not the least was his wife. Only one in a series of domestic crises was the occasion when Carmen Sylva emerged from a spiritualistic séance to start reorganising the dynastic succession with a triumvirate of herself, Miss Vacarescu and young Ferdinand. The sequel is described by Ghislain de Diesbach :[4]

"After ghastly scenes . . . the three protagonists in the drama were separated, held up to public ridicule and all sent about their duties, each to a different country . . ."

Miss Vacarescu settled in Paris, where she wrote admirable articles on Romanian life for the *Revue des Deux Mondes* and other journals. Ferdinand underwent the traditional cure for naughty princes : foreign travels and a taste of discipline in the Prussian Guards. Carmen Sylva, a tragi-comic prima donna, went home to mother and remained in exile for three years.

Over Sinaia the plump ghost of the Romanian Sappho seems to

[3] Queen Victoria: *Letters*, ed. George Earle Buckle (John Murray, 1931).
[4] *Secrets of the Gotha* (Chapman & Hall, 1967).

hover. (Von Bülow called her that, adding that "the poetry she wrote hardly matched the Lesbian songbird's".) In one of the pink clouds which float across Carpathian skies at sunset I seem to see the rosy face and swirling garments of one who passed most of her adult life in a world of fantasy, quite detached from the problems of her husband and her people. Like most of the Hohenzollerns she married into, Carmen Sylva was a compulsive collector of castles, the more inaccessible and fairytale-like the better. Carol indulged that taste : it kept her out of mischief. Peleş was her pride. The sliding sunshine roof was her own invention – to me it is her symbol, an extraordinary gadget which cost the earth and never worked properly. Remembering the dear Queen, I return to Peleş palace and go through the rooms again, thinking them more quaint than absurd, and more sad than quaint.

Beyond Sinaia an improved but still hair-raising road dips and surges to Castle Bran, formerly the property of Marie of Romania, a very different kind of person, though like her aunt by marriage she acquired castles and palaces as some women acquire lucky charms for bracelets.

Bran is a fourteenth-century stronghold, hung above a confluence of ravines and resembling a stork's nest on a chimney-stack. Today it houses another feudal art gallery and an ethnographical museum. There is a picture-postcard kiosk and you can join in a Dacian banquet with shepherd-waiters at the folk restaurant next door. Fifty years ago you would have seen gypsy families encamped near Bran, perhaps a Mongoloid veteran leading a huge Carpathian bear, a woman with a bodice full of snakes or a twelve-year-old peasant girl carrying two babies on her back – her own.

Marie felt she must have this "pugnacious little fortress" as soon as she set eyes on it. Its extreme loneliness attracted her. The hint was dropped and the township of Brasov presented it to her, the citizens taking payment in the traditional way by massing along the road and handing in petitions and complaints.

A crazed old architect was brought in to convert the place into a warren of spiral stairs, ghostly nooks and secret chambers. 'A person who never saw it,' Marie's youngest daughter says, 'can never be made to understand what it was like.'

The daughter of the French minister at the Romanian court about 1924 described to me the Bran of those days : 'It was decked out with antiques and flowers. I remember how the yellow nasturtiums hung down from copper pots. Marie often retired to Bran. A road was built for her; before that there were only paths for cattle. She would show her favoured friends the most wonderful collection of national costumes, more than two hundred, she used to say. She wore them continually. She had a small casement window beside the bed, she could open it in the mornings and feel the mountain breeze on her face.'

On account of Marie, this castle has a special appeal for British visitors. At Bran you are in touch with the intimate life of that "little English rosebud" – as misogynist Franz Josef called her – "far too precious" to be thrown away on Romania. Another royal marriage mystery : what political or dynastic considerations brought Marie and Ferdinand together? Her father, Admiral the Duke of Edinburgh, second son of Queen Victoria, wanted her to marry his nephew Prince George, afterwards George V of England. George himself was keen enough – at sixteen, Marie was clearly going to be the prettiest and brightest of the Royal Highnesses of Europe. But his mother laughed him out of it :[5]

"Well, and now about yr Matrimonial prospects ! ! ! ha ha ha ! You are quite right to think Grandmama has gone mad on the subject – and it is too *ridiculous* . . . the girl being a perfect baby yet – altho Aunt Marie, begging her pardon, does *all* she can to make her *old before her time* . . ."

"Aunt Marie" was Marie's mother, daughter of Tsars, pro-German and anti-British, wanting a Prussian alliance. She intended to see her eldest daughter a queen, and no one at that time could foresee that Prince George would one day be a king. But Ferdinand, adopted heir of an ageing, childless uncle and aunt, had an excellent chance of picking up the iron crown of Romania.

It happened in a flash, and Queen Victoria – who probably had more to do with it than was disclosed – expressed surprise :

"It seems to have come very rapidly to a climax. The Country is very insecure & the Society dreadful – & she is a mere child & quite inexperienced . . . Missy [Marie] wld *not* have Georgie . . . It was the dream of Affie's [Duke of Edinburgh's] life. I believe Ferd. is *vy* nice."

Ferdinand seems to have gone through the whole thing in a daze.

Rolled up in the ifs and might-have-beens of history are these thoughts : how might the course of life and government in Britain

[5] John Gore: *King George the Fifth. A Personal Memoir* (John Murray, 1941).

have run if Carmen Sylva, as consort of Edward VII, had imposed her eccentricities on society? and how might Britain have fared with Marie of Edinburgh, wayward and irrepressible, as Queen? About Marie, James Pope-Hennessy has no doubt :[6]

"She developed into a very theatrical person, authoress of an extremely clever book of memoirs, but as neurotic and self-satisfied as her cousin Kaiser Wilhelm II, whose character hers indeed slightly resembled. She would not have proved a satisfactory help-mate for Prince George."

Cameos of the early life of Marie of Romania, born Marie of Edinburgh in 1875, come up well coloured and clearly defined in that "extremely clever book of memoirs".[7] She toddles beside the lake at Eastwell in Kent, where she was born, and finds her way, awe-struck, into a ruined chapel. Among the firs of Balmoral she gazes, thumb in mouth, at her grandmother the Queen, who is all in black, seated in a pony cart, a faithful ghillie holding the bridle. At eight she sits for Millais : a round-eyed, full-lipped, well-shaped child with golden ringlets. At ten, at Osborne House on the Isle of Wight, she discovers her lifelong passion for flowers, especially madonna lilies. (Those stately, heavy-scented, vaguely Biblical plants expressed her own mystical yearnings. Wherever she lived she tried to grow them. The one place where they succeeded beyond expectations was at Balchik in Romania.)

She grows up "a tremendous tomboy" – decorative for all that, and ever conscious of masculine admiration and feminine envy. She rides and picnics at Malta, where her father is Commander-in-Chief and dear Georgie is a midshipman in the Fleet. She is spoken of as the most *chic* of princesses, most adventurous, most charming, most talkative . . . and most wilful.

Ferdinand of Romania was the third man, and Prince George the second, in her life. The first was Captain Maurice Bourke, R.N., commanding officer of the admiral's yacht *Surprise*. In that vessel Marie and her mother and sisters cruised in the Mediterranean, sightseeing and meeting relations on the French riviera and the coast of Greece. Captain Bourke told the little girls stories and pasted up their scrapbooks and at night he tucked them in their small white cots. On the last night he kissed Marie's cheek and

[6] *Queen Mary* (Allen & Unwin, 1959).
[7] Queen Marie of Romania: *The Story of My Life* (Cassell, 1934). The quotations which follow, unless otherwise attributed, are taken from this work.

made her promise that she would always be a good girl . . . "little did we know then, Captain dear, what pitfalls life has, and how difficult it is to be good."

Bourke, a promising officer, had his career cut short when H.M.S. *Victoria*, which he commanded, collided with H.M.S. *Camperdown* in the worst naval disaster of the century. He was not to blame, but he blamed himself. His nerve deserted him, his health failed and he died a comparatively young man in 1900.

"Maurice Bourke was my first love," Marie wrote. "He was indeed a hero to me and I have known fits of agonising jealousy when I was afraid he might care more for one of my sisters than for myself . . . To me he was a sort of God."

Letters which thirteen-year-old Marie had written to him were found floating among the *Victoria*'s wreckage, safely sealed up in a box. "Like a sign," she said, "that nothing could break the perfect friendship which bound us together."

Royal marriage conspiracies of those days were kept secret from the young ladies concerned, though the young men who had to do the proposing were brought into the picture at some stage of the negotiations. Marie paid little attention to the gangling youth who sat beside her one evening at dinner, except to make a little joke of him with her sister. He was Ferdinand of Romania and within a few months they were married.

Carmen Sylva, it was said, had carried a Romanian grammar for her bridal bouquet, immersed herself in Romanian folklore and made herself rather tedious to friends with her obsessive talk of the wonderful people of her adopted nation. In consequence, the wonderful people neither understood nor loved her. Princess Marie at the time of her wedding hardly knew what Romania was (nor did anyone around her : playing charades with young naval officers after her betrothal she was given the word "Romania" and the clue was "a town in Hungary").

She detested the country, the gloomy palace, the dirty rowdy streets, the disorganised provincialism of Bucharest, the introverted isolation and wicked gossip of the court. She stormed and wept, refused to learn the language and demanded to be sent home. As a result, the Romanian people adored her. She achieved a popularity which her husband and King Carol could only envy and marvel at.

Between wife and uncle, Ferdinand had a wretched time. More than once the King – "Onkel Karl" – had to step in to pay the

Crown Princess's debts. Ferdinand knew the depths of humiliation. Marie was afraid of no one, and it was she who bore the brunt of unpleasantness. 'You were a rebel,' Ferdinand told her. 'I was born obedient. You thrived on opposition, but I felt that in me some spring was broken. It was not necessary for Onkel Karl to be so severe with me.'

Carmen Sylva effusively welcomed her niece-in-law and introduced her at once to the famous salon. There was an emotional vacuum to be filled : "The Queen of Romania has fortunately forgotten Mlle Vacarescu and is beginning to devote herself to the bride of the heir apparent," wrote Baroness von der Hoven.[8] Marie at sixteen was already too bland and sophisticated to respond. The two were never great friends.

In middle age King Carol became as stern and cold as his iron crown. Constitutional matters were his whole life. He never relaxed and never smiled. 'The occupations of a monarch are grave, formal, important but never exciting; they have nothing to stir eager blood, awaken high imagination, work off wild thoughts,' he warned Ferdinand, who took it to heart, whose nose was for ever at the grindstone. "A man made for suffering," Ghislain de Diesbach calls him.[9] "The fact that he had married one of the most brilliant women in Europe was not the least of his misfortunes."

Marie meanwhile likened herself to a vigorous young tree, hemmed in by walls, probing and pushing with roots and branches until the walls fell down. Court women of Romania seemed to like their gilded cages, but she had to be free. She must realise, they told her, that Romania was not Britain. The monarchy was new, not secure in public affection, sensitive to scandal; "the monarchy must remain aloof." The tableau from this page of the memoirs must be the low-ceilinged drawing-room of the palace in Bucharest. King Carol, for some new extravagance or breach of etiquette, fixes Marie with a penetrating, deeply-shocked gaze. Marie gazes back, her blue eyes equally penetrating. Ferdinand quivers with apprehension.

'You have destroyed my childhood, you have thrown away the best years of my life,' she says.

'Only the very young,' Carol answers, 'consider their youth the best years of their lives.'

---

[8] *King Carol of Romania* (Hutchinson, 1940).
[9] *op. cit.*

Marie's disdain of convention, her spendthrift habits and ability to mix without condescension brought out the love of the nation. The Romanians, while liking the idea of a monarchy, had been disappointed with its representatives until she arrived. She was more their idea of royalty : a girl of panache and personality, warmth and colour, yet undeniably a *princesse de grande maison*. The birth of a son – the first Romanian-born royal prince – strengthened her hand. Taking full advantage of King Carol's delight, she broke through the wall of protocol and began to show Romania what panache meant.

She rode unattended in the streets (the first woman seen on horseback in Bucharest), drove a troika through the muddy avenues and stupefied peasantry of the royal parks, wore outlandish clothes, smoked cigarettes, assisted in the Bucharest carnival and pelted the citizens with roses, took on the colonelcy of a hussar regiment and arranged *fêtes champêtres* for her ladies and young officers. The road to Sinaia was her first avenue of escape and it stirred in her the beginnings of her passionate love for the land of Romania.

North, east and west of the palace of Peleş the forest marches away, fold upon fold. I see the miniature train in the valley, wriggling through rock tunnels, hardly making progress . . . vanishing and reappearing, vanishing for good behind a spur of the mountain . . . and reappearing again twenty minutes later, crawling on.

Fabulous panoramas separate out after a couple of hours' walking into distinct communities of mountain people, all with a smile and a good-day for the stranger. Hard winters, summer floods and no roads discourage intruders, each hamlet is a tiny kingdom remote from the rest. The shepherds and monks of that region were supposed to be in everyday contact with monsters and saints. Walking in the forest, I would not be surprised to meet the five dwarfish men with hip-length hair and tattered brown robes whom Marie discovered in a rock-dwelling. Made to understand that they were in the presence of royalty, they could only mutter 'Tsar Nicholas' – the First, they meant, the Tsar who extended his rule over the Danube provinces in the first half of the nineteenth century, when the monks had last been in touch with the world.

No rock-dwellings, however; and no sign of the monastery which, because it resembled the one on Mount Sinai, gave this district its name. The hotel proprietor has offered me a horse.

'I was told you were keen on riding. I have an animal for you, he's a little lively, he needs a good scamper.'

But I am not at all keen on riding. This big glossy bay looks much more ready for a scamper than I and, like a coward, I plead lack of suitable trousers.

Princess Marie had no such scruples. 'My Romania came to me on horseback,' she once said. Brilliant and fearless in the saddle, an enthusiastic tamer of stallions considered too rough for cavalry officers, she galloped a gauntlet of disapproval. She was among near-Orientals, the King said. She must remember that they didn't understand the practice of exerting oneself for pleasure. Riding made a woman barren, and Romania was looking to her to breed a big family . . . Marie scorned these arguments and the court fell back on tittle-tattle – that she rode her horses to death, she used them as an excuse for secret assignations.

Marie went on riding and when she had persuaded the King to give her and Ferdinand a palace of their own (the Cotroceni, now the Palace of the Pioneers in Bucharest) she renovated the stables and enlarged her string of gift-horses from admirers.

Through the Sinaia woods she rode astride, possibly the only woman in eastern Europe, in the early nineteen-hundreds, to dare to do so. Her favourite costume was Cossack, tailored for her in Saint Petersburg on the orders of a besotted grand duke : dark blue caftan braided with silver, scarlet underdress and baggy pants, a silver-chased belt and silver inlaid dagger at her phenomenally slim waist.

On warm days she would meet the old King on foot. When the court was at Sinaia everyone wore national costume by Carmen Sylva's decree. (Marie stopped that as soon as she became Queen.) But King Carol dressed in the black, red and gold of an infantry general, with old-fashioned képi and stout square-toed boots – his Plevna outfit. He plodded sedately through the glades with his walking stick, two sweating constables of the secret police trailing in his wake.

'Lovely day, fine weather.'

'Yes, uncle, and such beautiful woods. There are none so fine as Sinaia.'

'Where've you been?'

'Oh, everywhere, so many paths.'

'Yes, but take care. Your horse looks very wild.'

'But he goes like the wind' – and off she would go, like the wind.

He softened towards her as, at satisfactory intervals, she put out healthy shoots for the dynasty (six in all, and she outraged Bucharest morals by breast-feeding them). Her appointment as colonel-in-chief of the fourth Rosciori, the élite cavalry regiment, was Carol's instrument of surrender. 'The discipline will be so good for me,' she told him.

She chose the Rosciori because she liked the uniform : red tunics edged with black for everyday, all white for dress days; trousers sometimes black and sometimes white (It was a cheap sneer in western newspapers that corsets and lipstick were also part of the officers' uniform.)

Every young subaltern was desperately in love with her.

'Are we in black trousers or white today?' Carol would ask at breakfast-time, as Ferdinand requested permission to withdraw to his state papers and Marie took a look at the weather over the park. It was the nearest the old King came to making a joke.

She might go to the woods at the weekend, she would say, if the sun shone. Many square miles remained unexplored, she would lose herself on some wandering track and find her way home with the help of a wood-cutter.

The wood-cutter under the cliff of Bran is no child of the backwoods but a thinker of the régime, curious about what goes on beyond his horizons, as are many Romanians I meet. What do they think of Romania, over there in Britain, he wants to know. Is not the life improved, the ship of state steady, the population more enlightened, more educated, more broad-minded?

I tell him that most of us in the west carry a grey picture of eastern Europe in our hearts. We see workers' flats rising from fields of soya beans and in the streets a queue of depressed citizens shuffling towards their daily ration of black bread. In the queue, every seventh customer is a member of the secret police. It is hard, I tell the wood-cutter, to decide which is farthest from reality, our James Bond view of the east or your Dickensian view of the west. In the way people conduct their ordinary lives I see little to choose between us. The same hopes and fears motivate us all. One thing is sure, I shall find it hard to convince some people that I strolled round Romania without an escort, without embarrassment, and that I saw Romanians building their own houses, buying their own cars, taking their mothers-in-law for a day in the hills, criticising their deputies in parliament.

'Those motor-cars,' he says. 'That's one thing I condemn in Party Leader Ceausescu. He goes about in a Mercedes, he was up in these mountains the other day. They tell us everything in the east is superior, everything in the west is no good. Yet he prefers a western motor-car. I don't understand it.'

That apart, the wood-cutter believes Mr Ceausescu's heart is in the right place. He has received President Nixon of America, he has visited Mao in China, he has told the Russians firmly that they are on the wrong tack, he condemned the intervention in Czechoslovakia, he welcomes foreign tourists and makes everyone feel at home in Romania.

Terrible events occurred in the late nineteen-forties and early fifties, when the Democratic Bloc took power, led by Soviet communists and members of the wartime Patriotic Front. A reign of terror, the innocent suffered with the guilty, but that is past, only the old remember. Things became more settled when Gheorghiu-Dej was First Secretary. Under Ceausescu things are better still, everyone admires him. Romania has problems, that the wood-cutter will not deny. Great natural wealth, great poverty, much mismanagement. Romanians have enviable qualities but they are selfish people, listless in their response to the patriotic call, energetic in manipulating matters to their own advantage. 'Imagine what the Americans would have made of a country like ours.'

This country should be the richest of socialist states, with all her mineral sources and her agriculture; instead she is the poorest and most corrupt. There is still a Byzantine element in national affairs, a cruel, luxurious, intriguing element. It was always like that: Romania is too near the east. Much worse, naturally, in the days of the monarchy. The monarchy was the disgrace of Europe.

'Karl Hohenzollern,' says the wood-cutter, meaning King Carol I, 'arrived in this country with a single suitcase. When we abolished the dynasty in 1946 his descendants owned twenty-nine châteaux and a hundred and fourteen palaces. One thousand four hundred hunting lodges and country houses. Thousands of acres of crown lands, the best of arable land. Millions of acres of forest, in one day an eagle couldn't fly over them. Four million shares in the banks and the railways. Innumerable paintings. Heaps of jewels. A squadron of yachts.'

The wood-cutter owns a second-hand truck, but today he has brought an ox-cart for the brushwood on the steep bank of the forest. While we are talking his big white bullock has stood placidly

higher up, braced against the slope, twitching an ear. Its bell clanks
when it nuzzles among the fern.

'Do you call him Cassius or something like that?'

'Him? No, he's called Stefan. I have a calf at home, his name is
Nixon. Everything is Nixon in Romania since that visit of his. You
know the motorway from Bucharest airport? Officially it's the
Gheorghiu-Dej motorway, but since the American president drove
along it we call it Nixon Boulevard.'

11

Time and Tide at Constanza

The young ladies whom the Romanian Government provides as guides and interpreters for foreign travellers in that country are cheerful and knowledgeable – some of them. But it is a land where efficiency, in the western sense, is not regarded all that highly and you do sometimes find yourself stuck with a female dragoman who has evidently been chosen from the scatterbrained and specially trained in getting things mixed up. Magda, besides being one of that class, had the idea that her first priority was to minister to the needs of our chauffeur, a proud and sullen young man a good deal nearer her age than I.

Yet, infuriating as the girls can be, the moment they leave you is the moment when matters start getting out of hand. On the last lap of a trip from the painted churches of the Bukovina we passed through Constanza. Both Magda and the chauffeur lived there. It seemed a shame to drag them on to my destination, from which they would have had a thirty-mile journey home. I suggested they put me down somewhere central, Parcul Maksim-Gorki, say, and I would catch a bus. They could take the rest of the day off. They agreed. Better still, said Magda, catch a boat.

We checked with the timetable. A boat left Constanza harbour every afternoon at two. As the girl said, it was a lovely day for a sail.

In the past thirty years the shabby oil-impregnated port of Constanza on the Black Sea has pulled itself together. Few pre-war houses survive and those which do stand badly in need of a lick of paint. Modern shops and public buildings, on the other hand, are freshly finished in pinks, blues and yellows, which give the severe apparatus of communism a facetious aspect. Traffic lights, lane markings, Coca-Cola and Barclaycard signs put a western-capitalist gloss on the old Roman-Turkish-Slav-Democratic Bloc undercoats. For all that, most shops were closed, most of the traffic was making for the city exits and the place had a restful evacuated air. Perhaps it was just the time of day.

A long gentle hill, a long high spiked wall, a main gate with green-uniformed soldiers and tommy-guns, a long jetty with litter blowing about . . . the soldiers did not spare the intruder so much as a glance. I knew the Romanians were not a great seafaring nation, but had they nothing in that dockyard worth covering up, nothing to hide from an inquisitive westerner? There, for instance, in a dry dock not even roped off, lay a business-like nuclear job, something between a frigate and a submarine, in gun-metal grey and wearing the ensign of the Royal Romanian Marine, blue, yellow and red with a crown, and the gangplank positively invited you to step aboard.

A crown? Something amiss. The wearing of that flag is generally prohibited. The fierce little warship was set in cement. She was an antique, a torpedo-boat destroyer of a Black Sea squadron long disbanded. A plaque, unintelligible to me, commemorated an exploit of 1898.

Walking round her upper deck and peering through skylights at her straight-waistcoat of a wheelhouse and dungeons of messdecks I felt relieved that no accident of birth or circumstance had required me to serve in the Romanian Navy at the turn of the century.

The yard was thronged, active in an informal way. Its sheds and warehouses, like the houses of the town, wore matching shades of tinted concrete and the upperworks and funnels of the shipping were all colours of the rainbow. Love of colour is apparent in every walk of Romanian life.

Several passenger vessels were loading. Mine had not arrived, but a destination board showed where it would come in and the makings of a queue were standing about, chatting and spitting into the water. At the gangways of the bigger boats, more exciting destinations were announced: Belgrade, Budapest, Turnu Severin, Odessa, Sevastopol. One kaleidoscopic motor-ship with a cerise funnel and officers in *Merry Widow* tunics and epaulettes was bound for Vienna – a sight which, to someone who had not seen the Danube, gave a proper impression of the importance and navigable extent of that marvellous waterway (that accursed waterway, as nineteenth-century statesmen called it when bedevilled by riparian disputes) into the heart of Europe.

(Historians have smiled at Ali Pasha in his Albanian citadel, wishing the French envoys a fair wind to Vienna, and asking about the chances of getting a gunboat built in Paris – but the museum-

piece in Constanza dockyard was launched from the Seine, and it
was certainly possible in Ali's day to take a ship from Albania to
mid-Austria; probably more feasible then than it is now.)

Passengers stood about the decks of the big river boats. Some,
having seen their luggage on board, went ashore again and made
for the café. Bustle of departure was entirely lacking. The captains
had come to no decision, the passengers were wrapped in philo-
sophical calm or heated discussion about, I would guess, football.
Over a scene which would otherwise have been as near idyllic as
it can be in a dockyard, a Polish tanker, registered Gdansk, poured
black smoke and pop music.

Along the pastel-shaded waterfront of Constanza you cannot
easily visualise the Greek temples on the headland and the Greek
triremes in the bay . . . though they say the Greeks coloured their
temples red, white and blue and no doubt the triremes carried as
much scrollwork as a Carpathian cottage and wore big painted eyes
on their bows.

This was a port of call for gods, demigods and heroes. An army
of Colchis (far side of the Black Sea, but not identified with any
place known today) came in pursuit of Jason and the Golden Fleece.
There was a battle at Constanza. The survivors established the port,
which languished until argonauts from medieval Genoa erected a
lighthouse. (It still stands, but mind you don't trip over it – it is
only a few feet high.)

In the first years of the Christian era Constanza harboured a distinguished political exile. Publius Ovidius Naso arrived from Rome.
Propagandists for tourism say he chose the place himself, having
heard favourable reports of the climate and the cultural life. More
likely it was chosen for him, a dot on the outer perimeter of Empire.
What is known is that from the time he set up house on an island
in the lagoon north of the town, still called Ovid's island, he did
not cease to complain of the cold, the damp, the dirt and the neighbours.

Ovid died at Constanza and a monument which has stood the
test of shifts in political opinions and public tastes longer than most
stands in the main square.

A thousand years ago, Tartars, Kurds and other wild tribesmen
swarmed among Constanza's thatched hovels. The port was a kind
of metropolis of gypsies and beggars; this end of Romania has
always had a strong Romany flavour. "Very clever thieves," was
how Miss Vacarescu described them in one of her articles, "very

great cowards . . . naturally averse to discipline and training . . .
they repay kindness with ingratitude and are the scourge of our
villages and harvests. Their primitive instincts are as keen now as
when, centuries ago, they made their first appearance in Europe."

At the Ovidiu cannery on the shore (I thought it considerate of
Magda to buy me a tin of caviare, but it turned out to be for the
driver), we disturbed a gorgeous specimen of a gypsy girl. She was
flat on her back, having a siesta. Her white overall did not hide a
superbly sculpted body. Our driver prodded her with his foot and
she leaped up and showed us the blade of a knife. I motioned to
my camera – I wanted to capture the hostility in her blazing black
eyes, her stance, one hand punching the hip, the other upraised,
the high cheekbones edged with arrows of delicate black hairs, the
wild black hair which cascaded into a loop of string at the nape
of her neck . . . But she would not be photographed and I was
afraid to offer her money.

A young gypsy whom I met at the end of the jetty, where I had
walked while waiting for the boat, could have been her brother. He
glistened in the sun and his black curling locks were like black eels.
He was naked but for a pair of swimming trunks. He, too, had a
knife – he had been diving and he was crouched over a heap of
pink and yellow shells. For what purpose? The souvenir stalls of the
holiday resorts, no doubt. At the question his muscles tightened.
He took on the tension of a cat preparing to pounce. He did
pounce, and sprang to one side, and set off at a trot to a quieter
corner of the harbour, leaving his shells and some fronds of sea-
weed behind.

Magda used to say that gypsies were a moral people, but their
morals were not ours. Robbing each other, for example, was
criminal, but they could rob non-gypsies to their hearts' content.
She said the régime had done its best to integrate the gypsies and
awaken them to an understanding of their social duties, but had
not made much progress. About five per cent on that coast worked
in shipyards and factories, a few were cajoled into putting on dis-
plays for holidaymakers, but the majority would not, or could not,
join in and build socialism. Consequently a gypsy in Romania had
no rights, no privileges, no formal protection from the State. He
was an outlaw in the literal sense.

All the communist countries are plagued – if that is the word –
by gypsies, and it is there that the sternest confrontation between
modern society and the gypsy way of life is going on. In Albania,

the first rounds have gone to modern society : we saw new-built villages where gypsies had been compulsorily settled and had accepted the change. In other lands, the gypsies appear to be leading on points.

Where the gypsy dropped his sea-shells I read of the arrival of the heroic Soviet sailors at the end of the Second World War. It was written up on a black marble obelisk, but did not mention that this was the ninth occupation of Romania by Russian forces, nor that the Red Navy responded to an ally's comradely welcome by stealing their hosts' boots.

For most Russian sailors Constanza was a first glimpse of the western world. To them the dilapidated, badly-run city with its underfed inhabitants and wreckage of shipping was a funfair, a paradise of shops, restaurants, theatres and bourgeois decadence. *Pravda* in September 1944 approved the smartness with which Romania had got its banners and slogans up, and its pictures of *Maresalul Stalin, Genialul Comandant al Armatei Rosii*, but deplored the "jazz bands, the tinsel vulgarity and commercialism" of Constanza.

Pravda's war correspondent set the scene : "Well-dressed people are seated at the pavement cafés, traders and speculators sit on the high seats of horse carriages looking like old posters of the *burzhuis* . . ." Most of all *Pravda* condemned the "hearty cringing" of the citizens to the sailors of the Red Fleet. Romanians are realists, they do not approve of heroics when the odds are against them, and they are always ready to cheer the winner . . . characteristics inherited from the Romans, perhaps. Although they shared a frontier with Russia, although they had been nine times overrun by Russians, the Romanians were an enigma to their neighbours. The Soviet politicians and bureaucrats who moved in from 1945 onwards could not fathom that raffish, cocky, cringing, cynical people. And neither could the rest of the Slav nations around them.

Under the harbour wall a mass of silvery darts coagulated, broke up and reformed. A shoal of sprats, the gypsies of the sea, worked its way towards open water. On the jetty an angler kept pace with them. His net scooped up a few at a time. At that rate it would be dark before his wartime gas-mask satchel was full. He stopped and borrowed a match and lit a cigarette.

On this wall, he said, there used to be another memorial tablet. It must have been removed before the war. It referred to a rather serious crisis in Romanian-Russian diplomacy. Unexpectedly on the second of July 1905 there arrived from Odessa the battleship *Potemkin* and Torpedo-boat 267 of the Imperial Navy. Trouble on board. The outward sign of it was the red flag worn by each warship instead of the usual Saint Andrew's cross. No one knew exactly what that meant, but Constanza was not long in finding out.

The ships anchored one mile off the point and saluted the Romanian flag. King Carol's flagship, the cruiser *Elisabeta*, was in harbour and her captain returned the salute and sent an officer on board. The mutineers demanded fuel and stores. It was an awkward situation. Romania could not afford to offend the Tsar, but his rebellious sailors were ready to open fire on the town. The newly-installed telegraph worked overtime, relaying question and answer over the hundred and thirty miles to Bucharest. In those days it could take three days to travel from the Black Sea to the capital, more if the Danube was in flood.

The ships anchored a little closer. Bucharest eventually ordered the port admiral to let the mutineers know that fuel and stores could not be supplied but that the crews were at liberty to abandon their ships, come ashore and go in safety through Romania. Mistrusting that offer, the men of the *Potemkin* weighed anchor and took their battleship back to the Crimea to present similar demands to the townsfolk of Feodosia. They threatened to demolish the place if they were refused.

Feodosia stood firm. Back to Constanza sailed the *Potemkin*, her bunkers almost empty and her ship's company hungry. T.B. 267 parted company, returned to Sevastopol and surrendered. Over the next few weeks her men were either hanged or sentenced to life exile in Siberia.

The *Potemkin*'s committee of management hastened to enquire whether Romania's offer of a safe-conduct was still open. It was. The sailors rowed themselves ashore and scattered, some finding their way to western Europe and America. Five weeks after the mutiny, two Russian battleships arrived at Constanza. It looked like a punitive expedition, and timid burghers fled. But they had only come to escort the *Potemkin* away.

Denuded of his totally unnecessary sou'-wester, the fisherman revealed himself as a mere boy. He had studied English. He would like to visit that country, he said, he would like to see Las Vegas. 'We had your prime minister here. Harold Nixon. He drove down the new boulevard with Mr Ceausescu in an open car.'

The President of the United States, he went on, entered a café and ordered an egg, telling the cook to let him have the water it was boiled in. 'I want to give it as aid to an under-developed country.' The fisherman laughed heartily as he told the joke. I smiled, and he was encouraged to tell another.

The President of the United States telephones a black man. 'Can you come over to the White House right away?' – 'Yes, sir' – 'Well, how about tomorrow, can you come then?' – 'Yes, sir, whenever you like' – Can you come on Friday?' – 'I'm sorry, boss, I have to go to a funeral that day' – 'That's a pity, I wanted to see you on Friday, I wanted to give you your civil rights.'

I told the fisherman that during the famous State visit Mr Ceausescu had played a round of golf with Mr Nixon and the newspaper had reported the results as follows : "The Party Secretary, who had never played golf before, came second. The United States president, who plays golf every day, was last but one."

The fisherman said this story could not be true, as Romania had no golf courses.

It was past two o'clock. No sign of the boat. Everything in the harbour stagnated. A group of young people, mixed German and English, drifted along to join the queue and the Polish tanker signalled their arrival with a blast of Beatles music. The girls went barefooted, the boys had long hair and Afghan coats and one of them was stripped to brick-red waistline. He made a megaphone out of a rolled-up magazine and yelled across to the ship : 'Cut it out.' A figure appeared at the deckhouse door. 'Like, it's piercing.' The boy mimed with an imaginary volume knob. 'Too piercing, man.' The figure disappeared. To everyone's astonishment the music ceased and we heard no more from the Polish tanker.

From the talk of the newcomers and the attitudes of bystanders, I gathered that when the timetable of departures said two o'clock it meant three, or maybe half-past. Old Romania's clocks and calendars were the rising and setting of the sun and the passage of the seasons and something of the approximations of a far-off era are in her timekeeping today. The sun blazed down, but a breeze from the sea blew cold and goose-pimples appeared on the shirtless lad's red-skinned arms. Wavelets lapped the wall. In half an hour or so it would not be such a lovely day for a sail.

I took myself for a longer walk, out of the gate and round the point where the promenade, Bulevardul 16 Februarie, began. I was looking for something which came off a picture postcard with an Edwardian stamp : the dome, the scalloped arches and frothy woodwork of a pier-end pavilion. Though frail, it had been reported to be standing up to war and peace, time and tide, rather more successfully than the fortifications of old Constanza. It, and the oil pipe from Ploesti, and the stump of the Genoese lighthouse, were about all that lingered on, I had been told, from pre-1914 water-front Constanza.

On the street-plan it was marked casino, but as a pavilion it was built for Carmen Sylva. That cruiser had been named for her too, *Elisabeta*, and what is now the bathing station of Eforie down the coast was once the health resort Carmen Sylva. The dotty Queen was putting her signature on the Black Sea shores, and contemporaneously keeping the courts of western Europe in a titter.

In England she had failed to get Beerbohm Tree to produce one of her verse dramas in the West End of London, but the director of the Court Theatre in Vienna had succumbed, probably imagining he was carrying out the wishes of the Emperor. Nothing could have been further from the Emperor's mind. Profoundly suspicious of intellectuals and women, Franz Josef found the Queen's fat rosy cheeks, cloud of white hair, exotic clothes and arty conversation increasingly hard to take. 'She got on my nerves with her ecstatic delight,' he said at the première. 'I naturally grew colder and colder.'

His safety-valve was the wife of the British ambassador, a woman with a talent for making mischief :

Emperor : 'The woman is stark mad.'

Lady Paget : 'Poor thing, it is such a pity to think that so much talent should be wasted.'

Emperor : 'Talent? Have you read her books? I read one. I never read such things, such improprieties.'

Lady Paget : 'No doubt if she had had a dozen children she would have been quite sensible.'

Emperor : 'Yes, but for that you need two people.'

Lady Paget : 'So you do for one, Your Majesty.'

Emperor : 'Ah, but that one died.'

Lady Paget : 'Yet it comes to the same thing and I can hardly believe . . .'

Emperor : 'I assure you ! *C'est comme cela!*'[1]

On the journey to Constanza, Carmen Sylva wore diaphanous robes and a motoring helmet. She stood at the window of the royal

[1] Walburga, Lady Paget : *Embassies of Other Days* (Hutchinson, 1923).

train waving a napkin to cows in the pastures, whom she mistook for her loyal subjects. She and the King had to pay their annual visit en route to the salt mines and when it was over the Queen stood at the top of the lift-shaft and bawled tearfully at the convicts : 'My friends, we would release you all if we could.'

At Constanza she took over Ovid's isle and declaimed poetry to ships at sea through a speaking-trumpet.

It was June 1914. Nine years after the *Potemkin* incident the royal party awaited another Russian landing. King Carol, enthusiastically abetted by Crown Princess Marie, took personal charge of the arrangements, for the prefect of the Constanza police confessed that through worry he had not slept for three nights and was on the verge of a breakdown. By royal decree, every beggar and gypsy was ordered to report to his nearest police station and citizens told each other that, after years of election promises from successive governments, something was going to be done at last to rid Romania of the Romany nuisance. (Forty-eight hours later, since no one knew what to do with them, the beggars and gypsies were turned loose.)

Reception rooms were put up on the foreshore. To keep his Queen out of the way, Carol gave her a pavilion all to herself some distance from the landing-place. This was the building I was trying to identify.

Out of a midsummer mist, resplendent in black and gold, the two imperial yachts, *Standart* and *Polar Star*, steamed to their berths. A native of Constanza remembers how they settled among the miscellaneous little craft of the harbour "like a pair of black Tasmanian swans alighting on a common duckpond". With a telescope you might see a slim, short, composed figure on the *Standart*'s flying bridge, admiring the prospect of the bay. He stepped ashore where the *Potemkin* rebels had stepped before him : a person without pomp, but a Tsar. Against the urgent pleas of King Carol, who wore his general's uniform, he had put on a simple white linen suit. 'He looks like a cook,' the hero of Plevna muttered. Marie replied : 'Nicky is Tsar of all the Russias – and my cousin – but nothing can make him look like anything but a cook.'

Historically, it must have been the most interesting assemblage Constanza had witnessed. Tsar Nicholas had brought with him Alexandra, who appeared perfectly amiable while stifling a yawn from time to time; the Tsarevitch, a beautiful little boy of ten in a sailor suit, attended by the seaman Derevenko who never for one moment left his side; and the four young grand duchesses in stiff summer dresses and picture hats.

On the Romanian side there were Carol and Carmen Sylva; Crown Prince Ferdinand, ill at ease as always in public; the Crown Princess, sparkling; her eldest son Carol, aged nineteen, tall, lanky, suddenly grown up since he had done his stint of duty with his mother in the cholera camps of the Bulgarian-Romanian conflict, and preparing to set off for a spell in his father's old regiment of Prussian Guards ('Carol has reached a stage when he needs to be taken firmly in hand,' his mother said); her second son Nicholas, aged eleven, the Tsar's godson, delicate and spoiled, "almost too pretty for a boy" in his mother's view; and her three daughters Elisabeth, statuesque and artistic, Marie, plump, soft and sleepy, and Ileana the baby, aged five, blue-eyed with black bobbed hair, very pretty but having a comical idea of her own dignity.

The programme included a solemn Te Deum at Constanza cathedral, a banquet at the prefecture and a review of troops, at which Carol had the satisfaction of brightening up the Tsar's appearance with the green-and-gold sash of a regimental colonelcy. Gossip from the family tea in the black-and-gold saloon of the *Standart* reported a spitting contest between the Tsarevitch and his Romanian cousins, with grape-pips for ammunition and the lemonade jug for a target.

Carmen Sylva came into her own with a gala dinner at her pavilion, fireworks, dramatic readings and allegorical tableaux thrown in. When the final tableau – little girls with angel wings – proved too much for the set and the children collapsed in a tangle of scenery and broken limbs the audience agreed that it could not be helped. Art must be served, and the dear Queen was *so* artistic. Nothing could dampen Carmen Sylva's spirits that evening. 'Everybody must walk this way,' she said, mincing with her toes turned in as she led the guests to their carriages.

The object of the visit, the first and last by a Russian sovereign to Romania, was to examine the possibility of an alliance between young Prince Carol and either the Grand Duchess Olga (aged eighteen) or her sister Tatiana (aged seventeen). Olga, however, said she would never marry a foreigner, even if he was her cousin, and Tatiana liked only dark men. Carol did not seem to be bowled over by either of the girls and his parents were shocked – or pretended to be – by their immature conduct. 'Like young savages,' their prospective mother-in-law declared, scandalised by the giggling flirtations they carried on with the dandified officers of the imperial yacht.[2] (It would have been hypocritical in Marie to condemn flirting; what she objected to was the lack of style.)

After not much more than twelve hours at Constanza, the *Standart* and *Polar Star* sailed back to the Crimea. The Tsarina (no match for Marie in the moment of jealous bickering which broke out) crossed Prince Carol off her list, but the Russians in their wonderful ships had made it a day for Constanza to cherish. Rich barbaric splendour, the imperial theme, was calculated to delight the colour-loving Romanians. Their visitors' hauteur, their air of finding everything slightly distasteful but of being too polite to say so, did not at all offend the natives, though the outspoken townsfolk of Constanza, so appreciative of beauty and flair, so ready to condemn homeliness, groaned at the ugly sunburned daughters of the Tsar and complained they looked no better than peasant children, and sulky ones at that.

King Carol played one card that day in the game of regal one-upmanship and it was an extraordinary one. Prince Bibescu, pilot of the one-man, one-aircraft Romanian Air Corps, flew over the yachts and dipped his wings in salute. At that period, and in those circumstances, neither Russia nor any other country in eastern Europe could offer departing potentates an airman's farewell.

The shirtless youth called out and pointed. Round the harbour wall the funnel of a small steamship was moving. She dodged the breakwater and slid alongside our notice-board. She was the *Stefan cel Mare*, Stephen the Great. The queue reconstituted itself, the youngsters gathered round, rubbing their hands and asking the skipper what kept him. The sun had gone behind clouds and a wind from the Crimea was blowing in gusts.

But the skipper, descending from his perch, locked up the wheel-house. The deckhands, having made fast, picked up their plastic bags and jumped ashore. An engineer surfaced through a manhole, closed it after him and clamped it down. A man from the dock-yard went on board and walked round, locking up and collecting the keys of the different compartments.

'What is this, a strike?'

'The boat is late. The crew are tired. They are going home.'

---

[2] Elizabeth Narishkin-Kurakin, *Under Three Tsars* (Dutton, New York, 1931).

'And what about us? How do we go home?'

Passengers split into two factions. The Romanians, accepting it
as part of the normal inconveniences of travel, went off to find
alternative means. The foreign tourists started harrying and jostling
the dockyard man. They brandished timetables, he replied with a
rattle of his bunch of keys. I sat on a bollard and waited for the
outcome. The fisherman, picking seaweed out of his net, said something about a bus at seven o'clock. If not seven, than half-past, or
eight.

There was no hurry, then. I wandered into another part of the
dockyard, noting in passing that the big river boats were no nearer
departure and that the café was full of passengers, drinking coffee
and eating *mititei*, Romania's answer to the hamburger.

A shower of rain came on. I sheltered in a welding shop and
introduced myself to the charge-hand. He spoke excellent English.
'We Romanians have no difficulty, we got the gift for it.' What was
more, he had been eight years in Australia.

I asked about the wooden pavilion. It was gone, finished, he said,
they had built the casino on top of it – a more solid construction
altogether, like an opera house. Like an opera house on which a
mad chef had been let loose with an icing gun, I suggested, having
seen it.

The girls in the workshop were dumpy and suburbanish, with
a couple of disdainful, straight-limbed gypsies among them. The
sight of their coloured headscarves, carelessly tied, was like a
breath of the high Pamirs.

Jobs came from the sea and from the countryside, the charge-
hand said. They repaired ships and agricultural machinery. I asked
a girl if she worked on the ships. She said no, but in her rest period
she had been on board and compared the sailor's life with her own.
'Theirs is much harder.' I asked her workmate, a gypsy, the same
question. She stared and said nothing. I turned to the first girl.

'Your work isn't so hard, then?'

'It could be harder. I look for extra work to do. I know where
there is a tractor standing by the road in need of repair. It has
been in my mind for some days.'

'What about you?'

The gypsy girl stared and said nothing. The charge-hand patted
her on the shoulder. 'She's a great little sheila, this girl,' he said. 'A
good worker with a high sense of responsibility, you know? Only
she don't like talking to strange men, you get me?'

The rain came down steadily, but I had to go for the bus.
Cobbles and potholes in the yard, not much illumination, though
I could see over the wall the daisy-chain of lights on the new
casino, which was the old pavilion. The café was blacked out. Some
action had taken place while I was sheltering.

The river boats, without so much as a toot on a siren, had slipped
out of harbour. Where the Polish tanker had lain was an empty
berth. Constanza port was dim and silent, as though time and tide –
two unpredictable factors in any Romanian situation – had called
it back to a former era, as though it still awaited the coming of
Jason and Ovid, of the battleship *Potemkin* and Carmen Sylva, of
the Tsar of all the Russias and a newspaperman from *Pravda*.

12

Venice on the Danube

When last we voyaged in Dobrudja, it was hard to tell where the Black Sea ended and Romania began. The Danube was spread from horizon to horizon and the redbrick cottages sailed on the delta like flotillas of Noah's Arks.

This time, in autumn, the waters are back where they belong, between the towpaths, turning the odd grain-mill which is anchored in midstream, pushing the odd caviare boat down to Sulina and the sea. The mudbanks of spring are the steppe of late summer, undulating, bristling with stubble. The natives of the delta move slowly, forty miles by boat or on a bicycle is a long day's run, but they waste no time getting acclimatised to the changing of the seasons.

Julia the interpreter says that serfdom in Romania has been abolished, but until recently no one told the delta people. Farm workers in remote places knew no home but the long, earth-covered barrow in which whole communities slept like winter potatoes. Nor did they ask for one. In times of peasant rebellion these folk were always last to join the fight; and when it was over you would see them in the looted garments of their masters and mistresses, toiling away at archaic tasks, doing the bidding of those same masters and mistresses.

Agriculture is not the main industry. Even in the dry season, only ten per cent of the land dries out. Canal-like rivers, the fan-spread of the Danube mouths, carry much of the life and work of a thousand square miles, which have been Turkish, Russian and Romanian in their time but always a land of fishermen ("Sea Cossacks") and marshfowlers. Music, movement, colour and religion regulate their lives. Up to thirty years ago one would have put religion first. In a book of history and reminiscence by Marie of Romania,[1] she writes of exploring the Danube backwaters in the yacht *Regele Carol*, of anchoring in a lagoon and waking up next morning to find the ship surrounded by canoes full of Lipoveni,

[1] *The Country that I Love* (Duckworth, 1925).

as the Romanians called them – Raskolniki, Old Believers, fair-bearded, gigantic in stature, extremely polite. Their dark-robed priest brought on board a cross for the Queen to kiss.

We do not see any members ot this Old Testament sect, but Julia tells me they are to be seen, and she warns me not to offend them, if we do, by offering cigarettes. Tourism perhaps has driven them into inaccessible reaches of the delta, as it has driven the egrets and the pelicans. Tourism must change the ecological balance of a region which, one supposes, is poised on a knife-edge. Curtainland's *grand plage* begins on the skyline and a boat-trip among the creeks is an almost obligatory part of your holiday at Mangalia or Mamaia beach. Galati, the last big river port, a hundred miles from the sea, used to be notable for the ocean-going tramp steamers which penetrated to its jetties, but nowadays excursion steamers are the thing. They take you to, or bring you from, Constanza, Belgrade, Budapest, even Vienna, a twelve-hundred-mile journey up the Danube, and they are like small holiday resorts in themselves, with all the amenities on board, down to the ladies' hairdresser.

Excursion boats ply the main streams of the delta, but for the more intimate byways motor-driven fishing boats are provided. If you are attracted by semi-subaqueous surroundings and all the atmosphere of a mangrove swamp without the snakes and mosquitoes, it is not difficult to arrange accommodation with a fisherman and his family – one, of course, who is hallmarked with the Tourist Committee's stamp of approval. (In my experience it is not the cosy arrangement it sounds. Our fisherman's cottage was a brick bungalow on a new housing estate in Tulcea. Furnishing minimal, décor represented by an inventory of contents and an extract from the Blue Book of guest-house rules, stuck to the wall. We heard our hosts talking in low tones in another room, but hardly saw them. A snub-nosed little girl with pigtails sticking out round her head brought our meals, and to our questions she answered not a word.)

Near Tulcea, road and railway touch the delta and hereabouts the main stream of the Danube splits and spills and does its best to confound the mappers with rivers which become lakes, lakes which become islands, islands which turn into mudbanks and lagoons.

The main dredged channel to Sulina is the grand highway of Danube shipping. Ours is the northern branch, thinly trafficked, our boat one of the steep-prowed, light-draught canoes which are the temperamental workhorses of the Sea Cossacks. I would not care to be in open water in one.

Our pilot steers over mudbanks and tree roots with centimetres
to spare – not so much to cut corners as to avoid turbulence under
the banks. In the course of a few hours we pay several visits to the
Soviet Union : since 1945 a vast tract of Bessarabian wheatland
has gone back to Russia, and the national frontier runs down the
middle of the channel. Topographically little has changed. The
land is pancake-flat, pancake-coloured from last year's more-than-
usually disastrous floods. On the Soviet side a woman in a woollen
hood and wading boots walks along the towpath, scooping out mud,
fish or weeds with a net. There is a painted minaret on the skyline,
and a poppy-coloured dome . . . in these reaches, Islam and Russian
Orthodoxy met and mingled.

'Had not the Sea Cossacks the reputation of being hard fighting
men?'

'But they fought their wars against the sea and the floods, not
against each other,' Julia says. 'In a quiet country like this, everyone is peaceful with his neighbour. I think he has to be, otherwise
he cannot survive.'

Very Christian people on this bank, the pilot is saying. Some are
Catholic, some belong to rare ascetic and mystic religions, most
are Orthodox. (We shall land and look at a church; it is empty,
but the icon lamps will wink at us.) No, says Julia, the Moslems
don't exist any more. On the contrary, says the pilot, some of his
best friends are Moslems and if you visit his native village you will
hear the muezzin cry '*Allah akhbar*' daily, not from the minaret
because there is no minaret. He climbs a tree to do it.

I am struck by the ease and informality with which we enter
the USSR. No searching, no questions. No sign of anyone, in
fact. 'The rigmarole you have to go through before you can get
into Russia, even from another socialist land, and here you simply
step ashore,' I say. 'What's to stop me from walking to the nearest
railway station and catching a train to Moscow?'

We are still in the delta, among delta folk, Julia points out. One
would have to walk rather a long way, ankle-deep in the guano
of strange birds, and also take boats in places. One might be shot
at. 'They allow the delta people to carry arms, they have been useful against spies and foreign agents.' We shall see how hard it is to
get into the Soviet Union when we reach Valcov, Julia says.

Valcov, Vilkov to the Russians, is reached. All one can say about
it, approaching from the river, is that it looks a damp spot. At a
wooden jetty, attached to a television aerial on the roof of a hut,

the hammer-and-sickle is flying. A boat like ours is tied up at the steps and an old man is fast asleep in it. I would like to photograph him in that attitude. Our wash rocks him awake and he sits up and grins. Yes, he is willing and proud to be photographed, he will turn the boat into the sun, it will be a sharper picture that way . . . but as he is doing so a true son of the régime comes to the edge of the jetty, into the picture, shaking his fist at us and giving the boatman the rough edge of his tongue. They are the curse of curtainland, these self-appointed watchdogs of the proletariat who love pushing foreigners about and, if they see anyone doing anything, believe they are performing a patriotic duty by making him stop it.

Julia, ignoring him, skips on to the jetty and goes into the hut. She is out again in half a minute, looking a little pink. She is a buxom pretty girl, and I am not surprised that the border guards have been paying her compliments . . . nor will I be to hear that she has twisted them round her slim finger.

'That *moujik*.'

'Which one? In the hut?'

'No, on the jetty. Rude, vulgar creature. But you have that type in your country also, I think?'

'Is he some sort of official?'

'No, he's the carpenter. He's mending the jetty. I have told the police about him, and you can take pictures if you wish.'

'How about going ashore? No luck?'

'Of course luck. We may go, but we mustn't stay long and we must keep walking. They ask no questions, they are watching television, it's the Soviet Union and Yugoslavia football match.'

Valcov is – or was – the caviare capital of the delta, though not much more than a village on stilts. Again the atmosphere, without the humidity, of the tropical swamp; this might be a village of Burma or Thailand. The streets are boardwalks, the crossings rickety birchwood Bridges of Sighs. Women in white woollen hoods and muddy boots are laying wattle fences across a creek to net the sturgeon – a fiddling, tedious job which has to be done every year. Women are dredging clay from the stream bed for building material. Women are splitting wood for palisades. Young girls tramp the boardwalks shouldering buckets of what looks like cow-manure. Women and girls hammer nails into the planks of an upended boat in a front garden. Women and girls tie up the strands of a broken wire mesh net.

'I see all the women working, but where are the men?'

'Drinking,' the pilot says.

The black boats, with prows steeper than ours, are the gondolas for the gridiron of waterways which makes Valcov – if some neighbouring village has not copyrighted the title – Venice on the Danube. No *palazzi* here : the mud would not stand for anything of more than one storey. Clumps of reed-thatched cottages are embedded in gardens crammed with lupins, roses and hollyhocks. They have the smug look of English country gardens. I suppose these arrays of pink and blue plants are the blotting paper which sops up the Danube floodwater. I find it hard to believe that six months ago Valcov and riverside villages like it were inundated to their eaves, and four months hence they will be inundated again.

Every year in which the Danube freezes – it can happen overnight, defying weather forecasts – pack-ice jams the tributary streams and the delta branches. While that is melting and raising the water level in eastern Romania, storms of rain saturate hundreds of square miles of the Dobrudja countryside. Villagers save their boats by staking them to the chimney-pots. More than one child has had his first swimming lesson in the bedroom of his parents' house. What I take to be tree-trunks brought down by the river in flood are actually tree-trunks which will be chained up somewhere next winter for the benefit of random swimmers whose cottages are submerged and their boats lost. 'It doesn't happen every year,' the tavern proprietor says, 'but it's best to be prepared.'

Half an hour downstream a turn in the Grand Canal will disclose the world of State enterprise and collective endeavour. Wooden warehouses, corrugated roofs, stacks of crates, many Lenin posters, a refrigerated Soviet coaster at the jetty of the May Day co-operative, loading for some place on the other side of the Black Sea. This is where some of the big ships come to take on caviare, sturgeon and herring for the western world.

Meanwhile we shall sit on the verandah of this tavern and taste the caviare (red, thirty pence the pound) and drink what is known as English tea – black, scalding hot, with a slice of lemon. The custom of the delta, as demonstrated by the man on the corner bench, is to sip from the saucer and let the steam invigorate the pores of your cheeks. He finishes his tea and wipes a thick horseshoe-shaped beard. He is the nearest thing we have seen to an Old Believer and I stop fumbling for my cigarettes and decide to do without.

He stares in our direction, but not at us. He is staring, I suppose, at the old time, the good days, when the delta was really the delta, back about the time of Peter the Great – when the Tsar's bell clanged from the twisted onion-dome of that white church on the horizon, and the boyars passed by like doges under the narrow canal bridges, when the balalaika tinkled as evening closed in, picking up the song of the boatmen on the towpath, hauling their craft home against a slow current.

In that setting, the policeman looks out of place, and he looks as though he realises it. He flops down on the bench and pushes his cap back. It has left a red ring round his forehead. We can smell the policeman from here.

Julia talks to him. He does not want to know what we are up to, he is attracted by a new pretty face, that's all. It will be better if he accompanies us to the jetty, he suggests, the football match is over now and maybe they have changed the guard. No hurry, when we are ready will be time enough.

He is an exile from Odessa. He asks wistfully if all the girls in Bucharest are as beautiful as Julia. She says more so. I say no, Julia is in a class of her own. Ungallantly he quotes a Bessarabian proverb : 'At twenty, even the ass is beautiful.'

He would like to visit Bucharest. 'When the Russians go to Bucharest, it is the same as you Romanians visiting the west.' He admires Julia's little fur cap, contrasting it with the white woollen headgear of the Sea Cossacks' women.

'But I have a white kerchief at home exactly similar.'

'You should have worn it to come here,' I tell her.

'Why should I carry owls to Pallas Athene?' says Julia, a well-educated girl.

The policeman sighs. A quiet life at Valcov, he says. No life at all, really. 'No crime, no amusement. When you and I would say good-evening, these people are saying goodnight.'

Yet the rains will come and cottages will be swept into the channel, the population will ride on logs and maybe the carbide factory will explode again and the Danube will drown the injured or bury them in its mud, as it did in 1971. The policeman is unmoved, it will be time to consider those emergencies when they arise. Time enough . . . he is right. Here on the verandah, in the sunshine, time stands still and the calm days of autumn spin out to eternity.

13

Scandal at the Quiet Nest

"I found myself surrounded by a swarm of excited women in·
strange attire, prattling a language I did not understand. They
called me Sultana and each one wanted to touch me; they fingered
my clothes, patted me on the back, one old hag even chucked me
under the chin . . . amongst a labyrinth of mud huts did they drag
me with them, making me enter their hovels, put my hand on their
children, sit down on their stools . . ."[1]

Marie of Romania was recalling days of liberty as Crown Princess
when, a free person on a horse, she would canter past cartloads of
Turkish women huddled in dark wraps, being transported to some
unspeakable destination . . . past mud-built villages, howling dogs,
tiny churches and fat mosques and acacia groves . . . through
wretched towns where silent obese Turks eyed her, women crouched
like black crows in a line on a wall, entrancing children in baggy
cotton trousers raised their kohl-painted eyebrows and snapped their
red-lacquered fingers at her.

This is the land you see when you are stacked up over Varna at
the height of the holiday season, waiting to land at your Black Sea
resort – a scrub country of grey goat pasture, limestone outcrops,
the stalks of dead trees and the cracked earth of dry ponds. It is
still the Dobrudja, south of the delta, south of Constanza; a dispos-
able counter in Balkan politics. The old frontier, marked today with
a stone slab at the roadside, was some thirty miles south of the
present one. After 1940, that piece went to Bulgaria. Halfway
between old and new frontiers, threatened by the two prongs of a
blossoming vacationland, so far no more than threatened, sleeps
Balchik by the sea. Marie of Romania kept its picture in her mind
from the one brief visit she made as Crown Princess : tiny Turkish
houses scrambling down a gap in the limestone cliffs. As Queen,
when the time came to prepare the last palace in her collection, she
sited it at Balchik.

[1] *My Country* (Hodder and Stoughton for *The Times*, 1916).

It was 1926, only twelve years on from that sunny day at Constanza when the Tsar and all the Romanovs came down in their black-and-gold yachts. The Tsar and the Romanovs were gone, King Carol and his Queen were gone. (Amiable and witless to the last, Carmen Sylva died tuned in to the archangels, Raphael in particular, and she broadcast their messages to her people.)

Ferdinand was King, Marie his Queen. '*Ah, si j'étais roi*,' was her constant complaint. She believed that the nation would respond to her as to no other sovereign, that only she, manipulating the rulers of Europe as she manipulated her admirers, could bring the prestige and prosperity which Romania deserved. The slide of the Romanian Hohenzollerns into degradation and misery had already begun, with Carol, now Crown Prince, absenting himself from his regiment in time of war, marrying Zizi Lambrino and getting her with child and shooting himself accidentally on purpose to avoid the consequences. The marriage was annulled and Carol made handsome amends by offering a perfectly proper proposal to Princess Helen of Greece. They were married, but even before Helen's first child, Michael, arrived her husband's name was being linked with that of Madame Lupescu.

By 1926 the monarchy was in a tangle. Carol announced that he no longer wished to be considered a member of the royal family and his father, in the last year of his reign, at a solemn conclave, pronounced the destitution of the heir apparent.

Prince Nicholas, after an undistinguished career at Eton, had entered the Royal Navy and was serving in the Mediterranean Fleet, frightening the Maltese to death by tearing round the narrow streets on a Red Indian motor-bike. Stories are still told in naval wardrooms about the Valletta prostitute who set up in business for herself under the sign BY APPOINTMENT TO H.R.H. PRINCE NICHOLAS OF ROMANIA.

His mother was having better luck with her daughters. A dedicated matchmaker, Marie was determined to see the three girls nothing less than queens. Elisabeth had become Queen of Greece – a queen without a throne, it was true, and soon to be without a husband, for the marriage did not work out. Marie the second daughter, "Mignon", plump, soft and shy, the sort of girl mothers warn their sons against, had taken King Alexander of Yugoslavia for a walk in the forest at Sinaia and come back engaged. 'Mignon, my prosperous Queen,' her mother was able to cry a few months later, when she visited the newly-weds in Belgrade.

Life was smooth and pleasurable for the placid Mignon until the day in 1934, at Marseille, when her husband was assassinated.

Ileana the youngest girl was not quite of marriageable age, but it was understood that King Boris of Bulgaria would be interested when the time came. A *rapprochement* between the two countries which glared at each other across the Danube was centuries overdue.

Long before she started collecting kings for sons-in-law, Marie had collected palaces and castles, and she had also constructed a small fortress of affection in the hearts of all right-thinking Romanians. (A few wrong-thinkers existed : one might cite the militants who upset the royal train schedules from time to time, inflamed by a railway worker named Gheorghiu-Dej.) Though something of a Mrs Jellyby in her domestic life, arguably responsible for some of the sorrows of her children, she was the mother of her people, a Joan of Arc, a Florence Nightingale and a Catherine the Great rolled into one.

It had started in 1913 in the Second Balkan War, when Romania squabbled with Bulgaria over the spoils of the First and Marie discarded the pretty Cossack riding-habit and put on an equally becoming Red Cross outfit to organise the cholera camps. It had continued through the First World War, when she rallied a dispirited nation and marshalled heads of states, Allied and hostile, to support her on the principle that blood was thicker than politics.

Ferdinand pursued an indeterminate path throughout that war, half-heartedly leading his armies in the field, bemused by awful dilemmas and conflicts of loyalties. He failed to join the Central Powers, his name was expunged from the Great Book of the Hohenzollern and in his ancestral home of Sigmaringen he was mourned as dead. Up to the summer of 1918 it looked as though he had sacrificed his honour for nothing : Bulgaria attacked across the Danube, a crack German mountain battalion (led by Lieutenant Erwin Rommel) poured over the Carpathian wall and captured Bucharest, the Russians collapsed and the Bolshevists massed on the Black Sea frontier.

Marie's Rosciori, the Red Hussars, exquisitely accoutred, monocles firmly screwed in, trotted into action with admirable bravado and their colonel-in-chief's name for a battle-cry. '*Regina Maria!*' They were cut to ribbons in an afternoon.

Marie toured hospitals, handed out medals to the wounded, wrote her first best-seller (*My Country*) and gave the proceeds to the Red Cross, sustained morale behind the front, remained un-quenchably vivacious and became the inspiration of fighting forces trapped in a conquered land. The court had to flee to Jassy (now Iasi), the old capital of the Moldavian princes. 'We travelled over-night,' she put in her diary, 'and arrived in time for breakfast. I slept beautifully. I like sleeping in the train.'

All came right in the end. Capitalising on her fame at home and abroad, Europe being rather short of heroines, Marie appeared uninvited among the statesmen at Versailles. Could not Romania's delegates be trusted with the job? her husband asked. She thought not. The opening session of the Peace Conference suggested to her that Romania was being slighted, that all the little eastern states were being lumped together. 'Romania needs a face,' she told the press in Paris, 'and I have come to show mine.' At forty-two, it was still an astonishingly fetching one.

The French reacted with predictable gallantry. 'A Queen like that,' Clemenceau told the Romanian general Antonescu, 'should be received with full military honours, Marshal Foch at their head.' Crowds gathered to cheer her on her well-publicised "secret" missions to other western countries and chasseurs, lancers and foot guards provided her escorts. Paris and London were grand spec-tacles of the brave and the fair, pageants with casts of thousands, but Queen Marie of Romania stole a good part of the show.

She confided to the French leaders that the British lacked interest in Romania, because of their historical disdain of small nations . . . she told the British the same about the French. She returned to Bucharest more heroic than ever, for the Versailles settlement not only met Romania's claims to Transylvania, the Bukovina and the Banat in full but gave her the marvellous bonus of Bessarabia, more than doubling the country's pre-war population. From then on it was Greater Romania.

Some, including Marie, held that Marie alone achieved it. Official Romanian delegates have written rather sourly that her function was decorative and that, if anything, she hampered their work. The modern historian would point out that it was Allied policy all along to create a Greater Romania as a *cordon sanitaire* against Bolshevism.

H. Charles Woods[2] left a portrait of the metropolis of victories about the time Queen Marie returned from Versailles. Bucharest's

2 *Contemporary Review,* January 1921.

population is much increased, hotels are full and people continue to flock into the capital. All is dirt, disorder and poverty. Trains come and go sporadically, with unlit, unheated, windowless coaches. Only the Simplon-Orient express (Paris and Istanbul) keeps anything like proper time. The national finances are in an incredible mix-up. There has been no budget since 1914, paper money lies about the streets like snowflakes, the cost of living is two hundred per cent up on the previous two years. The index of corruption has soared in sympathy. "There is nobody and nothing who and which cannot be bought." Power is shared by the old gang and the newly-rich, but they will not introduce tax measures because the main burden must fall on themselves.

Marie, finding her country in a grim mood, swept off on further travels. She took England by storm, danced a quadrille with King George the Fifth and Queen Mary, took her seat in the *gorsedd* of the bards at Llangollen and wrote a piece for a daily newspaper called "My Ideal Man". Her fan-mail was delivered in a truck and it added up to one massive outburst of praise for her good looks, courage, charm, stamina, artistry, authorship, botany and tapestry-work. "As a dress designer," *The Times* reminded its readers, "Queen Marie might have earned, had it been necessary, a large income." And, it might have added, a fortune on the stage.

With her son Nicholas and daughter Ileana she hit America in 1926 and rode the crest of the wave called ballyhoo – which comprised flivver and sedan, Alphonse Capone and Babe Ruth, knee-length skirts and rayon stockings, Emily Post and Dorothy Dix, Florida real estate and Teapot Dome, the Dempsey-Tunney fight and the funeral of Rudolf Valentino.

Marie underwent the 'Hey, Queenie' of United States informality, the jokey impertinence of cartoonists and a lot of bewildering hospitality, and she figured in a quatrain by Dorothy Parker. Her good-natured readiness to take part in stunts brought out the worst in the impresarios of a tasteless era : Marylin Miller impersonated Princess Ileana in the musical *Rosalie*, a sillier-than-usual love-story about a foreign royal highness and a West Point cadet; thousands of gullible citizens paid good money to kiss the Queen's hand; Robert Sherwood wrote the play *The Queen's Husband*, a soppy comedy based on what he imagined life at the Bucharest court to be; civic heads mauled each other in the Queen's presence over the question of who was to sit beside her; somewhere in

Canada she stood patiently smiling while a whole city of thirty thousand people passed before her.

John Mason Brown[3] remembered her as "a handsome, strong-willed enervatingly energetic woman . . . dripping with pearls and diamonds, who whistle-stopped round the country from one red carpet to another on the luxurious trains which the railroads put at her disposal." Heywood Broun thought there were not half a dozen actresses in the States who could fill her role so well. A journalist on the *Toronto Star*[4] called her "a first-rate bridge-player, a second-rate poetess, a very high-grade puller of European political strings . . . who uses more make-up than all the rest of the royal families combined" – she was none of those things and she did not, but Hemingway relied on hearsay and he seems to have had an obsession about make-up – it was he who put about the story of the lipsticked cavalry officers.

Homecoming, 1926. The bells of Bucharest chiming, the formal reception at the railway station, the laughing, cheering mobs in the streets . . . it was a vivid memory for one young Romanian:[5]

'In the drawing-room at the palace the Queen was kissing her friends, greeting hundreds of people, handing out gifts from America – chewing-gum and marshmallows. We liked the marshmallows, but no one cared for the chewing-gum. Servants were carrying the big steamer-trunks through the corridors, each labelled in large white letters THE QUEEN OF ROMANIA. I had to stand in the corridor, there was no room inside. At a door at the far end, King Ferdinand appeared. I was shocked. I had not seen him for some months, and hadn't realised he was so ill. He wore his *robe de chambre* and shuffled along the corridor like an old man, thin and jaundiced. He heard the noise of the excited people round the Queen, and he stopped and turned and went back into his room. He carried a newspaper, I remember. It was the last time I saw the King.'

King Ferdinand died of cancer in July 1927. Towards the end he had a little joke for his ministers: 'Carol is a good boy really, a very clever boy. You know, he's like Emmenthaler cheese – excellent but for the holes.'

On his deathbed he wrote to the chief minister, another

[3] *The World of Robert E. Sherwood* (Hamish Hamilton, 1965).
[4] Ernest Hemingway: Article in *Toronto Star Weekly*, 15 September 1923.
[5] Georges Duca: conversation with author.

Bratianu : "I cannot face the future without thinking with a father's heart of the fortunes of my dear son Carol [who was then living abroad with Madame Lupescu] . . . I wish him a happy and honourable destiny. I have denied myself, in the public interest, the great joy of seeing him once more . . ."

Like Marie, we are surrounded by a swarm of excited women in strange attire. They belong to the egg-plant cannery of Balchik and they are giving us confusing directions for the palace, Tenka Yuva, the Quiet Nest. Round the ravine, under the trades-union chalets, down to the gatehouse which is smothered in American vine and has wartime mines at its portals, down through the deer-park, down past the waterfall on a track hardly wide enough for a pony-cart . . . it is all downhill to the Quiet Nest.

The gardens are in the care of the Bulgarian Academy of Sciences. Visitors may enter. Half a dozen gypsy women, in faded blouses and sackcloth aprons, are camouflaged among roses, michaelmas daisies, geraniums and cacti which overflow the herbaceous borders and the steep flagged paths. Evidently the gardeners cannot keep pace with the growth. Stop to speak to them and they slouch off to another job. It's unlikely that anyone remembers, anyhow.

We have been told to look out for the terraces, one for each of Queen Marie's children. The sixth is cut off short by the overhang of the cliff. Carol's terrace? No, Mircea's. Her youngest son died of typhoid at the age of two.

The Quiet Nest is not, and never was, a proper palace, it is more of a seaside villa. Within the park, which falls to the sea on a stiff gradient, Marie of Romania amassed enough treasures to fill several museums and enough junk to stock a few western antique shops and eastern bazaars.

Millstones on the paths, three decorative mills against the trees, echoing the Sans Souci of Frederick the Great; baths, fountains, stoneware, ceramic jars, Celtic and Oriental crosses, a rustic well, an alabaster throne, a row of white Illyrian pillars (contributed by Alexander of Yugoslavia) beneath a pergola of roses . . . crammed in this corner of Balchik bay are all the relics of a woman who loved curios, who was never afraid to ask for what she took a fancy to, and on whom admirers showered their gifts.

The house is well-proportioned, white plastered, with carved chestnut balconies and plum-coloured pantiles. From above, the spreading wings of the roof resemble the plumage of an exotic bird alighting on its Quiet Nest in the cypress thickets. The blue spike of a minaret out-tops the trees. Passing sailors could mistake it for a lighthouse and once they might have heard the sirens' song from an aeolian harp inside the weathervane. But the harp is blocked with swallows' nests, and the custodian says that as fast as he cleans it out they block it up again.

The building is a rest-home for artists and writers. We are spending the night there and, since it is a quiet time of the year, I am shown to the ground-floor apartment originally designed for King Ferdinand. It is bare and white, with one modern picture (strong-armed harvesters) and a frieze of madonna lilies. They are the only madonna lilies left at Balchik and a gardener says the others, which Queen Marie planted and which grew so profusely in the limestone soil and sea air, have been carted away to the Euxinograd palace, the Government guest-house thirty miles down the coast.

Ferdinand did not sleep here. He died before the Quiet Nest was completed. His widow did, and whom she might have slept with supplies legends for guides to entertain western tourists with. To be fair to the eastern Europeans, they are only retailing gossip which circulated during Marie of Romania's lifetime – gossip which is purged of its original malice for, as the manager of the Balchik rest-home says, 'What is the use of being a Queen if you can't take a lover?'

The boatman Hassan; the head gardener who cultivated for her a black rose (it, too, was transferred to the Euxinograd, where it died); the Italian architect Fabrice . . . in the Balchik story they join the list of lovers. The list is headed by the Crown Prince of Prussia before the First World War, and Waldorf Astor of Cliveden, whose wife Pauline did indeed complain that Marie was writing to him every day, and must stop it. It continues, according to various participants in the drama of Marie of Romania in the nineteen-thirties, with Rosciori hussars, Russian grand dukes (during visits to Saint Petersburg), a Polish count, a German envoy, Colonel Joe Boyle the Canadian paymaster who organised supplies ranging from a Rolls-Royce to bars of chocolate for the royal family during the grim part of their war, Prince Stirbey, from whose house Marie launched her Red Cross campaigns, two or three minor Romanian politicians, Colonel Eugen Zwiedeneck her major-domo at Balchik, a young aide at Balchik . . . The reports are not confirmed, and on this aspect of the Queen's private life her surviving daughter Ileana writes to me :

"I think you have to be very careful not to give the impression that Mama was a passionate woman. She was a great romantic and of course, being very beautiful, men fell for her, but she herself regarded this quite apart from a romantic point of view and was flattered but was seldom moved by these romantic attachments; she just accepted with a kindly smile. She hated hurting anyone's feelings . . . The only men we can say truly played a part in her life apart from my father were Lord Waldorf Astor, Prince Barbu Stirbey and Colonel Joe Boyle."

A younger member of the royal family says : 'Great-grandmama was *very* naughty. Stable-boys and everything.'

Queen Marie spent more time at Balchik as the years went by, eventually becoming almost a recluse there – or a prisoner. She retired from active interference in politics after her husband's death, when a regency council was formed (to govern for Michael, the boy king of the postage stamps) without herself in it. This was her reward for creating a Greater Romania, propping up a diffident monarch, making Romania's name ring round the world . . . The trouble was that, like many a central European and Balkan mother-in-law of this century, Marie was too fond of meddling with matters which did not concern her and which she did not properly understand.

In 1930 came the sensational return of the exile : Carol, the dispossessed heir. He landed in a private aircraft and was welcomed with acclaim, marched on Bucharest and accomplished a quiet coup against his little son.

History and the popular press have been hard on Carol II of Romania. He is the weak-chinned would-be dictator, a drunkard, intriguer and womaniser; a Byzantine character. Close to former royal circles, they speak with some embarrassment of the defect which destroyed the dynasty :

'I hardly know how to put it . . . Carol was . . . well, you know about Cleopatra's nose? Half an inch longer, and the history of the world might have . . . it wasn't Carol's nose, it was another organ . . . half an inch shorter, and our history . . . you follow me? Lupescu was the only woman who could . . . eh? You understand?'

His forty-year affair with Madame Lupescu required enormous sacrifices by both; and they remained faithful to each other; in different circumstances that would have been one of the world's great love stories. Carol was reasonably abstemious in those days, decisive, intelligent, hard-working, devoted to his country . . . western newspapers portrayed him as the exact opposite and King George the Fifth, who took some of his opinions from the headlines in the *Daily Express*, called him "that bounder".

Carol showed courage under threats from the Axis powers, while his mother made friends with Frau Goebbels. Governments collapsed, prime ministers fell like autumn leaves, the King made several clean sweeps of political parties and by 1938 he was leader of the National Front of Rebirth, a fascist régime.

So many heads rolled that Queen-Mother Marie felt insecure. She had to apply to her son for permission to travel, and sometimes he refused it. She was sixty, matronly, clear-skinned, with a beauty which would never fade, but she suffered from pernicious anaemia, with which is often associated a persecution complex. During a brief absence, her French gardener and her "man of confidence" died suddenly at Balchik – rumour spoke of poison. During another a devoted aide was struck down by what was described as a brain tumour. For the first time in her life Queen Marie knew fear and helplessness and looked about her for a protector. She found no one, only Colonel Zwiedeneck the morose old major-domo, who loved to wallow in alarmist propaganda. "I am absolutely defenceless," she wrote in her diary.

Morning on Balchik bay. A soft air from the sea, which is grey and murky, rolling baulks of timber and strings of onions on to the beach. Boats like the boat we travelled the Danube in are bobbing under the wall. A fellow-guest, a paunchy professor of philology, is already out there, up to his waist in water, swinging a rod. Fishermen lie back on a quadrilateral of net, like firemen on a blanket. Smoke rises from the cannery chimney and the thump of a pile-driver comes through the water from the new harbour extension. I look down on this from Queen Marie's little chapel, which has attenuated pseudo-Byzantine frescoes on its doors, one of the Queen with a church in her hands and the other of Princess Ileana with a boat. (As a young girl, Ileana was nearly drowned at Balchik.)

Female workers with raucous screams have settled like a colony of gulls among the dahlias. A Moslem woman from the town is peering into Queen Marie's silver well, the well of Allah, looking for the face of the boy she hopes to bear. In the shade, under a plane tree, his bald head like the dome of a statue, his olive-green pillbox hat on the bench beside him, sits Bai Simeon. He moves the hat, we sit down with him. He talks in a flat, complaining voice.

Bai ("Uncle") was gardener's boy at the palace and he is probably the only man left in this town who knew Marie of Romania.

'He says she was much loved,' the interpreter reports. 'He says they built a road for her, all the way from Tolbuhin, it was the first asphalted road in the Dobrudja.'

He says . . . he says . . . Among other things, Bai says that Ileana was to have married King Boris of Bulgaria, but when the King arrived at the Athenée-Palace hotel in Bucharest someone whispered that the princess was already pregnant and he left at once. (This is most unlikely.)

He says that Ileana's daughters are now washing dishes in a workers' café. (Not true : they live respectably, with their titles, in Germany.)

The Queen's illness, he goes on, was not an illness, it was a gunshot wound. I must know that both her sons were bewitched by Madame Lupescu. In the course of a quarrel at the Quiet Nest they raised their voices and the Queen heard them. She entered the salon just as Nicholas drew his revolver to fire at Carol. Instead of hitting his brother he hit his mother, who had rushed between them. She died of that wound. The cause of death was not an infection of the liver, as the newspapers said, it was the infection of some blood transfusions.

'Have you told anyone about this before?'

'No one asked me before.'

True or false? In 1937 the press scented a mystery about her illness, and an American interviewer[6] tackled her about it. Marie answered : 'I've heard anecdotes about myself, I hear all the stories, someone always comes and tells me . . . Shot by my son? No, I've heard nothing about that. My illness started with a haemorrhage and narrowed down to two controllable ailments, phlebitis and anaemia. Not cancer, thank God.'

That hardly amounts to a denial, but Princess Ileana calls the shooting episode "complete bunkum". "In cold historical fact my brothers never actually quarrelled face to face. Carol always used emissaries to do his dirty work for him. They never met at Balchik as far as I can remember, and they certainly never had words in front of their mother . . ."

Bai Simeon spills cigarette ash on his green smock, rubs at it and makes it worse, puts his cap on and salutes. The audience is over.

[6] Vernon McKenzie: *Through Turbulent Years* (Bles, 1938).

He stumps off to supervise the garden-women, for he is in sole charge of everything outside the Quiet Nest – the deerpark, the garden of Allah, the columns and statues and curios, the terraces and the alabaster throne on the ledge above the foreshore. He is getting on in years, his feet are troubling him, he wears the livery of the Republic and the shabby, unkempt air that goes with it; but he must have been a good-looking young fellow forty years ago and I wish I had thought to ask him whether . . . But it happened a long time ago, no doubt the old man's mind is clouded with more recent memories, what we are speaking of is pre-history for him, a legendary era of which the facts are dissolved in the fiction.

14

Disbanding the Monarchy

Halfway across Europe, at the Weisser Hirsch clinic in Dresden, much patronised by ailing royalty, Queen Marie knew she was dying and – as the London *Times* put it, maintaining the polite fiction that royal personages have no emotions – "expressed a desire to return to Romania". Her physician did not object. She had come to him too late. 'If Romania's medical men had been trying to kill her, they could hardly have done better than give her the treatment they gave her.'

If she did not reach the Quiet Nest alive, Marie stipulated, her heart was to be taken there, to the little Stella Maris chapel. And Balchik must wear purple, not black. And the flowers on the coffin must be all red . . . she had something of her grandmother Queen Victoria's morbid passion for the panoply of death.

The journey began, into the rising sun, across the interminable plains via Breslau and Lvov, through Poland and the southern USSR – a wearisome trip even for one who, in more resilient days, had said she liked sleeping in a train.

In the summer of alarm and despondency, 1938, Marie of Romania was hardly a newsworthy person, but one or two foreign newspapers copied the bulletins from the train which crawled day after day a few hundred miles nearer the Carpathian shield.

"To avoid travelling in the heat of the day, the train stopped at Cernovitz from nine in the morning to ten-thirty at night." We have no visa for Cernovitz, which is now Chernovtsi, a good way inside Russia; another piece of Greater Romania which melted away after the Soviet conquests of the Second World War. In 1938 it was the frontier town, a silent outpost shimmering in the haze of the wheatfields; a bare platform and sidings without shade; at one end the red flag hanging limp, at the other the blue, red and yellow of Romania and a brave show of uniforms and top hats, into whose protection the two-coach invalid train, grey with dust and running late, glided and stopped.

The single pair of rails from Cernovitz to the horizon was all that broke the undulations of the Ukranian steppe. The landscape was stunned by heat. The locomotive gave a sigh and expired, they rolled the coaches by hand into a siding and the townsfolk came and hung branches on them and poured jugs of water on the roofs to cool them for Regina Maria. Stationmaster, doctors, aides and equerries and civic councillors, douaniers, soldiers and landlords sweated with perplexity and self-importance. It was not every day a queen visited Cernovitz.

In Bucharest that day the temperature was ninety-two; not a day for travelling long distances, still less for lying cooped up in an airless wagon-lit. The bulletin had been another polite fiction. The truth was that Marie had suffered another haemorrhage and for thirteen hours the doctors did not dare risk the slightest jolting.

Late at night the train moved on. It rolled at little more than walking pace along Romania's torrents, past her lonely monasteries, round the bluffs of the Transylvanian Alps which had been wrested from Hungary at the Peace Conference twenty years earlier. Marie was not aware of them, nor of the display of uniforms and the weeping crowds of ordinary people who gathered at wayside stations to see the Queen come home.

King Carol and his son Michael, then aged seventeen, and his sister Elisabeth, Queen of the Hellenes, waited at Bucharest station. The Prime Minister was there too, and the full cabinet, and the chiefs of the armed forces. Absent were Mignon, in Yugoslavia, Ileana, in Austria, and Nicholas, disgraced and in exile in Switzerland, but hurrying home.

The following day they took Marie on another journey, the eighty-mile ascent to Sinaia, and carried her from the train to the Peleş palace. She died within a few hours of being put to bed.

At the lying-in-state, mourners pointed out to each other the masses of madonna lilies and the wreath bound with two ribbons and the words Carol and Nicholas. The brothers, temporarily reconciled, followed the cortège to the mausoleum of the kings at Curtea de Arges, under the Carpathian snows.

Ileana the youngest daughter, her mother's favourite, arrived next day. She had had trouble with her passports. She had motored for nineteen hours through Hungary and western Romania and, passing through Cluj in the early morning, had seen the flags at half-mast and known that she was too late.

With the timing of a great actress, Queen Marie issued her last message to the nation on the eve of her last day on earth :

"I was barely seventeen when I came to you. I was young and ignorant, but very proud of my native country, and even now I am proud to have been born an Englishwoman . . . but I bless you, dear Romania, country of my joy and my grief, the beautiful country which has lived in my heart.

"I entrust my children to the hearts of my people. Being mortal they can sin, but their hearts are warm, as mine was. Love them, and love one another. Maria Regina."

At Balchik they wore purple, and the aeolian harp of Tenka Yuva was silenced for several years. On the rough road to Bran the same year a traveller saw a procession of peasants. The majority were women, dressed in the gaudy local costume. A priest in mauve vestments walked at their head. Behind, a smaller procession was made up of men in tight-fitting trousers of homespun wool, with broad leather belts and embroidered smocks open at the throat and dark felt hats. These sunburned peasant folk had come for the *pomana*, the forty-day rite, and they celebrated the departure of Marie's soul with fiddle music and dancing and a feast at the roadside.

Marie's heart was duly deposited in the Balchik chapel, in a jewelled casket. A few years later, when the southern Dobrudja was ceded to Bulgaria, a former aide hurried to the Quiet Nest and took the casket to Bran, where Ileana placed the heart in a marble sarcophagus and cemented it so firmly in the rock that when the communists arrived and she had to flee the country she could not get it out again. A local tradition says it is still there, but the authorities confirm that it now rests with Queen Marie herself, in the tomb at Curtea de Arges.

Dying in 1938, she was spared the humiliations of seeing her country once again backing a loser in a world war, and the final degradation of the Romanian Hohenzollerns.

King Carol II, forced to abdicate, joined a whole flock of royal birds driven from their nests by the war. He alighted on Spain, on Mexico and Bermuda, before finding a resting-place in Lisbon. In the battledress of exiled celebrities – dark glasses and headscarf – Elena Lupescu accompanied him and was at his bedside when he died of a heart attack in 1953. Twenty years later she was living quietly at Estoril and a few years ago a visitor[1] found her "a very intelligent as well as a good-looking woman. Conversation with

[1] Nubar Gulbenkian.

her was always a great pleasure, for she had had a large experience of life . . . and she displayed a good deal of wit in the way she recounted it."

Perhaps Mr Ceausescu in harassed moments envies those tragic figures, the victims of ruined dynasties, who manage to enjoy status without responsibility, who keep their titles, courtiers, memories and jewels, and who remain comfortably off, though not so comfortably as the lawyers who handled the shocking tangles of their affairs.

The life of Nicholas, Queen Marie's second son, has been one of almost perpetual self-indulgence. He was stripped of his royal rank for a morganatic marriage, but in his seventies he remains an Honorary Lieutenant, Royal Navy, and has successfully laid claim to a new title : Prince of Hohenzollern. Two marriages have brought the prince two little nests, one in Madrid and one in Lausanne.

Elisabeth Queen of the Hellenes, divorced within two years of her marriage, described by acquaintances as a mean, cold, grasping woman, died unwanted and unwept at Cannes in 1956. Her beauty as a child was astonishing ('It was unnatural to be so beautiful,' a friend says) and for a time, in Romania, she experimented with agriculture and is said to have grown the first rice crop in that country. But she grew fat, vicious and careless of her appearance and old courtiers remember her almost with disgust.

Marie ("Mignon"), left a widow at the assassination of Alexander of Yugoslavia and turned out of her kingdom in 1940 by Axis invaders, spoiled her children as her mother had done and let no regrets or affairs of state divert her from a restless search for pleasure and entertainment. She died in 1961.

The youngest daughter, the closest to her mother's heart, was Ileana, the bobbed-haired little girl of the Tsar's visit and the Red Cross campaigns of the First World War. Ileana took her royal duties seriously and while still in her teens helped to found the Great Legion of Girl Guides of Romania – first of several innocent youth movements, soon to be absorbed in Carol's national guard "to preserve them from the influence of party politics".

Ileana married the Archduke Anton of Austria and bred children rapidly. After the Second World War she went to Buenos Aires and then the USA and in 1954 she divorced her husband and married a Romanian doctor named Issarescu. The second marriage did not last either. A few years ago Princess Ileana founded an Orthodox monastery in Pennsylvania and entered it as Abbess. Few daughters retain such devotion to their mothers for so many years, and there can be no one better fitted to have the last word on Marie of Romania (I have asked her to say what were her mother's faults) :

"Her faults, I would say, were the result in many ways of her virtues and her overtrusting nature, which made her believe in people who were unworthy of her trust. I should say she was to a certain extent blinded by her own charm and the effect it had on others . . . It may be that my daughter's eyes can with difficulty focus upon the faults of a beloved parent, but even now, after thirty-six years, and now having myself passed the age she was when she died, I am still convinced that she was a very rare human being . . ."

King Michael of Romania is the son of Carol II and he was once known to stamp collectors as the "boy king". Wearer of the iron crown at seven, then forced to hand it back to his father, then restored on his father's abdication by occupying Germans in 1940, he was finally driven out by the Russians in 1946. Today, in his fifties, he is a portly stockbroker of Geneva.

Queen Helen of Romania, a princess of Greece, first wife of Carol II, a queen who was never crowned, ends her days surrounded by old retainers at Fiesole in Italy. From the time she first allied herself with the unhappy dynasty, Helen was subjected to smear and insult. An innocent divorcée, manoeuvred into impossible situations, she did not hesitate to sacrifice herself more than once for what appeared to be the best interests of her adopted nation. Several characters in the complex saga of the Romanian Hohenzollerns engage one's sympathy. There is Ferdinand, the diffident king, manfully tackling jobs he was temperamentally unfitted for, there is Michael, valiantly standing up to Germans and Russians much too ruthless and powerful for him, there is Queen Marie of course, who did nothing small or mean and loved making people happy . . . but the one person who emerges with most credit and with dignity unimpaired is Queen Helen. She alone seems to have known what it meant to be a sovereign, with a sovereign's loyalty and sincerity, and she was torn to pieces for it.

The family is not extinct. Ex-King Michael has five handsome children – all girls, and at the last count Princess Ileana had twelve grandchildren. None of them have set eyes on Romania, and none of them are likely to.

Courtiers and their ladies, a more numerous band than might be imagined, keep the royal fairytale going – a fairytale with a dragon which breathes Stalinist tyranny and atrocities. They do not know that life in Romania is normal now. They do not want to know.

'She writes like a communist,' a former lady-in-waiting says.

'She writes like that, poor thing, because the letter may be intercepted,' says another.

By some devious and totally unnecessary cloak-and-dagger route the letter has been smuggled through from Bucharest. It could more easily have come through the ordinary post. The old friend writes that her grandson is entering the university, that she is having a new bathroom put in with the money she has won in a lottery, that the children have been ski-ing at Predeal, that they saw the archduke on television the other night, being grilled about the case for a monarchy by two Hungarian interviewers . . . I fail to convince the old ladies that it might well be true.

They remind me of the philologist whom we met holidaying at Balchik. He, too, had had a letter – from his son in New York. The young man had found a nice job with a radio network, a nice girl, a nice country cottage. His letter was full of admiration of the Americans and their way of life.

'Of course,' the philologist said, 'he has to write like that, or they wouldn't let him send it.'

15

Moonlight and Roses

The tourist map which the Bulgarians give to motorists nowadays is a gridiron of thick red lines which connect all the major towns and represent main roads and stretches of motorway. Although the policy seems to be, as with the travel brochures and hotel prospectuses, to describe a situation five years from now, not exactly at this moment, the map does not lead you wildly astray. And when you come to what I call Spaghetti Junction, the interchange outside Golden Sands on the Black Sea riviera, you see that eastern Europe, not renowned historically for its communications, can match the west for civil engineering when the incentive – in this case tourism – is there.

The map I travelled with on my pioneer journey in Bulgaria had one red line on it, a line which connected capital city with principal seaport and divided the country neatly across the middle. This was Highway One, Sofia to Burgas.

It seemed the obvious route to take. It followed a valley between the two parallel mountain chains, Balkan Range and Sredna Gora. On that map your finger made short work of a string of alliterative townships (Klissura, Kalofer, Karlovo, Kazanluk) and dots of villages (Rozino, Rozovo, Rozavec) whose names were given to them not to confuse the traveller but to proclaim the staple industry, which is rose-growing. You skipped over an inch or two of broken line – an unfenced road or gravelled road, you assumed – and there you were, on the Black Sea.

But a dotted line on a Bulgarian map of the nineteen-fifties often meant no road at all. The best route from Sofia to the coast was a more roundabout one, and what looked the best road on the map was travelled by go-it-alone innocents like myself, ignorant of and frightened to ask for local knowledge; and by few others. In Bulgaria, when you left the city behind, you were back in the old etymology of communications, when Journey was a day-long ordeal, and Travel was synonymous with travail.

The Bulstrad (motoring organisation) hints to drivers said ominously: "Inhabited places lie at short distances from each other, and each has a medical centre with trained staff and supplies of the necessary drugs." It was true for the first couple of hours. Though narrow, the road was asphalted or (rather too often for the liking of a driver with a timetable to maintain) in course of being asphalted. The first leg of Highway One crossed a broad fertile valley and pointed due east like an arrow at its goal three hundred miles away. There were villages and State farms, fishermen beside a lake, blossoming towns and a few trucks which left cement trails behind them. Women workers dug the fields, a railway track crossed and recrossed the route (but never a sign of a train).

Vitosha, mountain of Sofia, lost its violet cap in the violet haze of a sunny afternoon. The blue-grey ramparts of the Balkan Range, which Bulgarians call Stara Planina, "Old Hill", seemed to close the road ahead. The topography on the ground was not quite as straightforward as it looked on the map.

Nor was the road. It ran out of tar and started taking sharp bends, winding inconsequentially through a forest like the track of a drunken mule, climbing every little foothill to see what was on top. I would have liked to stop and see also, but I had to keep going. I had slowed down, alarmed by the pinging of marble chips on the undercarriage. The smoke-screen of dust I raised kept catching up with me. I had hoped to reach Burgas by dark, but at that rate I could hardly expect to get to Kazanluk, roughly half-way.

Col succeeded col. The railway line disappeared into a tunnel under the Konitsa spur from which, as far as one could tell, there was no emerging. The green forest fell away, the road straggled among thin poplars. Places marked in heavy type on the map turned out to be ramshackle collections of unplastered cottages which might have dropped off a lorry. It was hard to tell whether they had inhabitants or not.

(Over the years I have come to know that road better, and I know that this village is celebrated for its yoghourt, that for its chestnut purée, another for its millet beer and a fourth for its black-currant brandy. Every village, almost every cottage, has fruit orchards, hop gardens, clinging vines and strings of red and green peppers round it, every district is celebrated for something, usually something to eat. Bulgaria is one big salad bowl, if you take the trouble to explore it; fruit salad and vegetable salad.)

But the petrol was poor stuff. They have improved it in the past twenty years. Your tank emptied at an alarming rate and the map, though well sprinkled with monastery signs, battlefield signs and historic site signs, showed no motel or petrol station sign. Coasting down the loops of the pass, economising, I listened to the crunch of the tyres and wondered how long they would hold out. The answer came immediately : a pop-pop-pop which grew louder as the blister inflated and scraped against the wing. It burst. I slid to a halt beside a half-circle of black and white stones which out-lined the precipice edge on the hairpin bend. One could not say they protected you from it.

The landscape was silent. No other vehicles attempted Highway One that afternoon, and I did not blame them. No village roofs broke the pale surface of the beeches and poplars below the road. Two storks, two black points circling and climbing, were all that moved in a clear sky above their nest in a poplar tree as slim and straight as a radio mast. The interminable hills marched on. I felt lonely, and rather worried. The new arrival in eastern Europe is like a new boy at school. He is conscious of being an outcast until he has learned the rules and proved himself an acceptable member of society. He can do without accidents, because he has a shrewd suspicion he will be held to blame for them.

While rolling the spare wheel into place I had a curious sense of being watched. One does, when acting suspiciously, and it was a suspicious act to linger on the highway. Bulgaria, most faithful client and imitator of the Soviet Union, was not then the tolerant, tourist-welcoming land she quickly became. It was understood that a foreigner travelling alone and using his own transport would make his way efficiently and expeditiously from approved hotel A to approved hotel B. No roadside picnics, no forest walks or moun-tain rambles, no hanging about villages trying to get off with the girls or strike up conversations with picturesque natives. Two minutes here to stretch the legs, two somewhere else to wipe the dust off the windscreen – that much was permitted and no more. So, at least, the young man in the Sofia office of Autoklub had implied.

I could see no one and hear nothing. Even the storks had departed. The noise of the car had disturbed them and now the female had returned to her nest and her mate had floated away over the hill. The white road on the mountain had all the desolation of a no-man's-land – not rough country, not barren, but like so many places in eastern Europe simply left alone, a track on which no traveller pauses for fear of being benighted.

I rolled the punctured wheel off the hub and rolled it straight into a policeman.

He was not the first I had seen. Sofia, to western eyes, was stiff with uniforms and I took them all for policemen although they may have been soldiers or militia or bus conductors. All the colours of a military tattoo paraded Sofia's streets – blue tunics and white breeches, khaki suits and green caps, gold-frogged scarlet tunics and white trousers and riding boots, grey battle dress and red forage caps . . . being new to iron curtain society I had thought it best not to look too closely, not to risk getting involved. An American in the Balkan hotel in Sofia, however, had told me that it was those not in uniform whom one had to steer clear of.

My policeman at the roadside wore a grey blouse with red-green-and-white flashes and he carried a rifle. My first reaction was to pretend he was not there. But when I bent over the wheel spanner he gave two sharp hisses and I sprang up. He backed away and unslung the rifle. He was a mere youth, a grimy, thin-faced lad with cropped hair, in a coarse ill-fitting uniform. He made some remark. I could only reply by shrugging my shoulders and spreading out my hands in the universal gesture of non-comprehension. I did not know enough Bulgarian even to say 'I can't speak Bulgarian.'

'You will find,' my Autoklub friend had briefed me, 'that we speak chiefly the Slav languages. With our friends from other lands we use that unwritten language which all persons use when they are young and afterwards forget. It is called the language of the heart. By that I mean that all Bulgarians speak the language of brotherhood and love, with which all persons should be familiar.'

From the start I had felt inferior in the presence of the people. They commanded my admiration because they tolerated a system which, from all I had been told, was intolerable. Their natures, more sensitive than ours, were more in tune with real values. I saw the oceans of misery which had been poured into their deep-set eyes and I felt I had to make it up to them for being the under-dogs of history, locked in their mixed-up, much-fought-over little land. Their capacity for pride and humility, cruelty and tenderness, passion and apathy, for being plunged in despair and trans-figured by a gust of gaiety all in a moment, baffled and impressed me. My knowledge of Bulgarians dated back a full seventy-two hours, and my acquaintances numbered about four, including the policeman.

The grey forage cap was squashed down on his head, the long rifle gripped with both hands. Its uncomfortable-looking butt was grounded between his boots. Had this sorry-looking specimen stepped back another pace he would have tripped over the sling which, frayed and too long, trailed in the dust.

I packed the tools away, moving round nimbly to let him know that I realised it was a crime to stop on the road. The language of the heart is all very well, but how do you initiate the dialogue? How avoid those fatal misinterpretations which sound hilarious in retrospect but are no joke at the time? I put no trust in the language of gestures either. Country people of lands once under Turkish rule give you a nod for no and a shake of the head for yes — that is, some of them do. When you think they are waving you good-bye they are telling you to come closer, and vice versa. Consequently, when I climbed into the car and the policeman hissed again and signalled "I am ready to be overtaken" in the manner once recommended by the British Highway Code, I assumed he was forbidding me to leave and I climbed out again.

He began to talk, using the same word over and over and re-inforcing it with slaps of the hand against the rifle-barrel. I could only guess his meaning. Where did I come from? 'Sofia.' I pointed west. Whither bound? 'Kazanluk.' I pointed east. For the moment it satisfied him.

He tossed the rifle in the air, caught it and rattled the bolt. He began waving it wildly about and squinting down the barrel. I shivered. But he was only drawing a bead on the stork, which had reappeared and was wheeling over the nest. '*Takataka*,' he said, then returned to the "At Ease" position and roared with laughter, displaying broken teeth, some brown and some metallic. I shivered again. A breeze was rocking the poplar tops. In a couple of hours it would be dark and I had nowhere to sleep. How to get this to a trigger-happy policeman on a lonely road in Bulgaria?

He propped his rifle against a thorn-bush and came up to me to feel the stuff of my jacket. He seemed interested in the pockets. It dawned on me — it ought to have dawned earlier — that he wanted to see my papers. Always keep your papers handy, foreigners had impressed on me in Sofia. In three days no one had asked for them. I offered him the passport. He frowned over it, turning it round and round to reveal all the visa stamps. He pointed to the photograph. Yourself? Yes, believe it or not. He went over the document page by page and came back to the photograph.

'Hey, you can't do that.'

He was trying to tear the page out. But the cry startled him. With another grin, slightly more ingratiating, he closed the passport and handed it back. Then he fumbled in his blouse and produced a snapshot and presented it to me, indicating that it was mine to keep. I have it still : a plump girl with black braided hair and roses in it, wearing what was either a wedding dress or a choral group folk-costume. For a *quid pro quo* I found a snapshot in my wallet and presented it to him. He accepted with a slight bow. We were getting on splendidly. Not, unhappily, in the direction of Kazanluk.

I ought not to have shown the wallet. He demanded it. Never argue with authority was my first resolution on entering Bulgaria. I surrendered it, hoping he would not make too much fuss about the British banknotes under the purple *leva* currency. I carried them for emergencies but it was against the law.

They were the first things his fingers lighted on. He grinned with triumph and I felt my face going hot with embarrassment. He extracted a pound note, found a crumpled ten-*leva* note of his own and held them up side by side. A swap? I nodded vigorously, not stopping to work out the relative values. When I did I realised that my policeman was corruptible, which is naturally what one expects, first time in curtainland. He was offering two pounds for one – the black market rate, no doubt.

He took mine, I took his, he returned my wallet, we were all square. I could go.

But again he made the overtaking sign, picked up his rifle, shoved it in the back of the car, pushed past me and got into the driving seat. The dreadful significance of the whole deal was at last clear. I had just sold him a nearly new one-and-a-half-litre Riley. Too stunned to protest, I stood aside and waited for him to drive away.

But who can fathom the police mentality in iron curtain lands? Who can predict their next move? Having stolen the car, he was in no hurry to start the engine. After a moment, evidently remembering some necessary courtesy of the country, he got out again and cordially waved me good-bye. Good-bye or . . . gradually I was catching on. Not good-bye, but hop in. And now he went round to the passenger side, making signs that right-hand-drive motor-cars were a novelty to him. Rolling down the mountain, I understood everything : all that he had been trying to communicate in the tense confrontation was 'Going my way?' – all the business with passports and wallets added up to a friendly exchange of souvenirs.

At the foot of the pass we hit tarmac and began negotiating a series of riverine plains, sealed within the walls of the hills. Long shadows leaned over the valleys, but I could see cornfields flowing like rivers of gold and pale islands of beech trees in proliferous leaf. The scent of lavender hung over the road and was replaced by the scent of roses. '*Rosa*,' said the policeman. At last we almost had a word in common.

I had planned to be in the Roses Valley in mid-morning, before the girls finished picking the rosebuds and loading them on trucks. I wanted to detour among those villages where you may still inspect clumsy copper stills and heavy wooden presses, cracked and juice-stained, and perhaps see a bearded farm-worker in a wrinkled Turkish cap, sucking his pipe on the stoop of a cottage . . . relics of days when attar of roses was called peasant rose-oil, when it was a cottage craft, not a national industry.

But there we were, the policeman and I, hurrying in half-darkness through forty miles of roses, and if it had not been for the perfume in the air I would have mistaken them for potato plantations.

Bulgaria's national flower is the rose. Nowadays all the railway stations and airports are planted out with red roses. On any boulevard which tourists walk down, it is roses all the way. The sign above the schoolhouse door at Rozino says ROSES ARE THE GOLDEN CURRENCY OF OUR LAND and that is no exaggeration, for Bulgarian attar trickles round the globe and the country's earnings abroad amount annually to about £30 million – a big credit item in the budget of a small communist state.

Distilling the concentrate was for generations a casual disorganised process carried out by hundreds of smallholders who farmed two or three acres of plantation apiece. Nowadays the rose-growers are the darlings of the economy and the planted area covers thousands of acres in the flat sheltered plain along the Tundja river. Every acre yields three million rosebuds; three million rosebuds yield one pint of attar; and a pint of attar, in 1974, was costing the foreign perfumier about £1200.

For three centuries there have been roses in the Roses Valley. The first arrival was the red oil-bearing Damascus variety, *rosa damascena Mill*, which you also see depicted among the arabesques on Persian palaces. Later came the white rose, *rosa alba*. The two strains live in harmonious Yorkist-Lancastrian co-existence and I am told of – but have yet to see – a bush in the Valley which bears red and white blooms on the same spray.

Modern automated distilleries have sprung up round Kazanluk and in the experimental gardens the director challenges you to name a rose he has not got. (I said : 'Marie of Romania' – he produced it.) There are laboratories for pesticides at Kazanluk, and factories which turn out rose eau-de-cologne, rose jelly, rose toothpaste, rose jam and rose soup.

I learned all that on subsequent visits. Possibly the policeman tried to get it across to me – I remember he said '*Rosaliika*,' and smacked his lips – but we did not reach a proper understanding on that journey. I learned that he was called Boris. Everyone I had met in Bulgaria was called Boris.

'Boris Hristov,' I said, and hummed a few bars of *Eugene Onegin* for him. The name conveyed nothing.

He gave me his identity card to look at. *Militer*. A soldier, not a policeman after all. A civilian, in fact, a national serviceman. I drove him up to the barracks at Kalofer, a decrepit country house at the end of an avenue which had seen better days. Going out of my way was not exactly altruism. I thought the army might have a gallon of petrol to spare, to get me to the official camping park at Kazanluk. Maybe it would even have a meal and a bed. Reacting against all the unpleasantness of the day, I was beginning to feel myself among dear friends in Bulgaria.

The sergeant saluted the foreign saloon with profound respect. He spoke a little French, not much. He told me where petrol might be picked up in the morning at Kazanluk; he himself had none, the detachment or whatever it was had not been fully mechanised. We sat on a patch of grass and squashed mulberries in front of the guard-hut and assessed the merits of American (that is, British) tobacco aganist Turkish (that is, Bulgarian). We drank a glass of *rosaliika* which, the sergeant said, would ensure my return one day to the Roses Valley. I left him at eight p.m. The moon on the Balkan Range, rose-red in a cloudless sky, lit up the ribbon of asphalt between the dark low growths of the rose bushes. Twenty-five miles to go, fuel gauge at zero.

The moon was higher, brighter and more silvery when I ran out of petrol, but it failed to shine on the cluster of roofs which ought, by my calculations, to have appeared ahead. There was no telling how far away Kazanluk might be, and no one to ask.

I rolled the car on to a dry rutted track which opened a passage among the bushes. Along avenues like this the rose girls walk, their wicker baskets slung at their hips. It takes them two or three hours to reach the end of the row and then they turn and walk back, gathering the roses which have bloomed behind them. The slow dance of the rose maidens, up, down, change baskets and start again, goes on every morning for six weeks in May and early June.

"Bloomed" is not quite right. They pick only the tight buds, in which the perfume is imprisoned. Quite quickly, in the warmth of the sun, the petals open and the moisture evaporates. I suppose the directors of the rose-attar operations get no pleasure from the fragrance which spreads over the Valley when the sun is high : to them, it signifies so much essential oil gone to waste.

My car was not designed for sleeping in. I climbed into the back seat, but could not get comfortable. I was lying on a strap of some sort. I hauled it out and Boris's rifle clattered to the floor. In his hurry to clock in, he had gone away without it.

This brought back the familiar tightening of stomach muscles. To be found camping out illegally behind the iron curtain would be bad enough, to be found camping out in possession of arms was probably asking to be put against a wall and shot. The main thing, it seemed to me, was not to be found. The car gleamed horribly in the moonlight above its bower of rose bushes. No passer-by could fail to spot it. But the rifle at least might be hidden and I took it out and stumbled into the plantation, looking for some thick bush to prop it against.

An owl raised a derisive hoot, a distant dog barked. The moon gazed down on an apparently deserted landscape, a scene of true tranquillity, but to anyone stranded in it the Valley was full of life and movement. When Bulgaria sleeps, the night creatures stridently take over. Winged insects crashed into the briars and struggled to extricate themselves, small animals shuffled among the weeds. I listened for footsteps on the road, or the sound of a vehicle; but the curfew which the régime imposed on foreign motorists evidently applied to the population also. Across the Valley, towards the river, a couple of lights flickered. Not Kazanluk, it was too far from the road. (Had I known what I learned next day, that a hydro scheme and barrage were under construction I would have trotted a long way in the opposite direction and put a few thousand rose bushes between me and the bloodhounds and anti-saboteur patrols.) At least I knew better than to go knocking on people's doors in the middle of the night.

Scratched by thorns and pestered by insects, I gave up my idea of sleeping under the roses, away from my car. I sneaked back and locked myself in. Drawn out by the night air, perfume hung over the interior like a chloroform mask.

Far away another dog barked. Cuckoo and bullfinch notes had replaced the owl's cry. I rubbed condensation off the window and looked out. The moon had set, smoke-rings of cloud floated like aureoles on the peaks of Stara Planina, the sun was hesitating on the lip of the forest, as though wondering whether its appearance would be counted an intrusion. Dawn was at hand. I wound the window down and sniffed, as though for the first time, the memorable scent of the roses.

I awoke in high spirits. A long night, disturbing in parts, but we had defied authority and got away with it, we had contravened the sternest State law and . . . Self-congratulation was premature. Close at hand a policeman hissed, like Boris.

Or was it my imagination? I was wondering, when a second policeman hissed. Then a third, from across the road. Then others, more faintly. It was their signal : any second they would spring the ambush. Either that, or all four tyres were leaking air.

The sun burst through the mist. All the birds stopped twittering. The hissing continued and it was accompanied with faint popping sounds, as of unstuck bootsoles on soft ground. The law was out in force, biding its time. Why prolong the agony? I stepped out and lifted a white handkerchief.

Closer to the flowers, brushing them, I detected the source of those sounds : the hiss and pop of myriads of rosebuds as they opened to the morning sun. In ten minutes it had all died away, the green buds were pink-tipped, ripe for the pickers, and down the road they came, behind two cantering donkeys, a cartload of young boys and girls. They were singing *Bulgaria My Homeland*, a song full of sunrise hopes and the springtime of youth, a song I was to enjoy hearing many times.

An old-fashioned khaki-coloured motor-bike and sidecar was travelling in their wake. It pulled in beside me. The driver was the sergeant of Kalofer, rather dashing in cavalry breeches, and his passenger was Boris. I led them into the roses and, after some to-ing and fro-ing, placed the rifle in Boris's arms. The sergeant's eyebrows made a question-mark.

'To frighten the birds,' I explained.

Boris looked chastened. The sergeant was disposed to sit on the car bonnet and yarn for a while, man to man, about the short-comings of conscripts, the need to wet-nurse them. 'Who gets into trouble when one of my men loses his equipment? Not the culprit, I assure you.' I nodded sympathetically and said it was the same with us, the same with military outfits the world over.

'We telephoned Balkanturist at Kazanluk,' he went on in his execrable French. 'We learned you had not arrived. I would have come and looked for you last night, but Boris said no. "He's an Englishman," he said, "he's resourceful, nothing frightens him, he'll make himself comfortable before everything else, that's the first lesson an Englishman learns." '

He stopped a passing truck and commandeered a can of petrol for which I paid with a packet of cigarettes. He said I should call again when I passed through Kalofer on the way back. I did, and we drank some more *rosaliika*, to be certain of meeting a third time.

We have not yet done so, though I often travel that way. It is a fine fast drive now, over the saddles of the hills and through the vales of lavender and roses, past the new Georgi Dimitrov dam and reservoir, along a good section of the motorway on which the signs point confidently at Vienna in one direction and Istanbul in the other.

Nowadays we think nothing of driving from Sofia to the Black Sea in one day. The new map is dotted with petrol stations, caravan parks, breakdown service areas and roadside telephones and in the season a steady procession of touring coaches files through the Roses Valley. Plenty of trains on that once-abandoned railway, if you should be stranded somewhere. But there is really no excuse for being stranded, hardly a possibility of so arranging it that you were stranded on a May night, in a world of moonlight and roses, and that you woke up to hear the buds whispering to the sun.

16

The Tears of Radka Boboshevna

When I saw her my heart sank. Had the stone steps of the Balkan hotel in Sofia caved in and swallowed her, had I been required on the strength of that first glance to describe her, I would have said she was chunky, mannish, snub-nosed, sullen, black-eyed and slightly oil-streaked, dressed in a sort of grey flying-suit with a woollen head-scarf. A Soviet pilot or engineer, a cliché curtainland woman, or a spy-writer's idea of one.

The hotel steps, however, remained firm beneath her wooden-soled boots. I was right about the snub nose and black eyes, wrong about the oil. The flying-suit was her official uniform, tunic and skirt of some grey canvas-like material, with a small red star, her Komsomol button, on the lapel.

'Good morning, I am your guide,' she said. 'My name is Radka Boboshevna, you may call me Radka. First we shall visit the church of Saint Petka of the Saddlers. We shall walk, please, and the car will follow.'

On the parapet of the old church, which is sunk to its barrel roof in Lenin Square at the level of the city-centre tramway junc-tion, Radka halted and began reciting its history. Thirty feet down, a policeman was kicking a bundle of rags. I moved over for a better view. Radka followed, still talking. The rags clothed a body which lay on its side, head propped on elbow. It was an elderly citizen and he was comfortably arguing with the young police officer who, after all, was only stubbing his toe in embarrassment against the coping.

'What's going on down there, Radka?'

'The man is gypsy or Armenian, he is not from Sofia. Inside the church is most interesting . . .'

I moved away. Radka stayed at my side. I studied in profile this guide of mine who had roped herself to me for the tortuous ascent through Bulgarian history and wondered how I could lose her. She might have thrown off the head-scarf, given her jet-black hair a good brushing, touched up her sallow complexion, smoothed out the wrinkles in her brow and her skirt and been a passable-looking girl.

'Are you Sofianese, Radka?'

'Yes, we say *sofianitsa*. Inside the church is most interesting, not so much for its architecture as for the frescoes, which date . . .'

'What's it like, living in Sofia?'

'It is very good. Sofia is a beautiful city of many parks and wooden places. The frescoes of Saint Petka date from the sixteenth century and . . .'

'Can we see them?'

'No. The damp air would damage them and they are kept locked up. Now we shall take the car and visit the church of Saint Sunday. It has a vaulted basilica-style dome, built in the sixth century on the site of . . .'

'What is the name of that big mosque down the street?'

'It is called the Big Mosque. We shall visit it later. The church of Saint Sunday is built on the site of . . .'

'Must be quite a view from the minaret of that mosque. I'd like to climb to the top.'

'It is not possible. The church of Saint Sunday is built . . .'

'Forgive me interrupting, but Saint Sunday doesn't sound right. Wouldn't you say Saint Dominic's, or something like that?'

Radka opened her handbag and peered into it. 'It is Saint Sunday, it is written so. The church is built on the site of a small fourth-century church. On the way we shall see part of the Roman city and part of the Thracian city which lie under the modern city. Sofia is one of the oldest capitals in Europe. It is also the highest, except for Madrid. It was orginally Serdica, the crossroads of Europe. It attracted attention because of its geographical location and its mineral springs . . .'

Later I said : 'You know, Radka, I don't want to be a tourist in the ordinary way. What you're telling me is very interesting, but it's the kind of thing I can read up for myself in the guidebooks. I have only a few days to spend here and I'd like to soak up the atmosphere. In Sofia, for example, instead of churches and museums I'd like to visit the fruit-market and some of the big shops, and take a ride on the tram and so forth.'

She consulted the driver of the car. 'We shall pass the fruit-market on our way to the museum of Bulgaro-Soviet Friendship. The shops for tourist souvenirs are near Saint Petka's, we shall not return there today. We have the car' – she fumbled in her hand-bag, which appeared to be packed with hand-grenades, and waved the programme at me – 'and you may go where you wish, it is written so. There is no need to take the tram.'

Later I tried again. 'This Turkish prison you're taking me to, how old is it?'

'Five hundred twenty years, I have told you, it is built in 1562.'

'Four hundred and twenty.'

Radka compressed her lips. 'It is four hundred twenty years old.'

'Well, I've had enough history for one day. I want to see how Bulgarians live now, not how they lived then. Instead of the old Turkish prison, couldn't we see a new Bulgarian prison?'

She talked with the driver. 'I am sorry, it is not possible to visit a modern prison.'

The best time I had in Sofia was when Radka had to go to the dentist and I gave the driver the afternoon off. No Thracian or Roman remains obstructed my route. I gave all the monuments to Russo-Bulgarian Friendship a wide berth. The only church was one I found by accident, a small Byzantine place in Sofia's kitchen-garden suburbs, crammed with medieval paintings and humming with life. A small choir sang in it, aged inhabitants clumped round, kissing images and inaudibly murmuring. A wedding party trooped in to have its wreaths and bouquets consecrated, a young priest recited his office and simultaneously gave all the ikons and silver screens within reach a brisk rub with a polishing rag. All took place in a compartment not much bigger than the inside of a Sofian tramcar.

When I told Radka about it she said : 'But of course. Bulgarians are very religiously people.' She herself had been to church that day, to pray for her toothache. Socialism and religion, the twin sources of life's energy . . . they seemed to run smoothly in harness throughout Bulgaria.

I took a tramcar, the first that stopped, and rode to its terminus at Red Village, КРАСHO СЕЛО as one learns to read it; and noted that, frown as they might in the city centre at the careless disposal of a cigarette-end in a gutter that was hosed down several times a day, there was in the working-class section much the same amount of litter, noise, general untidiness and drunkenness (though of a more good-humoured kind) as you would find on a housing estate in London or Leeds.

I went to the State Opera, paying ten *stotinki* – two and a half pence – for a seat. (If you wanted to do the thing in style and take a party, it cost thirty pence for a box.) Among the principals were names well to the fore in the international lists, Ghiaurov and Raina Kabaivanska. (I boasted to Radka about having seen La Kabaivanska leaving the theatre, and Radka said she saw her every day, the diva lived in the same street and they met at the bus-stop.)

Such names, and the opera titles, are posted up at Bulgarian theatres in the impenetrable disguise of Cyrillic lettering. The smeared printing of the bills and the poor-quality gum which allows them to flutter in draughty streets like handkerchiefs on a departing troop train make the code no easier to crack. Guesswork gave me *Tosca* and *Carmen* from ТОСКА and КАРМЕН – but that was last week's programme. The choice seemed to lie between БЬТЕРЭЛАИ and КАВАЛЕРИЯ РУСТИКАНА. I nearly did not go : middle-European folk drama is too parochial and jolly for my taste. But an Italian journalist, claiming only a few hours' acquaintanceship with the Cyrillic alphabet – and that only from road-signs and restaurant menus – read them off fluently : *Butterfly* and *Cavalleria Rusticana*. Printed capitals, he said, presented no difficulty. 'Wait till you see the Bulgarians' handwriting.'

I told Radka how impressed I had been with the enthusiasm and size of the audience, the professionalism of the principals and the power of the bass singers . . . not however with the production as a whole, which lacked inspiration.

'And the seats were so cheap, it was unbelievable . . .'

'Music and works of art and books of all kinds are very cheap in Bulgaria. For a recording of Nicolai Ghiaurov, how much do you pay?'

'Perhaps two pounds, ten or twelve *leva*.'

'I have such a recording, long-play, twelve tracks, it costs me one *lev*.'

'Are you fond of music, Radka? Do you go to the theatre? What do you do with yourself in the evenings? Do you have a boy-friend?'

'I have several friends, not one particular friend. I like very much to walk with my brother. In the evenings I am working.'

'You mean you have another job?'

'No other job, no. I am working always as tourist guide. It is rather hard for me, the work and studies is very long.'

'But you must get some time off? At week-ends, for example?'

'Sometimes, yes. Now, please, I must tell you about the Sofia theatres. In Sofia are thirty-five theatres and twelve symphony orchestras. The Ivan Vazov National Theatre has well-established traditions and fine actors . . .'

Radka that morning wore a navy-blue jacket and skirt and a starched white blouse. Severe enough, but an improvement on the flying-suit. Her shoes were flat and comfortable-looking, she seemed to have washed her hair, and from time to time she put on a pair of large round sunglasses. She was dressed for out of town, for the first day of our provincial travels. We motored over the old faded coat-of-many-colours of farming and forest lands, which even big cities like Sofia have managed to shrug off only as far as the suburbs. One has the feeling that the countryside is taking over the towns, not the other way about.

At the first sign of authentic people – a gang of deep-chested peasant women hoeing between rows of tobacco plants – I stopped the car and went across to photograph them; a display of independence which provoked a slightly strained situation in the car. We drove on for a mile in silence, and then Radka said : 'It will be allowed for you to take pictures.'

The plain ended, the foothills began. Through gaps in the pine-wood we could see the Rila massif, the great southern barrier. Groups of triangular summits were scattered like the encampments of invading armies from Macedonia. Alexander the Great slept there. One huge snow-white tent dominated the rest. 'You're keen on walking, Radka. How about us climbing that mountain this afternoon?'

'No, it is not possible. It is Moussala mountain. It is the highest Balkan mountain, two thousand nine hundred and twenty-five metres high. That is . . .' She opened her notebook of decimal equivalents.

'Nine and a half thousand feet.'

'Nine thousand, five hundred, ninety-six feet, point four.'

Instead we traversed its shoulder and came to that Rila monastery which travel books make such a fuss about. One sees why. It is staggering, up there amid the gloom of the snows, the pines and the pack-donkey trails, to enter a walled citadel and receive full in the face the blaze of pink, white and black arches, colonnades, stairways, balconies and towers. As when, after a house in which terrorists are hidden has been under prolonged siege and bombardment, a single window-pane remains miraculously unsmashed amid the débris, so the fragile painted woodwork of the Rila monastery stands intact, virtually the only survivor of its kind, near the military highway into what has been for wars, for a thousand years, the most distressful country in Europe.

A village-full of peasants had come to pay its devotions. In the scramble for admittance to the painted chapel – where every saint admonishes you, 'Believe – or else' – I slipped my chain and took refuge up some pinewood staircases, to the top of four storeys of balconies round the monks' quarters.

There one could look down with an agreeable detachment. The irreverent analogy came into my mind of the view from the bridge of a Mississippi stern-wheeler, the sunny Rila courtyard being the crowded landing-stage of a Louisiana river port. Only one person, however, waved to the showboat's pilot. It was Radka, and she took her revenge with a punishing chapter on Bulgaria's religious struggles, and a museum. I tried to spell out the Cyrillic inscriptions. For the first time, she smiled – a scornful smile, but a smile nonetheless.

'But this cross is gilded, not golden. You can see the wood-carving at the corners.'

'No, it is gold. It is written so.'

'Are you sure? Because, look, where the gold leaf has rubbed off. It's olive-wood, I would say.'

'Wait. I will ask.'

She summoned the curator. Her expression told him that here was a foreigner, arguing, contradicting, all the time knowing nothing – I deduced the words from the tone of her voice. A female attendant, built like a chucker-out, nodded understandingly and kept glancing at me with iron-curtain hauteur. The curator delivered a five-minute lecture, to which Radka listened attentively.

'The cross is carved wood, pine and chestnut. It is covered with gold.' Her expression added : 'There – what did I tell you?'

In Rila village, below the monastery, I escaped again. In one of her rare off-the-record pronouncements, Radka had informed me that it was the Kingdom of Storks. Storks had taken long leases of all the chimneys, and sub-let the lower parts of their nests to colonies of swallows. Up the side of one house I saw a path to the stork's nest, an old black wooden monastic-type staircase.

From the rooftop I saw my guide disconsolately roaming, clutching her big bag and sunglasses, pestered by gypsy children. It was noon, hot and dusty. I felt ashamed of myself.

'Radka, I'm sorry. I suppose the storks are a bit temperamental on their nests, aren't they? And if I get pecked, it's you who'll get the blame, isn't it? Let's move on.'

'It is not possible. I must show you the Partisan monument. It is on the hill. We shall climb on foot.'

The hill was a miniature Moussala. Halfway up I stopped and said : 'You're tired. We'll go back to the car.'

'No, I am not tired.' She turned her head away, but I saw a tear on her cheek.

'Is it toothache?'

She nodded – I did not know her well enough to know whether that meant yes or no.

'Am I being difficult? Always arguing and contradicting and running away?'

She said nothing. She started to follow me downhill at a distance, but after a while the sound of her footsteps ceased. She was sitting on a log, having a little weep.

'I am not a good guide,' she said. 'I shall never be a proper guide. My English is not good enough. I did not work hard at it, I regret it now.'

'That's not true. I wish I could speak a foreign language as well as you speak English. No, it's my fault. Be honest now, am I not the worst tourist you have ever had to deal with?'

She said : 'The worst? You are the first.'

She could not find a handkerchief in the bag of hand-grenades, but she refused mine. At the foot of the hill the driver looked sharply at her and narrowly at me. In his place, I would have jumped to the same conclusion. We drove on, locked in the individual compartments of our inhibitions, through the calm, orchard-lined, aimlessly-wandering lanes.

Radka spoke no more of monuments and churches and cultural landmarks. Perhaps, in that quiet land, there were none to speak of. Instead I began to draw her out – for her sake, I hoped her teeth were easier to draw – on the subject of a tourist guide's education. Two years Russian and English, she said, then six months in a Black Sea resort, in a hotel specially fitted up for training waiters, couriers and receptionists. Hardly any conversation in the language, apparently no supervision ('It was holidays for us, believe me we spend our time playing on the beach') – but after it was over a lot of homework, learning parrot-fashion the touristic descriptions of Bulgaria's scenic routes. The examination consisted of a coach tour through all the places of interest, during which each guide-to-be gave the others a recitation on the stretch they were passing through, as though she had a bus-load of foreign visitors. The real business of couriership – the shouldering and solving of the foreigner's ninety-nine little anxieties and problems – was not touched upon.

'They'd do better to put it on tape and play it as the bus went along,' I told her when she showed me the eleven rolls of notes (which cleared up the hand-grenade mystery), economically written up on both sides of the paper, with no margins, in her tight neat hand.

'But would you know what to do if I lost my passport?'

She looked scared. 'Have you lost your passport?'

'No.'

'I would not know what to do.'

She had never handled a tourist before, never seen a foreigner, except in the distance at Sunny Beach. She did not know it would be like this, the job frightened her but, having done the full course of training, she must stick it for at least three years. 'It is written so.'

'Did you have a job before this one?'

'Yes, I was a nurse at the Sofia polyclinic.'

'You liked it?'

'Yes.'

'But not at first?'

'No.'

'There you are, then. You will like this job too, when you settle down.'

Radka's tears had pitted the ice, and I began to melt it when I asked for some instruction in the language. Her eyes sparkled again, but not with tears, at my efforts to pronounce the unpronounceable. The driver, a silent and vaguely menacing figure, tilted the rear-view mirror to grin encouragement. ('You have met our driver? His name is Vladimir,' my guide said, after we had been sitting behind him for two days.)

It started as a joke, Bulgarian without tears, and I was a slow pupil, but I tried hard because acting as teacher did wonders for Radka's self-confidence. She made me learn ten words a day. Every evening, over *slivova* or rose liqueur, a word-test was conducted with great formality and solemnity. Vladimir sat in on it, he absolutely refused to be dismissed, it gave him such pleasure to mouth the answers behind Radka's back. Restaurant waiters and customers joined in, full of admiration for a westerner who had actually learned to say yes and no, 'Shall I close the window' and 'Another piece of bread, please' – though he fractured the vowel-sounds in doing so. Something like mass hysteria broke out among a party of schoolchildren, having supper at the same country inn, when they heard me going over the numerals; a word from their slip of a teacher quelled it instantly.

From one source and another I picked up new expressions, so that when the driver accepted a cigarette and said *'Blago darjà'* (thank you) I could reply *'Gnama dzashtà'* (don't mention it) and when Radka retired with her *'Leke nosht'* (goodnight) I could call out *'Priatna putchifka'* (pleasant rest) . . . and make a coachload of British tourists stare. Radka beamed and came back to shake my hand. 'You are *totchno takà, otlitchno,* my best pupil.'

The Bulgarian courier on that coach, a dapper extrovert youth who had studied his job with Radka, the bright boy of his year, she said, came over to ask my impressions of the country. Entirely favourable, I told him.

'Jolly glad to hear you say so, sir.'

I reminded Radka how lucky she was, having only one customer to cope with, while young Lenin ('Frightful name, sir, don't you agree?') had forty. But both insisted that individuals were more to be feared than groups. Lenin was just back from a tour with the Italian journalist I had met in Sofia.

'Not a minute's peace, sir, not one jolly moment. I show him a a factory, he wants to know every blessed thing about it. Frightful, sir, what? I told the chap, they make cutlery at this factory. "How many knives in one day? How many spoons? How many forks?" – every blessed time. I'm not a jolly industrialist, sir, what? I was frightfully glad to see the backside of him, I can tell you.'

Bewildered by her colleague's grasp of the vernacular, Radka looked glum again. But before Lenin left us ('Cheer-ho, sir, must get back to my blessed party') I whispered to him – knowing it would be passed on – that Radka was a jolly charming girl, jolly conscientious, a frightfully good companion. When Radka asked my opinion of his accent I said : 'He's certainly fluent, but your English is more correct.'

We stopped on the E.5, the dead-straight Istanbul highway, at a level crossing. Field-workers got up off their knees, women appeared at the verandahs of cottages, gypsy children streamed out of some half-underground settlement and congregated at the rail-way fence. It was the hour at which the Orient express passed through. So in rural England, two centuries ago, farm workers laid down their forks and tramped to the roadside to salute some Tantivy or Telegraph stage-coach and to set their turnip watches by it.

The car cooled off in the shade of a double avenue of cherries. Several pickers descended from the trees and poured their choicest fruits on us. It is a characteristic of the agricultural Bulgarian that he wants to share the delicacies of his land with the stranger who stops to admire them.

A wide load – it looked like the half-section of a new Danube bridge – came hurrying down the international race-track and the rest of the pickers tumbled out of the trees. The juggernaut hurtled past, ripping off branches, leaves and fruit. The pickers philo-sophically turned up their thumbs; to them it was just one of life's little ironies.

Radka sat knee-deep in cherries, forcing them on me. 'I know why you're keeping my mouth full, you've found the way to stop me asking questions.'

Trivial remarks like that reduced the driver to helpless laughter. But Vladimir was by no means the moron he pretended to be. With gestures, rudimentary English and my own rudimentary Bulgarian, he imparted valuable snippets of information. His passions were football and motor-cars. The car was a British Ford Cortina; it had done two hundred thousand kilometres and it purred along like a sewing-machine; the tyres were Czech, before that India, he said, *otlitchno*, excellent. The next set would be British again.

This make of car, he maintained, was the sturdiest in the world. The Sydney and World Cup rallies had proved it. Every year, round the outskirts of Sofia, they had an Old Crocks race. The British ambassador entered his ancient primrose-coloured Rolls, but Ford always won it.

I asked if he had a friend in the Army. 'That uniform cap under your seat?'

'It's mine. Last year the State orders that official drivers must wear the uniform cap. The drivers refuse to wear them. There is a new law this year, drivers must carry their caps but need not wear them.'

We hit the Roses Valley at the right time, eight o'clock of a May morning. When we stopped and opened the door the old fragrance, and thoughts of Boris, drifted in. Young workers mobbed us, thrusting bouquets of roses at Radka. The picture books which deal with that region are full of smiling, shapely girls in national costume, tossing roses into overflowing baskets, but such figures are about as likely to be met with on the spot as the nursery-rhyme milkmaid in a modern English dairy. The reality is down-to-earth : gypsy families, children, hessian sacks and donkey-carts.

Our besiegers were small boys. The schools had just closed for the summer, and every schoolchild was doing his fifteen-day stint for the State. A little put off by the gallantry of a twelve-year-old who was trying to twist roses in her hair, Radka launched into her lines :

'The oil-bearing rose of Damascus was almost destroyed by German capitalistic interests before the anti-fascist war of liberation . . .'

'This brings back memories, Radka? Not so long since you were working on your school holiday tasks?'

'No. The German chemical manufacturers, producing synthetic perfumes, were envious of the Bulgarian attar and tried to exterminate . . .'

'In the rose gardens?'

'No. Listen to me, please, and then I will tell you. The Germans uprooted the rose bushes and planted parsnips . . .'

Radka had boxed peaches. Children generally went to the pleasant, sweet-smelling jobs, packing and canning fruit, bottling cherries, picking strawberries, gathering lavender and roses. 'Everyone enjoyed it. No pay, no, but a free meal every day and at night we slept in an empty school. We travelled the countryside like gypsies, crowded in trucks and carts. We had the opportunity to see different parts of our land. It was a happy time for me.'

Since schooldays, her brightest adventures had been walking and mountain-climbing. On foot she had conquered Vitosha, the 6000-foot peak of the Sofia suburbs. 'We went up and down in one day, my brother and I. Afterwards I was in bed for two days, I couldn't move my limbs. Many young communists attempt that climb, but not everyone succeeds.'

'I was admiring your Komsomol badge. When will you be a full member of the Party?'

'Not yet. Perhaps not at all. For me it is not too interesting.'

'Our driver, is he a Party member?'

'No, he is agrarian unionist.'

'Isn't that the same thing?'

'No, it is opposite. They complain about the bad things the communists do. But at present the communists are stronger, they have about two-thirds of the seats.'

'You have two political parties, then?'

'Two main parties and some others. Bulgaria is a democracy, it's not like the west, where you have only one party.'

'But we, too, have two main parties and some others.'

'Yes, I have read of that. They are called by different names, but they are the same party, I think. They are the capitalist party, isn't that so?'

'I suppose so. But in Britain even a communist can stand for parliament and if he is elected he can take his seat.'

Radka conveyed this to the driver, who commented on it promptly and concisely.

'Yes, it is as I thought. Vladimir says that the wealth of the arch-capitalists determines the ruling section of the parties. The communists of Britain have no money, therefore they cannot gain power. They are admitted to the elections for propaganda purposes. I think they have to pay some money?'

'To stand for parliament? Yes, a hundred and fifty pounds each candidate.'

She consulted her diary of monetary equivalents. 'Ah, that is dishonest. It is not possible. That is a worker's pay for three months in the mines or heavy industries.'

One saw Radka at her liveliest when the sun was high. Her tears still flowed, not from remorse or self-criticism, but from a natural spontaneous vitality which, until I got to know her, I would not have associated with the snub-nosed, tight-lipped girl whom I first met on the steps of the Balkan hotel.

'You must know,' she said, 'when we first meet, I tremble very much.'

'I trembled too.' It had not occurred to me that behind the stiff tunic of iron curtain woman there might beat a quaking girlish heart.

As the sun sank, Radka's chatter died away. Her thoughts were turned into deeper channels. Then one had to be prepared to grapple with sombre themes, the pressures of darkness and the unknown, the sadness and introspection to which the Slav temperament is addicted. Evenings I tried to leave to my guide and driver, to give them a chance to relax. But often we found ourselves to-

gether late at night in hotel lounge or folk restaurant, watching a
dancing bear or listening to the drone of the fortune-teller. Anything, as far as Radka was concerned, to defer the bedtime hour.

Fortune-tellers abound in rural Bulgaria. Radka had a mysterious
fascination for them, and they for her. I would have been more
suspicious of their readiness to read a hand if they had charged for
it – but our fortune-tellers, ordinary-looking women, regarded the
offer of payment as an affront. Clairvoyance was a gift from heaven.
You got it freely, you must make it freely available to others.

Radka herself told fortunes, from the grounds in a coffee-cup,
the gritty *tursko kaphè* which is being ousted all over Bulgaria by
the powdered packet. The simple rites one performed reduced it to
the level of a party pastime, but she made some disclosures that
were uncannily close to the mark about my past – 'For you are
growing old,' she said innocently, 'and the cup tells more about
your past than your future.'

'You really believe this, don't you?'

'Of course. Every Bulgarian believes.'

Vladimir, a cynic about most things, took it seriously too. Anything fantastic or fabulous was sure to grip my companions' imagination. They affirmed the existence of witches, of Little People, of
the Indian rope-trick and the monstress of Loch Ness, as Radka
called it. They accepted the literal truth of legends, favouring par-
ticularly those which demonstrated the inevitability of retribution.

We spent a night at a lodge in a deer forest and I told the tale
of the medieval lord of whom it was foretold that he would meet
his end on the antlers of a tame stag; so he shot the stag. 'He had
the antlers mounted in the hall. One day, as he passed through,
they fell on him and pierced his brain.'

The story made a profound impression on both my hearers.
Radka muttered to herself the phrases which had struck her most
forcibly, to fix them in her memory. The old tale accorded well
with the Slavic philosophy of life. 'And so that *vojvodin* could not
escape his destiny.'

'How do you feel about ghosts?'

'Ah, yes, I am very much afraid. Believe me, the stairs I climb
are paved with ghosts. I am afraid to sleep alone, at home I always
sleep with my sister. Yes, of course I have seen them. Two weeks
ago I saw my grandmother, who died in April.

'This is the hard part of my life as tourist guide. Three nights
ago, when we were at Plovdiv, something heavy dropped on my

bed. I screamed and put on the light. It was nothing, the room was empty.'

Bulgarians believe that the souls of the dead linger on earth for forty days, during which period they can appear and give messages to loved ones.

'It is worse for my mother, who was the favourite child. She has met grandmother several times since her death, even at the grave-side in broad daylight they have met.'

'Radka, I never saw a girl like you for tears. What is it this time?'

She pointed down at the chain of rounded summits in the Stara Planina, whose snows were bathed in moonlight. 'I think of the sufferings of our sad country. I think about the Russian armies and Bulgarian volunteers in their ragged coats, in winter, without shoes. You remember, we have been on the Shipka pass and I have told you of the campaign of 1877, when they turned back the Turkish invaders and saved Europe.'

'Tell me again. Then we'll have my examination in Bulgarian.'

'Yes, I have an examination for you. It will be a hard one, because it is the last.'

We were on the late-night flight from Burgas to Sofia. In an hour we ran through the Bulgarian vocabulary and some pidgin conversation about books, in the course of which Radka told me that the most dramatic moment in English literature was for her the moment when Jane Eyre, on the point of marrying another man, hears the anguished cry of her lover, many miles away.

The scenes through which we had spent ten days wandering passed beneath, intermittently glimpsed through moonlight and cloud. The E.5 highway, entwined with the Orient express route; the Roses Valley; the Rila mountains, in which the monastery was locked . . . the aircraft hit a rough patch at the end of the Sofia runway and came to a halt, shuddering from wing-tip to wing-tip. 'Women drivers.' (I had noticed that we had a female pilot.) But Radka was not in a facetious mood.

'I shall not say goodbye. I shall ask permission to come to this airport with you tomorrow.'

'But it's midnight now. You'd have to get up at five o'clock, and probably you have a full day's work ahead of you.'

'I think I shall have permission for this.'

Precisely on time she arrived with the taxi. The rather frivolous polka-dotted red blouse of the past few days had yielded to the grey outfit she had worn when we first met. She looked like a young prison wardress.

I had cured Radka of the habit of seizing my luggage while porters propping up pillars of hotels gazed on indifferently and taxi drivers sat wrapped in their private fantasies. But this morning I dared not object. 'It is written so,' she would have said.

The streets glistened under an early-morning drizzle, the first for more than a week. The white-uniformed guards at the Dimitrov mausoleum were cloaked in green. 'You will remember that Sofia has wept for you' – she spoke with professional reticence, and continued in the same tone : 'You will remember that the boulevard is named for Botev, the great revolutionary poet of Bulgaria. In autumn the plane trees are very beautiful.'

'Did you sleep last night?'

'Yes. Today is the fortieth day. I think my grandmother will not come.'

Sofia airport is a dreary place at the best of times, a transit camp on the regimented routes of the socialist airlines. Six o'clock on a rainy morning showed it up in its least flattering light. We had half an hour to wait. Throwing open a door in a row of mud-coloured unlabelled doors, we sat down in the cafeteria, at that hour a sort of canteen and doss-house for the night staff of Balkanair and fitters on overtime at the Bulgar-Renault car factory. We stirred lukewarm water and powdered coffee in cracked cups. I remembered Pasternak on airports : 'Where the skyline of departures ends the history of situations.'

The ashtrays overflowed. A listless fat girl in blue overalls pushed the previous night's garbage up and down with a broom made of birch twigs. The door behind us kept blowing open and shutting itself, groaning on its hinges.

'Even the door is sad.'

I had put an extra handkerchief in my pocket, prepared for tears. But no white bud in the Roses Valley was firmer than Radka's snub nose that morning, and no young Russian hero sculpted in granite on the Shipka pass could have looked more determined about the lips.

'Next time I come to Bulgaria . . .'

'You will not come, I think.' From the disagreeable way in which she spoke I might have been declared *non grata* and going home in disgrace.

'Yes, I shall. Not this year, but probably next.'

'No, you will not return. I have seen it in your coffee-cup. I did not want to tell you. I have seen your journeys through Bulgaria, they do not continue, they are finished.'

A loudspeaker announced the flight. We made our way to passport control, where you surrendered various documents to faceless men – I think of them as faceless, for all you see is the tops of their heads – who shuffle them and pass them to one another under the counter, in and out of pigeon-holes, comparing them with heaven-knows-what dossiers and black lists. You cherish this as a typical memory of communism, forgetting that the little states of eastern Europe always did have a name for bureaucratic tyranny.

'Anyway, you'll come to England one day, and there I will be your courier, and will describe all the churches and monuments to you.'

'It is not possible,' Radka said. 'That I think is dreams, which cannot come true.'

Formalities concluded, I was free to board the flight.

'What will you do,' she asked, 'travelling to London?'

'I shall sleep. What will you do?'

'I must go to my office. The Committee has another job for me, starting at eight o'clock.'

'Another tour? Another tourist?'

'They do not say. I think perhaps yes.'

'Perhaps British?'

'They do not say.' Radka paused. 'I hope not British.'

'My dear, was it as bad as all that?'

'Not bad, no. But soon the journeys are over, and then it is hard to say goodbye.'

17

Beside the Seaside

First came Varna and Burgas, two fishing ports sixty miles apart. Then, spreading north from each, the coastal settlements of rich Bulgarians – stucco villas on low cliffs above the sea, hedged in with orange, lemon and dwarf cypress. King Boris took the Euxinograd, a palace near Varna, for his summer residence. One small colony, Drouzhba (it means Friendship), was thrown open to the west in the nineteen-fifties and it became Bulgaria's prototype international resort. A lot of people think the Black Sea coast would be all right if they had called a halt at that point.

But the whole coast is eager to please. Bulgarians – hotel staff, camel-ride concessionaires, folk troupers – are responsive if you treat them right. The uncouth attitudes some holidaymakers complain of often conceal shyness; and a bit of disenchantment would be understandable, considering what the Bulgarians have to put up with from their guests. It is sad to see the patronising superiority of our fellow-countrymen when they get among the people of socialist lands. They cannot answer back because argument with westerners is frowned on. If they could, some would surprise us by saying they feel sorry for us, because we have not yet accomplished our revolution.

Not all of us do it.

I sat under the pines at Golden Sands and read a letter from Radka, who was touring with an excursion party :

"I missed to tell you that there was a very sweet English girl in my group . . . Afterwards she rushed up to me and gave me a beautiful bunch of red carnations, telling me that she and her family thanked me for the cares I had bestowed on them. I cannot explain what happened to me, but I began to cry like a small child in the street and could not stop my tears for 15 minutes. Her mother came to express her gratitude and I saw tears in her eyes. Oh, believe me, I began to cry again.

"It was very solemnly when we got off the bus, all began to ask for my address. I saw them off at the very plane (it is not allowed!) and everybody began to kiss me. At the end were two old men and one turned his head to the other and scolded him that he was enough old and kissed me several minutes . . . I was happy and unhappy at the same time."

At Golden Sands and Sunny Beach the tower-blocks of hotels, a miscellany of inspirational architecture, each year's instalment a little more outrageous than the previous year's but all pretty much alike inside, have sprung up like dragon's teeth on a shoreline which, according to my pre-1945 map, bore not even a name. It was rarely frequented because of poisonous snakes. When an early Five-Year Plan scheduled it for development, they imported hedge-hogs to deal with the snakes, and for a long time they were plagued with hedgehogs. The rich flora of the coast, which once spread wild through swamp and forest, blooms now in captivity in formal gardens of a promenade. The geraniums, begonias and roses are healthier and taller than they used to be, so who can say they are not happier? Something like this has happened also to the Bulgarian people. 'The only thing I envy these foreigners for,' says an off-duty waiter to his girl-friend, staring at me, 'is their freedom to travel.' This young man wants to have his cake and eat it : he wants the security of the zoo and the liberty of the jungle.

I inhabit a hotel traditionally reserved for the British. I have heard it called the English castle. Across the park is the German citadel, on the slope the Russian fortress, hidden among the pines a Belgian kingdom and a Turkish empire . . . the Bulgarians have given the hotels these names. Bulgarians on holiday are content with the sort of barracks accommodation the tourist authority would not dream of offering to foreigners, and they think Golden Sands is marvellous, a dream country. For them it is holiday experience enough to walk the promenade and gaze up at the ziggurats of angled balconies (more Babylonian than Hammurabi ever knew), the mineral pool attached to one hotel and the undersea restaurant (not completed : they have struck snags) attached to another.

Even on the beach the nations stake out their frontiers. Fraternis-ing breaks out when you go for a camel ride, a motorboat trip, a meal in one of the folk restaurants which have seized, sterilised and served up palatable dollops of old Bulgarian ways, from fire-walking to dancing bears. All the lore and legend of the Near East have been ransacked to make the foreigner feel anywhere but at home.

From the white cliffs of Balchik, where the Quiet Nest's minaret lifts its pointed cap above the shrubbery, the riviera creeps down to Albena, the new Babylon. There the planning errors of the pioneer developers (they were many, and these days it is fashionable to acknowledge them) are being corrected and new architects of the People's Republic are apparently taking leave of their senses. Then comes Golden Sands, with stone pines and oleanders and undulating acres of evergreenery behind, then Drouzhba, nowadays looking charmingly outmoded, then the commercial and naval port of Varna, then Sunny Beach . . . a gradual descent into bucket-and-spade country.

By way of Burgas and Nessebur, sea-girt, a complex of picture-postcard timber cottages and small Byzantine ruins, you continue south to the estuary of the Ropotamo river and the Turkish border. By that time you have outdistanced tourism. Under a Ropotamo headland a banner is flying. It marks the site of a new holiday ground, destined to be the biggest of them all. You visualise the entry of the folk-dancers to the peaceful dunes. 'Come unto these yellow sands, and there take hands . . .' – How does it go on? Something about a knell.

Fifty thousand tourists, they tell us, will be down here by 1984. But the lonely paradise is putting up a fight, and it won't all be plain sailing. Stepping into this country from the Black Sea resorts is like stepping back into the picture some of us have of the rustic world of childhood, before the wild life departed and the fish floated away belly upward.

There are gravelled lanes, tall grasses, buttercups and butterflies. Near the river the vegetation grows dense and exotic. These broken fan-belts lying about are actually snakes, though harmless. From the reeds, when you disturb them to get a sight of the river, clouds of white admirals and swallow-tails rise up and scatter. The hedgehogs of the reclamation drive higher up the coast did not exterminate their fellow-creatures; they chased them all down here, to flourish on the banks of the Ropotamo.

Winding through a rift valley between low hills, patrolled by squadrons of dragon-flies and surfaced with its own botanical speciality, a large waxen water-lily, the river comes to the sea. Nothing advertises its attractions. No town stands at its mouth or on its sides, not even a village. It flows with a majesty which suggests a fairly impressive pedigree, but that is misleading. The Ropotamo is barely twenty miles long. You can follow it most of the way from mouth to source on foot, or in a boat. Of the two, walking is quicker.

A superannuated fisherman, left over from another age, lets his craft drift downstream, then pulls back to where he started from. He will row us up to the first or second oasis if we like, five miles in five hours against a cloudy green current, all through the white porcelain of the lilies, whose cups are big as frying-pans. Nothing else moves on the Ropotamo. The dirt paths along which Greeks and Tartars prodded their donkeys are desolate. We leave reeds and water-lilies behind and enter a reach where the banks have a fringe of oaks, willows and vine and a display of big convolvulus-type flowers, blown over maybe from the sub-tropical gardens of the Crimea. The butterflies are a positive nuisance. Ashore, wild bees are swarming and the ants raise pyramids to their Pharaohs.

Galleries of variegated foliage hide Jasnapoljana . . . but Jasnapoljana has nothing to hide, it is only a name on a map. We are eight miles from the sea before a no-fishing notice indicates that we are approaching society. Round the corner is a landing-stage and a soft-drinks kiosk standing back among the bushes. This one day will be the very heart of the new Sunny Beach – a replica of the fun town, Brighton-on-the-Euxine, where at this moment, on stage or in a café, some group is beating out a pop-song of the day, celebrating the imperturbable tranquillity of the Ropotamo :

> "Far from society's
> Mad syncopated rhythm."

An open truck disembarks a party of countrywomen on a Sunday-morning outing, and they make for the jetty. 'Room for one more?' – 'Why not?' says the skipper. It is a long black boat with curving prow, a design as old as the coracle but, unlike the coracle, adaptable to outboard motors.

We set off upstream. The driver knows his river. He works the tiller from side to side, to the full extent of its traverse, avoiding obstacles concealed from all but him. At times the engine splutters and dies, at times the boat drifts to a stop and turns broadside, at times the driver growls and all the women start rocking the boat with mad syncopated rhythm. There is a frenzy in their performance which a stranger might associate with venerable rites due to the river spirits. But we are only aground on tree roots.

Underwater oaks and their trailing branches lurk everywhere.

Water snakes spin away in the wash, the bleached ends of the trees are covered in black turtles, some not much bigger than ladybirds. This part of the Ropotamo is supposed to be the last haunt of the Thracian hyena, but its cry cannot compete with the cackle of women on a boat-trip.

Our farthest point is on the edge of the forest, near a motor road, thirteen miles from the sea. On the bank, under a notice which says STRICTLY NO FISHING sits a fisherman. He hails us and tells the skipper that boats are not allowed so far up the river. The skipper replies with an open-palm gesture at the notice-board. In that exchange there is for me something typical of Bulgarian life and character.

Change, then, to the motor road and follow the rest of the Ropotamo to its infancy in the canyons of the Strandja plateau. Oak and beech are matched with box and cypress. The botany is more exposed and more brilliant : autumn crocus, marigold, gentian, and the branching yellow flower which Bulgarians, after thirty years of socialism, still call king's candles.

From the high point of the ridge there is not a cottage in sight and the nearest town, Malko Turnovo, is twenty-six miles away. Nothing, as far as one can see, is to prevent the traveller from walking into Turkey across the Strandja moor – nothing but the thought of those hyenas.

To complete the pastoral scene it only needs a shepherd, and here he comes, tapping his black umbrella, swinging his wallet, leading a flock on what must be an old drove road.

I am lying on the turf with my head propped against a boulder. He stands over me and grins.

'Putchifka?'

'Da, putchifka.'

'Russki?'

'Ne.'

'Germanski?'

'Ne.'

'Ku kourski?'

'Angelski.'

'Ah.'

Infuriating, that that conversation, which just happened to contain most of the Bulgarian words I knew, should take place with no third party within earshot. It lasted for about as long as it took us to smoke a cigarette. The sheep, at least, speckled and wiry, with topknots of coloured ribbon, seemed to appreciate it, from the way they stood and stared. Then he took up his umbrella and trudged on, the flock followed, pattering along the sacred highway, and the bitter scent of wool fat hung for a long time in the air.

To be judge of a beauty contest was never included in the programme of my ambitions, and I would have thought Bulgaria one of the last countries to have approved such decadent goings-on. But an ever-obliging press officer nominated me. The event is included in the instant folklore catalogue of the Black Sea resorts, along with the *koukeri* dancers, the rose-maidens' chorus and the bagpipe-and-balalaika band. It was a continual irritation to the press officer, that Americans claimed to have invented the beauty contest in Atlantic City in 1921. At that date they were all the rage on the Black Sea, and the press officer had pictures to prove it.

And what more appropriate setting, on historical grounds alone, than this fabled coast? Was it not within bowshot of these shores that the Judgment of Paris was delivered, when at the fatal marriage feast Helen's lover-to-be awarded the golden apple to Aphrodite and set the Trojan war in motion? Like Paris in that primal beauty contest, I wondered if I had the tact for it and the necessary grasp of the international situation.

Sunny Beach attracts girls from east and west as well as a lot of native talent. Experience had shown, the press officer warned me, that it was unwise to let the same nationality appear twice in the first three places. 'There is no sense in it.' And one had to bear in mind that Bulgarian girls did not enter to win, only to provide local colour and encourage the others.

Power politics being what they are, I decided we could rule out the Swiss and Scandinavians as well. But that left plenty of headaches. A NATO-Warsaw Pact confrontation was inevitable; Arab-Israeli too, as like as not; Greek-Turkish almost certainly; maybe even a clash between Ulster and the Republic of Ireland. They were a cosmopolitan lot on the Black Sea that year.

Consulting the precedents is a *sine qua non* in a situation of ticklish diplomacy. The press officer had all the files in the Burgas bureau, he had been annoyed by something he read in the *New York Herald Tribune* and was collecting ammunition for a *démenti* through the Bulgarian press agency and a bid for the antiquity of Black Sea beauty contests.

The previous year's Miss Beach came from Belgrade, the one before that was Austrian.

I turned back over the years. Wien, Wien, Wien . . . all the prize-winners were Kirstens and Erikas and Gabrieles, all were Viennese, with here and there a German girl intervening. 'Most of our tourists come from those countries, so it is natural,' the press officer said. 'Besides, the publicity is important for us.'

'Don't the communist countries object? You have a fair number from Russia and Romania.'

'No, no,' he said irritably. 'You people have communism in the brains. For us, we do not give two shoots.'

Rules and records over the years made good reading. "Rich prizes were distributed," the announcement for 1966 said, "including excursions and free trips for the best-developed and most harmonious bodies."

Miss Beach 1967 (Vienna) told reporters : 'This is my favourite summer resort. I never dreamed of winning the contest. My mother forbade me to enter, but a friend put my name down.' Munich-born Erika Lang, winner of the 1962 contest, said : 'At first my husband would not allow me to take part, but now he is glad I did. I have grown so fond of Sunny Beach that I never want to leave it.'

Yes, I see that the Miss Beach stakes have taken on a mythical colouring, they are almost a part of the folk traditions of the coast. In the archives time's parabola falls back to the days when the beach was a swamp on the sea's edge, unnamed and untamed. In the nineteen-thirties, Youth and Beauty competitions were the thing and they took place beside what are today the oil-slicked waters of Varna's commercial harbour. Males, with patent-leather hair and short-sleeved bathing suits, stand up to their ribs in sea-weed, applauding the beauties who parade on a sort of pontoon arrangement.

Varna, 1935. The Italian ambassador presented prizes. "The seventeen-year-old Fraülein Hilda Förster of Vienna, in the most daring, most transparent and most expensive bathing dress ever seen, was proclaimed Venus of the Varna beach." Fraülein Hilda said : 'I never dreamed of winning such a contest. My father, who is director of the Bank of Austria, sent me here because I graduated with excellent marks at school. I dare not tell him I have entered for the prize – I want to come back next year !'

Varna, 1934. "The Queen of the Beach was elected today. To

the strains of Aïda and acclaimed by 40,000 people, fourteen beauties with graceful tanned bodies marched over a specially-built platform in the sea . . . Miss Bertha Benbassat of Constantinople was proclaimed Queen . . . Many holidaymakers protested, insisting that the Viennese singer, Miss Fanny Gebhar, should have the prize. Certainly she made a good impression with her beautiful body. Several contestants burst into tears."

The lovely Turk was reported as saying : 'I am very happy. I was about to refuse to take part, because my mother objected. It is my first visit to Varna, and already I am in love with it.'

In the nineteen-twenties they were called sea-nymphs, and in 1905 sea-hyenas, possibly on account of their long striped bathing suits. The enveloping garb of those years looks more suited to the Serpentine on Christmas Day than to the Black Sea in a blazing August. Kimonos, sailor suits, satins and beads pass tremblingly over the rickety boardwalk and every girl wears a picture hat or a bandeau. The scenes are blurred, but the blurring brings out the classical form of the compositions. They might portray the slow dance of captives round a Grecian urn.

"Phthia, 1000 BC. Aphrodite said : 'I never dreamed of winning this golden apple. My husband would be furious if he knew I had entered, I shall not tell him because I want to come back next year.' "

My own event went off smoothly and is now in the record books. I attended as a spectator, for when I went to take the vacant seat at the judge's table by the swimming pool a heavily-built case of sunburn said he was keeping it for a friend. The friend turned out to be some kind of gynaecologist from Kiev, attending an inter-national congress at one of the hotels – not the most appropriate choice, I would have thought, for a judge of virgin beauty. The press officer was not available for comment, but I gathered that the real Miss Beach struggle centres on who will make the panel of judges. The minor contest ended with Miss Austria leading (fur coat), Miss German Democratic Republic second (compendium of ladies' accessories) and Miss Czechoslovakia third (free trip round the bay).

18

Looking Back

Plovdiv is looking back. Above the city a brown silk balloon lifts into view. Some curly-moustachioed hero of the Russo-Turkish wars is about to bestride the lazy-pacing clouds and sail upon the bosom of the air. Coming closer, we see it is unmanned and tethered with ropes, rather the worse for wear after last night's thunderstorm.

Floods have washed away that milestone of travellers to the Orient, the bridge on the Maritsa. We cross a terrifying pontoon job, of which the only reliable piece of woodwork is the notice-board which announces that the Bulgarian Army built it in four days. I would rather they had given themselves more time. The Maritsa river, chocolate-brown, nags at the stanchions and hurls branches on to the platform. Crossing, we dip the axles under and push the whole thing out of shape. Behind us a low-sprung American automobile takes the temporary bridge with that lurching confidence American cars have, and the two rear-seat passengers, bald men in dark suits, do not lift an eye from their newspapers.

The Fair is spread over the meadows beside the river. The guide is a middle-aged dwarfish woman with flat feet and a sweet, humble expression. What do I wish to see? I am not sure, everything looks waterlogged. 'What would you recommend?'

Why did they choose Plovdiv for the international Trade Fair? It is a pleasant, low-lying town on banks of green willow in what is ordinarily a placid river valley. It is noted for bookshops and by-ways and some splendid painted mansions. It has a well-camou-flaged industrial section. The football team used to be Lokomotiv, but now it is Maritsa.

When Bulgaria achieved independence from the Turks, this was the first city and chief route-centre. Nine foreign consulates were established in Plovdiv and the first inter-continental train, Vienna to the Orient, was soon to pass through. Bulgaria cemented her new unity by calling a trade fair to Plovdiv and if western visitors expected something on the lines of Nijni Novgorod or Samarkand they must have been reassured to see a stock exchange and a Crédit Lyonnais and a booming mercantile section. Behind the extravagant bay windows of those painted mansions, Greek and Armenian businessmen had for some time been writing letters to Paris, Manchester and Odessa.

The Trade Fair opened in 1892. A stationary steam-engine and a flagon of peasant rose-oil were the best Bulgaria could offer. Czechoslovakia, then Bohemia, sent beehives, Austria sent river barges, Hungary contributed a threshing machine which attracted wondering attention, for "in twenty minutes it dealt with a hundred rice bundles all by itself."

That year, in the German pavilion, Plovdiv saw its first electric light bulbs and the Frenchman Godard ascended in a balloon, a replica of which floats above the fairground today . . . but America stole the show with a demonstration of Edison's phonograph.

From what we have seen so far, America is on the way to stealing it again with that long black Cadillac and the two arch-capitalists inside.

'It is for you to decide,' says Mrs Gavankova politely.

Out of politeness, then, we kick off with Bulgaria, a pavilion divided up into neat little furnishing layouts, fur coats and tufted rugs and sportswear, commodities which Bulgarian visitors inspect with interest because they will not for some years be seen in the shops. That woodwork : Mrs Gavankova says that far away in the marshes round Leningrad there is a country so cold and unhealthy that Russian lumberjacks will not work in it. Bulgarians do the job, they get extra pay for it and social privileges, when they come home on leave they are heroes; and most of the timber comes to Bulgarian furniture factories. The bit I like best in this pavilion is the little show of colour slides through a projector, Beautiful Bulgaria, synchronised to a recording of the radio and television children's choir singing *Bulgaria My Homeland.*

Whichever way we turn it we cannot make sense of the Fair map. Every passer-by to whom Mrs Gavankova appeals for help is a Russian who is himself lost. They run excursions from Moscow to the Trade Fair. It costs £60 for fourteen days, which includes £8 spending money. Five of those days are spent sitting up on thinly-padded, straight-backed benches in the train.

Not a train like this super-chief which stands on a hundred metres of track outside the Soviet pavilion. This is a cold monster of railroad perfection in crimson, with a real driver in the cab of its

diesel locomotive and a real conductor at the door of each coach –
an inquisitor he might be, from the reluctance people are showing
at going in for a look round. The pavilion is forbidding too : a vast
machine shop, blocks of grey steel, crucibles, convertors, transform-
ers, a tremendous monument to Labour and Production. I am awe-
struck at the transportation miracle they have accomplished in
planting this lump of heavy industry on soil a thousand miles from
its habitat. Bulgarians shrink a little : they are wondering whether
it is here to stay.

For light relief, we stumble into North Korea : pathetic little
cotton shirts in cardboard boxes, laid out as they might have been
under the gas lamps on a Saturday-night market stall in the England
of last century; packets of tea which, from the look of them, are
veterans of many a trade fair; a melancholy slant-eyed girl with a
visitors' book of which the pages, on this tenth day of the Fair, are
empty.

West Germany and Romania emulate the USSR, but more
subtly. Greece is blue and white, decked out with tourist posters
and wooden platters and amphorae, such as you buy on the waterfront at the Piraeus. France exhibits wines, farm produce, electrical
goods : uninspiring. Italy has gone in for female demonstrators,
elegantissime, in off-the-shoulder sweaters and microscopic skirts.
The machinery they preside over suggests an allegory of sex – the
plunge and recoil of pistons, the arcing of electricity across a gap –
and the Italian pavilion seethes with men spectators, a vortex of
furtive excitement.

Over Great Britain's contribution to the Fair I draw a veil. Mrs
Gavankova is embarrassed for me, and agrees that one should go
into trade fairs with money and enthusiasm, or stay out.

She picks up the trail of the black Cadillac – the only vehicle
permitted in the fairground, for some reason – and it leads to an
astrodome. The Americans did not rent a pavilion, they have set
up this lovely unearthly thing studded with pastel discs in a meadow.
We join a queue : our first queue. Brows are unclouded here, eyes
lit with anticipation. This is one's reward for plodding round the
Fair.

In the astrodome they are giving doughnuts and hot dogs away.
Dreams also. Restock your fantasy world. A chic miss with all the
languages at her finger-tips is cajoling little boys into conversation
with a cartoon lion on a closed-circuit television screen. The cross-
talk is above my head, but the audience guffaws continuously. As

no other nation, the Americans have remembered the first principle of showmanship : get your audience involved. You can play parlour games, indulge in an orgy of button-pressing and electrickery, spin the golf-trolley of 1984, tinker with racing motor-bikes, rock a Chris-Craft cruiser in a custom-built marina, a shapely lagoon of Florida sapphire . . . shake hands with life-sized models of American presidents and watch the all-American travelogue unfold in a comfortable little cinema – race riots and baseball parks, gunfights and tuna fishing, remote lakelands and automobile graveyards, Fourth of July parades and Watergate hearings . . . all the colour and richness of American life, the bad with the good, a dramatic indictment of the bloodless uniformity of eastern Europe.

Near the exit, where people are running to get on the end of the queue and go round again, noses are flattened against a glass case. It is Edison's phonograph, nineteen-seventies version : on a mirror, a piece of pinkish stone about the size of a walnut, labelled with two words in English which need no translation : MOON ROCK.

The south road from Plovdiv to Greece takes us to Bachkovo, third or fourth of the grand ecclesiastical sights of the Balkans. Founded about 1066, it remains like the Rila intact within ramparts above a torrent. Unlike the Rila, it is a mixed bag of buildings – chapels, ossuaries, cloisters, cells – daubed with frescoes more naïve than artistic.

Thirty long-haired, wild-looking monks give the place an otherworldly touch. They must be old men, and the driver says they are all harmless lunatics. Yet Bachkovo is a place where one might sit out the evening of one's days quite comfortably. Rustic benches, a trickling fountain, a flowery courtyard, the sunshine on the cobbles . . . maybe the monks have more sense than Bulgaria gives them credit for.

Bachkovo is as far as most visitors go, but a well-shod road continues south, uphill, tracing the river to its source, blasting through rock in places on a gradient which seems no gradient at all until you reach the watershed and find you are at 5000 feet. From the air and the botany you would never suspect it. The ravines are clothed with oak and chestnut, beech and sycamore. In pockets of the hills you can see tobacco plantations and vineyards. The village gardens, which slope down from cottages of the purest revival style, white plaster, dark oak balconies, pink pantiles, bulge with overblown roses.

Near the topmost ridges, where the hills melt away into the Aegean, the landscape is still parklike and kindly, perfect in peace and simplicity. It is as though Orpheus, when he tamed the wild beasts, did something for the countryside too.

A few miles from Greece, from Pamporovo or Smolyan, you can walk in summer and ski in winter to the Orpheus Rock. He was a native of Bulgaria, and that is precisely where he emerged from Hades with his half-regained Eurydice – and, looking back, lost her for ever.

I puzzle over Orpheus and his message. What is wrong with the backward glance? Or does it mean that he who hesitates . . .? I put it to the driver, an ignorant fellow who does not even know the story of Orpheus. He listens, and says promptly that obviously it is a question of faith, the myth means that without faith there cannot be love.

They still celebrate the Orphic mysteries in these mountains which the Bulgarians call Rodop, though no one seems to know what the mysteries are. Rodop himself was a god, petrified for some misdemeanour and permitted to look on his goddess, Heme – another mountain – only from afar. Some say this myth sublimates the deep-rooted ideal of unity which Bulgarians clung to throughout their history.

Without dispute it is a proper land for myth and legend. Natural bridges, stone forests and sandstone sphinxes abound. The geology is a blend of lime, sand and granite, spiked with semi-precious pebbles and streaked with lead, zinc and manganese. The people have no like elsewhere in Europe. The lost tribes of the Rodop, the first to be ottomanised, cling to Islam still. And the region has been chosen for the most costly hydro-electric development and the most extravagant winter sporting. So memories of the Rodop comprise donkeys and turbo-generators, Alpine flowers and tropical foliage, bikinis in winter and thick Turkish woollens in summer – and the day you walked through a dry hinterland of high pasture and rock pinnacle and heard, far from the sea, the bellow of a ship's siren on a huge, invisible, artificial lake.

West of Smolyan the traffic was hydro scheme trucks, which made dust tunnels of the mountain passes, and walking haystacks of donkeys with astrakhan-capped men on top and veiled women in print smocks and woollen jackets trudging behind. Our driver went up close behind a cart, grinning. Father and children, swathed in hot garments in midsummer, rode in it. Their mother, like a deserted bride in white calf-length veil and *haik*, submissively brought up the rear. Our driver nudged her with the front bumper. She did not look back.

Villages, poor and derelict, with wretched little mosques, rise in tiers above bends in the torrents, in complete harmony with their surroundings. Men in black, in a field far from nowhere, assemble for some incomprehensible purpose, gabbling in a dialect our driver does not pretend to understand. On the Vasil Kolarov lake a steel and concrete barrage has succumbed to oriental influences and there is a mosque within sprinkling distance of the water blown off the dam.

This mosque is operational. The driver urges me into its court-yard, where a few old men are washing their feet at a fountain. He stares brazenly into a humble room full of women, to whom the *hoxha*'s wife is reading the Koran. The *hoxha* himself arrives, a sad Turk in a black suit, and the old men follow him into the mosque and kneel on a frayed carpet. So does the driver, dragging me by the hand . . . none dare object, it is understood throughout the Rodop that the old faith survives only as long as the faithful do not make a fuss.

These people are not very forthcoming. Their history, I suppose, justifies a jaundiced outlook on strangers. Where to lodge becomes a problem that not even the driver's effrontery can solve. We have to cross the western ridges, into the harsher country of Pirin and the town of Melnik, smallest in Bulgaria, whose one thoroughfare is a mountain stream and ribbon of quicksand, crossed by rope bridges. Lanes are in much the same state as when a traveller of last century passed that way : "so narrow that one donkey cannot pass another."

When darkness falls, and the wilderness is full of strange sounds, our driver mentions as an encouraging item of news that not many years ago the brigands held captive Miss Stone, an American missionary, and would not let her go until the government paid out ten thousand dollars in gold. 'You hear what this old mountain-eer says?' – 'I can hear but I don't understand' – 'He says the bones of the rebels are lying white among the rocks. That is why the wind moans.'

We dine in the lead miners' canteen off raw cabbage and cold gristly sausage and wine like diluted pickle vinegar. The long low room, the extension to a wine cellar which stretches back into the

mountain, is noisy with miners, grimy and grizzled, all drunk except
our nearest neighbours, a red-bearded gorilla and a pale-faced slip
of a youth. It is the red-bearded one who speaks of the bones of the
rebels. Maybe the youth is middle-aged, but in Melnik, stronghold
of the ancients, he seems a stripling. He has little to say. It is some
time before I learn that he speaks English, and that is when he
asks if the driver and I are prepared to share a room.

'I am, I don't know about the driver.'

The landlady comes to escort us to the *hanche*. She wears grey
ankle socks to protect her feet from a pair of crippling wooden
shoes. I look more closely and see that they are socks of grey mud.
By the time we cross her threshold we are wearing them too.

The beds are woven mats on the floor of a cold jutting embrasure
in a timber shack. One has an occupant already: someone fast
asleep, wrapped in an overcoat with a fur collar. Through the floor-
boards you can see the river swirling down from Pirin's snows.

The two miners are coming back to the *hanche* to sleep with us.
That makes five in the room – five and a dog. The dog very nearly
did not make it through the quicksand. She is a decrepit wolf-
hound, all skin and bone, and when she flops with a sigh on the
mat she reminds me of Ulysses' dog, stretched on the dunghill,
feeble with age and tormented by flies.

Our friends are in no hurry to retire. They have cigarettes, I
have whisky, they talk and I listen. Like miners the world over,
they are not much at home with surface matters. They are happiest
with subterranean subjects, they like talking about the potential of
their mountains, the lead and the nickel, the zinc and cobalt and
magnesium. The sleeping financier puts in a word now and again,
but does not deign to roll over and face us.

Our friends know the Orpheus Rock. They can outline its geo-
logical character, for they have surveyed it from top to bottom, but
what the Orpheus myth is saying they cannot tell. 'Forward,
forward, mankind must march forward,' says the sleeper from the
depths of his fur coat. 'It is fatal to look back, it is vain to seek
precedents from the past.'

The red-bearded man agrees. 'For the days are short and the
hours are few,' he says enigmatically. Realising that we have an
educated person among us, he makes it clear that he and his colleagues are not common workers, they are mineralogists. With these
rough types as the cream of Bulgarian mining society, what must
the rest be like?

The dog bleats in her sleep and her tail thumps the mat. I did not think she had the strength. 'She's chasing a hare.'

'She is dreaming,' says the youth with unexpected gentleness. 'She dreams of her puppy days, when she was a young dog, do you remember that?'

The red-bearded one remembers. 'Bounding through cornfields. Like a dolphin. Like a boat on a stormy sea, you could not fatigue her.'

'Red deer, fallow deer, the hare . . . an aurochs, once . . . yes, in these same mountains and in the Rodop. She was young then.'

The older man steers the dog off the mat with his steel-capped boot, and prepares for sleep.

Next day, brigandish in their heavy boots, fur-tipped jackets and fur-peaked caps, the miners awaited their truck. The dog, after one sniff at the mist, had curled up under the balcony and gone to sleep again. The truck came up the bed of the stream, avoiding the soft sands, and we went down in the ruts it had made. Before we parted the red-bearded man came over and, on behalf of all the lead miners, asked me to convey fraternal greetings to the lead miners of Great Britain.

They went upstream, we went down. The engine raced, the wheels spun, the driver cursed and the mud spurted to roof-top height. Probably the same was happening to the miners' truck, but I did not look back and I imagine that they, sons of the Orpheus homeland, did not look back either.

The sleeping stranger came with us. No, of course he was no financier, the landlady addressed him as 'Professor', and he told us he was a sociologist and several other things at the Academy of Sciences in Sofia. We passed through Siroka Laka and made for the Dospat reservoir. The main road had been cut up by pipe-laying traffic, and we had to make detours. What was more serious, Professor Barev had forgotten his red passport – he had the blue but not the red – and where the road wound to within ten miles of the Greek frontier we entered a military zone and were turned back. A shame, the professor said, he wanted to show me where the Tsar lived.

'Which Tsar?'

'Tsar Nicholas of Russia.'

'The one who was murdered at Ekaterinburg?'

'He wasn't murdered. He and his family escaped. They found a way. Through the Urals. Down to the Caspian Sea and up the Volga. Down the Don. Into the Black Sea. They arrived at Varna. From Varna they made their way to Plovdiv and received sanctuary. After a year or two they moved again. Settled in the Rodop. I could have shown you the community.'

'Do you believe all that?'

'I neither believe nor disbelieve. I only tell you what the peasants of the Rodop believe. Legends are legendary, as you were saying last night, but there is a basis of fact. Your British Foreign Office has documents about it. Your King – who was he, the one who looked like Nicholas, wore a beard? King George the Fifth, yes, he knew of it, he kept in touch with the Tsar.'

'But wouldn't the Tsar be about a hundred if he were alive? I know the Rodop is famous for longevity, but . . .'

'No, the Tsar is dead. Died twenty, twenty-five years ago. The Tsarina also. The Tsarevitch, the boy who was never healthy, died a long time ago. The four girls are alive. Not as girls, of course, they are aged women. Indistinguishable from peasants. Married to peasants, two of them. Two remained single.'

'Is this known to the régime?'

'Everything is known to the authorities.'

'Why, then . . .?'

'It is ancient history, there is no need to remember it. The grand duchesses are old women. They have forgotten their previous existence. It was necessary to forget. How otherwise could they have survived?'

'I read something about an American book recently, which claimed that the Tsar's family was alive and well and living in southern Bulgaria.'

'If it is an American book, then I am inclined to disbelieve,' the professor said. 'No nation has produced more stupid post-mortems on Ekaterinburg.'

'They had a wonderful exhibition at the Plovdiv Fair, though.'

The professor dismissed the astrodome with a wave of his hand. 'Childish games, childish toys.'

We roam another tract of the land of Orphic myth and romance and come to Jundola, a small health resort in a world of rounded hills and clumps of trees like feather dusters. The professor describes it as a centre of longevity, one of several in Bulgaria. That country's 1969 census claimed two thousand centenarians, two-thirds of them female, or one centenarian per four thousand of population – easily a world record. The common objection of sceptics, that middle and eastern Europeans reached their centuries faster because they added on years as young men in order to avoid military service, obviously doesn't apply to the women. I tell the professor that I have never met a centenarian; he replies that I am about to meet several.

The woman curator of a revival-style country house designated national monument trips up and down stairs, pointing her wooden pointer with a steady hand. She has a pinched white face with strongly-marked veins but few wrinkles. Taking off her skull-cap puts years on her, for she is as bald as the marble knob on the bedpost. Her reputed age is a hundred and thirteen. Barev says deduct ten from that. 'After about eighty, the old folk start counting eight months as a year.'

He converses with the woman. It is a tough life in the hills, she reports. Extremes of climate, a spartan diet. Nature takes the years off the weak and adds them to the strong. If a mountain shepherd reaches fifty, he is fairly certain to go on to be eighty-five or ninety.

The curator puts us on the track of Zaviska, herdswoman, now unemployed through sciatica. She has been offered a room in a social home, but prefers her lean-to shack. Soon she will celebrate her hundred-and-ninth birthday. Being accustomed to visitors, she recites her history. As a child she pastured sheep in the Thracian plain, a privilege won from the Sultan himself. She is Christian and despises the Turks. They give themselves airs, she implies. When she was a girl they knew their place, they dared not enter her village, if they had to pass through they would do so at night, with sacking round their ponies' hoofs.

In her time she has been Russian, Bulgarian, Turkish, Roumelian and Bulgarian again. Bulgarian is best, she says, with an uneasy look at my notebook. Well, what poor old granny would not be uneasy when two city slickers descended on her, asking questions and copying down the answers?

The patriarch of the village is out on the mountain. Active but toothless, sharp-eyed but . . . Barev, translating, taps his forehead. His sister, a few years younger, a mere hundred and twenty or so, is still around. This woman could tell tales of Alexander the Second, Tsar Liberator, how they spread straw for his carriage, how soldiers lined the route, one for every five paces of many miles, how the Don Cossacks distributed largesse and her parents, not knowing what paper money was, gave it to the children to play with. When was this? No one can say. If true, it must have happened soon after the Crimean War. I suspect the old lady is telling tales her grandparents told her – getting them mixed up too, for Alexander never came near these mountains.

We do not meet this woman, but we see the graves of the five husbands she has buried, lined up neatly in the backyard.

The *Guinness Book of Records* is severe on longevity. "No single subject is more obscured by vanity, deceit, falsehood and deliberate fraud." You can number the properly-attested centenarians of any nation on the fingers of one hand. The most accurately-documented group of human beings in history – the British peerage – has produced one centenarian in a thousand years.

Professor Barev dismisses the British peerage as he dismissed the astrodome. Centres of longevity are centres of harsh living, peasant regions, highlands like the Caucasus and Hindu Kush and Rodop where one does not expect accurate record-keeping. They are where "scarcity of oxygen stimulates heart action, increase of red corpuscles and the sensitivity of the thyroid gland, which consequently controls blood heat more effectively and destroys cholesterin, the chief guilt factor in diseases of the aged".

Seeing that I am not convinced, not even with the story of the man from Azerbaijan who has satisfied Soviet gerontologists that he was born in 1805, the professor will send me a paper about it, in English, stamped with the authority of the Bulgarian Academy of Sciences.

(I am interested but still not convinced. The paper, full of misprints, puts my feelings in a nutshell with its opening sentence : "Many Bulgarians lie to be a hundred or more.")

19

Scrap Iron Curtain

Radka waits in the customs hall, beyond the barrier. She is not alone. She has an escort of young men, some in Army grey, some in the civilian uniform of dark drape suits with long lapels. The soldiers want the flower she carries, a white rose. She laughs. I see that she is aware that I have arrived. That rose, I take it, is for me.

The young men melt away. Radka inhales the scent of the rose. It is not for me, she has brought it along to give herself confidence. That, I would say, is something she abundantly possesses already. The customs man, chalk poised, awaits her nod. She bestows it, regally. He clears the baggage and a twitch of Radka's forefinger brings a bright-blue-suited official out of the shadows to carry it away. It is not many months since I was in a tangle and Radka in tears over simple manoeuvres like that.

She is happy to welcome me back to her country. I am happy to be back. She finds me not at all changing. Nor is she. Truly? Perhaps a little changed, more grown-up, more . . . I was going to say schoolmarmish. More confident. But then, it is more than a year. It is one year, five months and eleven days, says Radka.

Outside she relaxes, laughs and cries. Her English forsakes her, she cannot find words to express her feelings. That a foreigner should say farewell to Bulgaria and then come back! The rose-petals are saturated. 'Believe me, I can explain but I am enough ashamed.' Before coming to the airport she drank two hundred grammes of vermouth for courage, and now her head is a little bit spinning. She takes command of herself ('Now we must be very solemnly') and orders a passing soldier to go and see what keeps the driver.

And who was that peasant woman in the red shawl, who giggled over Radka's shoulder and looked so out of place among all the people coming off the aircraft?

'It was my mother. She wanted to see you, to see what my Englishman looks like.'

Grinning, the driver jumps in and starts us off. He has been watching the Japanese tourists, rarities in Bulgaria, getting themselves weighed for the flight. 'Forty kilogrammes. I couldn't believe it. Not one weighed more than forty. Me, I weigh a hundred and forty.'

Radka translates, shaking with laughter. 'They should travel . . . should travel two . . .'

'To?'

'Two. Two for the price of one,' she gasps. The driver, catching on, bursts into a raucous howl of laughter. We are back to the place I was getting acquainted with when I left last year : Bulgaria, land of smiles.

The driver fires questions at me in about five languages, and I hardly know how to reply. Radka, uncovering her flushed face, is suddenly stern. Pay no attention, she says, those are the only foreign words our driver knows, he is merely showing off.

On the way into Sofia I take up the commentary where Radka left off . . . Park of Liberty, Boulevard Botev, Hotel Pliska.

'Hotel Cognac. You have forgotten, I told you before, Pliska is the name of Bulgarian brandy. You remember how the Russian visitor could not find the hotel and in the street he asked, "Where is please the hotel Cognac?" – and now all Bulgaria calls that hotel the Cognac.'

I remember, but find it freshly amusing. Radka and the driver are convulsed.

We are spending one night at Hotel Cognac. It swarms with Russians, flocks of them, shepherded by guides. They must be a joy to handle, these Muscovites and Leningraduates. They stand like statues, shoulder to shoulder in dumb apprehension, awaiting orders. When one moves, they all move. But each small flock avoids contact with the other. Join the wrong crowd and you may find yourself going home to Tiflis, when you actually live in Archangel.

Men are solidly built and grim, the women homely, down-at-heel, thick-set. Staring at their faces in the elevator mirror you see them as cartoon characters and do not instantly distinguish masculine from feminine. Clothes, make-up, the normal display of the sexes toward each other are not among their priorities.

Radka confirms that the Russians' guides are to be envied. Tell a Russian tourist to stay put and he will stay until the Danube runs dry. Whereas the Germans, worst of all the Romanians . . . with those nationalities the guide is for ever turning her head to scold. With them she must stop and count her party every five minutes. With Russians it is enough to count them first thing in the morning and last thing at night.

Radka and her superior, Mrs Kostadina, come to dine with me in the pectopaht. (Restaurant in Cyrillic is РЕСТОРАНТ, which western tourists pronounce as it seems to be written. And now : 'All Bulgaria calls it the pectopaht.')

We are hemmed in by Russians. Mrs Kostadina, a young woman with bright button eyes, several languages and a lively mind, tells me that Radka, last year a frightened simpleton, is now the shining light of the English-language interpreters. Radka is feared and admired by hotel directors from here to the Bosporus. When a British shipowner came to Bulgaria last spring to have a ship launched it was Radka who took care of his wife and helped her launch it; Radka that day was seen on television. Radka has travelled with the British ambassador and the United States *chargé d'affaires* . . . she has trodden where it is permitted to few Bulgarians to tread, she has attended a reception at the British embassy.

'My heart was beating very fast. It was a big test for me. I carried flowers for the ambassador's wife, at first they were reluctant to let me in, they thought perhaps I had a bomb hidden among them. It was so nervously for me I forgot to show my invitation card. Our minister was there, it was very solemnly when the ambassador put his arm round my shoulders and said some high things about me. Afterwards his wife sent me a beautiful handbag. My brother begged the invitation card, he has put it in a frame and hung it in his room.'

Subdued cheerfulness breaks out over the Russian tables. The service is poor, half-cold food comes and goes to the wrong customers. No one minds. The Russians are loosening up. Good-natured chat, rapid and interrupted with shouts of laughter, but never loud or dissonant, is interchanged. A part-song for about twelve voices is sung next door to us, so softly as to encourage rather than distract our conversation.

Personalities establish themselves. A Russian Jew, the photographer of the party, marches from table to table, exhibiting the pictures he took today and jotting down orders for them. A procession of diners follows the pictures round the restaurant, enlisting the opinions of each table, until half the company is on its feet. The pictures are presented at our table. Silence falls. The Russians, impassive, wait to hear the stranger from the cold side of the iron curtain pronounce judgment. A camera cannot portray, I say, the charm of the ladies, the virility of the men. In short, everyone is much better-looking than these photographs make out. The opinion, relayed round the tables, offends none but the photographer. Without my noticing where they come from, two bottles of vodka appear on our table.

The Russians have swung into the rhythm of their natural gaiety. They sing songs, dance to the music of the gypsy band, gossip and exchange jokes. Like children who have heeded the warning before they left home, they enjoy themselves while remaining on their best behaviour.

Radka teaches four young men the old tavern song which begins :

> "If you have good wine, give it to us,
> If you have bad, keep it for yourselves"

and goes on from wine to women to song, to another twenty verses. Mrs Kostadina sets up a dialogue with an adjoining table which puts me in mind of the shadow-plays and puppet-shows of Moscow and Sofia because it is nonsense stuff, a conversation of the absurd. Yesterday, her neighbour is saying, the bus went so fast round a corner that the driver saw his own rear number-plate. Mrs Kostadina asks in return if her neighbour noticed anything of the accident on Stamboliiski street. A lorry was carrying a load of holes. One hole fell off, and another lorry ran into it.

I am reminded of the story of the Englishman, the Frenchman and the German on the motorway . . . The story is rather a long one, the Russians laugh in the wrong places and at the end they ask for some points to be cleared up. I hear them all round the restaurant explaining the English motorway joke to one another.

> ' "If you have nice girls, send them to us,
> If they are ugly, keep them to yourselves . . ." '

The hefty Muscovite next to me specialises in political jokes. I cannot understand any of them, but I appreciate that they concern the relatively safe topics of China and her satellites.

We are to see Mrs Kostadina home. We walk the cool, lily-scented streets of this extraordinary city of Sofia, which has a million citizens and ten million aromatic trees to put them all to sleep at nine o'clock every evening. We walk in the shadows of lofty monuments, grey lifeless palaces, onion-domed cathedrals, black-bricked Roman arches worn nearly into the ground, a marble mausoleum, a statue to the Tsar Liberator, the first kingly statue I have seen beyond the iron curtain.

We enter a skein of city-centre alleyways in which, when the late-night tram clangs behind you, you have almost to flatten yourself against a shopfront to let it go by.

An escort of Soviet tourists, well-fed and contented, walks with us. The oldest member wears a miniature crimson-and-gold medal ribbon. He seems to think that I too should be a veteran of campaigns. He is ready to proclaim eternal brotherhood, but has no word of English. Several times, grasping me by the shoulder, he opens his mouth to speak, sighs and closes it again and shakes his cropped head. At length he stutters out : 'Stalingrad.' On the spur of the moment I cannot recall any Allied victories of the Second World War.

'Smolensk?' he asks.

'Smolensk, *da*. Alamein.'

He has not heard of Alamein. 'Smolensk. Taganrog.'

'*Da*. Dunkirk, Matapan, Narvik, Normandy, Sidi Rezegh, Tunis, Arnhem, Midway, Guadalcanal, Iwo Jima, Anzio, Knightsbridge, the Ardennes . . .'

The names mean nothing to him.

'Leningrad.' He points to his medal. 'Ladoga.'

'Ladoga, *da*.'

He beams and comes out with : '*Adios, gringo*.' Radka, dropping back, explains that it is the title of a television serial popular in eastern Europe just now. We exchange the names of television serials.

The Russians are quick to take on the protective colouring of their environment, or perhaps create an environment round them which suits their colouring. They are in high spirits and I wonder how soon we shall have a demonstration of that Asiatic barbarity one reads of, or the notorious *kabatskaya melankholiya*, tavern melancholy, that Slavs are supposed to be addicted to. But in the gardens of the National Library our friends are as carefree as schoolboys on a nature ramble and, like schoolboys, they hang back, form cliques and nudge each other. They are making disrespectful comments, I know, about the heroes and politicians on the monuments. Under those obstinate, close-cropped skulls there are minds capable of soaring flights of satire.

One who studies English asks us up to his room for a nightcap. The night-cap is Moscow champagne. He enquires : 'What is to mean that expression, that east is east and west is west and never shall the twain meet?'

I cannot tell. May he ask another question? 'What is the price of the Rolls-Royce motor-car?'

I name a figure, adding on a thousand or so for luck, and mentioning some of the optional extras, such as back-seat billiard table and swimming pool. The Russians discuss the information among themselves. I start to explain that this is an English-type joke, then let it go.

A Moscow toyshop last winter, he says, had on display a doll which walked and talked. A London toyshop, I reply, sells a doll which walks, talks, drinks milk and wets its nappy. The Russians are perplexed.

Through Radka one of them suggests that it was a black day for Europe when the term "iron curtain" was coined. It was the west, not the east, which coined it. Gospodin Tsourtsill. I agree. Another says : 'That is the past, let us forget the past.' I agree. The iron curtain has rusted away, he says, it is a scrap iron curtain. He is so right, I say.

Next morning the hotel forecourt is besieged with Russians, segregated once more by groups. They are departing and so are we. Waiting for Radka, I sit unrecognised, leafing through the foreign newspapers which have just arrived. There are copies of the *Morning Star* and *The Times.* One or two people glance through the former, no one bothers with the latter. The English-speaking Muscovite sits opposite with *Pravda.* He shows me the feature on the sports page : БОБИ МУР - МОМУЕТО ОТ ''ИСТ ЕНД''

I have seen enough of the alphabet to decode this as "Bobby Moore – East End Kid". The footballer is portrayed, London's East End is pictured too, but the drawing is based on Cruikshank, out of Dickens.

I offer my friend *The Times.* He rustles the pages, grimaces at its flimsy quality (it is the Air Mail edition) and hands it back. His group is called for. *Adios, gringo.*

'Have you counted your passenger and made sure he is correct?' Radka has done so. It was a hard task for her, but she did it. She has doubts, however, whether we are adequately provisioned for the journey, for the gap between breakfast and lunch. She arranges the box of halva, the shopping-bag full of apples, the carton of Turkish delight and the packets of walnuts and biscuits on the shelf under the rear window. Before we slip out of town on one of those ill-paved minor streets which give you a clear impression of the immensity and emptiness of central Europe by having signs pointing down them reading Moscow, Istanbul, Belgrade, she stops at a pastry shop to buy *banitsa*, hot flaky rolls dripping with cheese and grease. We shall be all right now, since this is the season for fruits along the road. She halts the car again as soon as we are in the country, to collect grapes from a vineyard and an armful of egg-plants from a co-operative depot.

Not to be outdone, the driver pursues a company of gypsies through the reeds to the edge of a lake and comes back twirling a string of fish.

Last year we travelled in a Ford, this year's car is a Volga, a weighty, resilient vehicle, bristling with nuts and bolts. The doors are strongroom shutters, the upholstery is elephant-hide. I have inspected the tool-kit and it seems to be made up of crowbars and monkey-wrenches.

It rides the pavé sluggishly, like a tramp steamer in an oily swell. Rowan, plum and pear rise and fall to starboard and port, heavy with fruit, flaming with October colours. Distant plantations of oak and chestnut, wild cherry and copper beech flash their red and orange signal flags across the valleys. The autumn fashions of Bulgaria's northern forests this year are vivid in the extreme. The mountains, clothed to their summits, are like clouds in a stormy sunset.

That flat-roofed building on the left, the driver tells us, is an establishment for extracting snakes' venom. Radka goes on peeling her apple with a pearl-handled penknife. That cairn, the driver says, was the result of villagers flinging stones in a heap : it was how they worked off their frustrations under the Turks. Radka shrugs and does not comment.

Cottage gardens, cottage crafts, melon patches, strings of peppers . . . the country is an assemblage of the smallest agricultural units. Even Sofia suggests a conglomeration of individual cottages in a forest. Over there, the driver says, is the village of dancing donkeys. To make a donkey dance, you take a hot pepper and shove it . . . Radka asks if the driver would prefer to be guide, if so she will take over the driving.

Petrokhan pass. Petrokhan is Peter's Inn, a ruined hostelry on the summit of a saw-cut in the Balkan Range. The pavé stops short, the pass is chopped up with frost and flood. The road must crawl in submission to the highest summits before it is allowed to escape through the gap. Resistance country, Radka says. Scene of the anti-fascist rising of 1923, harshly suppressed. Thirty thousand martyrs have their plaques along this road on the face of rocks and springs. On this hallowed path Georgi Dimitrov, who sleeps in the marble mausoleum in Sofia, and Mihailov, who has a city named after him, and other patriots travelled in a solid-tyred lorry to command the rebellion. As we negotiate the bends of this road, Radka is silent and fasting and the driver puts on a typically Slav expression, sombre with a lurking grin, which seems to say : 'We have suffered, we suffer, but our turn will come.'

Bulgarians are a patient people. That is never more evident than at table. We sit in the mountain restaurant awaiting food – our own fault, they are cooking the egg-plants we brought, stuffing them with garlic, bay leaves, lemons and various vegetables. The dish is called *imambaldiyà* and is worth waiting for. In Turkish the name means "the priest fainted" – presumably because he ate too much.

One of Radka's colleagues comes in with another privileged traveller, an American biologist, a rather withered specimen. After twenty-four hours in eastern Europe he is bemused at the sight of people driving about in automobiles, getting on and off buses, shopping in supermarkets and sitting in bars, much the way people do in Illinois. From what he has seen of the countryside (eighty miles of highway) he suspects the Bulgarian peasant is not making the best use of his resources. He explains how they whipped that problem in Decatur, Illinois. Public-spirited citizens, housewives and suchlike, took crash courses in agronomy and horticulture and then went out and showed the farmers how. Where Decatur leads, the professor thinks, Bulgaria may follow. Radka says it is possible, Bulgarians are always willing to learn.

Why, he complains, don't they have clocks in public places? He has seen only one, and that was stopped. Radka refers him to *Gulliver's Travels*, the passage where the Lilliputians decided that Gulliver's watch must be his god, from the frequency with which he consulted it. The professor finds it amusing that an iron curtain maiden should be familiar with a western classic he has never read. Oh, we are not so dumb, we Bulgarians, his escort says. Who was Shakespeare before he anglicised himself? Spiro Sheker, none other, he came from the old Jewish family of sugar-boilers. *Sheker* means sugar.

And your American politicians, says, Radka, include some sons

of Bulgaria, like Spiro Agnew for instance, who was Agniev before
he left Sofia . . . not to mention Palev Malev, our driver chips in,
inventor of cigarettes.

The professor puts it down in a black leather-covered notebook
with spiral binding. He has already covered a dozen pages and now
he turns back and with Radka's help fills in some answers to queries.
'The mosque? The pink and white one? Yes, I know it, that mosque
was built by Sultan Imambaldiyà the Second . . .'

Sated with egg-plant, ankle-deep in walnuts, our caravan pulls in
to Berkovitsa, amphitheatrical red roofs in a horseshoe ring of the
hills. It is commemoration day. Red, green and white banners
decorate the yellow marble facades, the martyrs' memorials are
strewn with roses, brigades of schoolchildren are advancing, heap-
ing up floral tributes and gathering round plinths to hear a lecture.
In Berkovitsa, graveyard of heroes, hardly a day must pass without
a *putsch* to remember.

The town is a climatic station, where Bulgaria's weight-lifters and
wrestlers come for training. That is the modern section, like a spa
town, where sparkling waters burst out of the ribs of Kom, a famous
mountain and a brand of cigarettes.

The old city is pure Ottoman empire, a corridor of loose paving-
stones between high walls capped with pantiles. Nail-studded doors
open on to gardens of Allah. A house is dedicated to Ivan Vazov,
author of *Under the Yoke*, the national classic. He came to Berkovitsa to die of tuberculosis, but could not make it. The climate, the
townsfolk, the wine conspired against him. In Berkovitsa, Radka
says, they honoured him so much, they knew his tastes so well, that
twice a week they would catch a young Turkish girl and tie her
up in a sack and throw her over his wall as a token of their esteem.

That was eighty years ago. A little earlier, in the same winding
street, the Jews nicknamed Shekergevi ("sugar folk") began making
strawberry wine from the wild fruits they found on Mount Kom.
It was much sought after : it had a kick and a bouquet all its own.

No one enjoys a glass of wine more than Radka, and eventually
we find our way to the State cellar. Why so late? the president,
Kostadin Mihailov, wants to know. 'Most visitors come here first,
some of the trades unions don't trouble to go anywhere else.'

Fifteen years ago old people and children went fruit-picking on
the hills and brought their wicker baskets to the cellar. Now the
business is collectivised and fruit comes down by the truckload. The

State has introduced new lines : raspberry, blackcurrant, grape-and-blackcurrant.

We sample them all. Mihailov has a trick of hooking the stem of his glass under mine and tilting it, so that you have to drink to avoid getting it in your lap. It is heady stuff – strawberry sixteen per cent alcohol, brandy-and-blackcurrant up to twenty. 'Drink up, drink up to be a strong man,' is our host's refrain. 'There are half a million bottles left.'

Are they wines, cordials or what? 'I often ask myself that question. They have no category, we have to pay maximum duty when we export them, fortunately there's no need, except for a tiny shipment to a customer in Moscow, Bulgaria drinks all we make. Even in Sofia you'll find it hard to buy a bottle.'

The big food and wine store in the main street – a marble palace, appropriately sited where the old bazaar used to meander – is scented with strawberry wine. I buy a couple of bottles but the assistant who wraps them tells Radka we ought to go round to her house, she has better stuff at home.

From Kom to Lom takes in Vidin, the citadel on the Danube. Then dirt roads, black earth, maize country. At Lom the watermelons hang by their stalks on the steep bank, if they are not harvested soon they will all end up in the Danube. The opposite shore is Romanian, low and reedy, spotted with sheets of stagnant water. When God made the Danube, the saying goes, he scooped mud from the channel and dumped it all on the Bulgarian side.

The Bridge of Friendship across the river from Roussé in Bulgaria to Giurgiu in Romania is probably the most impressive visible piece of civil engineering in the post-war Balkan catalogue. Radka is primed with the specification : two tiers (one for road, one for rail), two miles long, the biggest bridge on the Danube. The ugliest too, I tell myself. Like our motorcar, it is a strictly functional job, matter-of-fact and no frills, tough and straight as a bar of iron. It was a remarkable achievement for its era, an act of faith in its way, for back in 1950 there were no roads on either side of the Danube. Those long-time enemies, Bulgaria and Romania, wanted a symbol of socialist interdependence and solidarity, and that is what they got.

Mostar na Drouzhbida, Bridge of Friendship, is the only crossing, except for insignificant ferries, on a river frontier of three hundred miles. But a single carriageway suffices. We walked over it, Radka and I, late at night. In the hour, three vehicles passed us. Underneath, no trains ran. As to the Danube, "that accursed stream", it was a black silent boulevard planted with weeping willows, and it flowed indifferently on. At times, Radka said, in flood, bridge and river were closed to traffic. One would scarcely know the difference.

It was Radka's second crossing of this bridge. The frontier guards remembered her and raised no objection to her strolling for a while in Romania. She had accompanied a Bulgarian party to Bucharest earlier in the year – first time abroad for her and for them. When they came to *Mostar na Drouzhbida* her heart was beating very fast.

The group consisted of bank clerks who got round the regulations and took no less than twenty *leva* apiece into the foreign land, more than four pounds sterling, for a stay of five days. Radka had that privilege too. She bought earrings, some cloth for her mother, some Romanian confectionery, and she sent twelve picture postcards. 'I didn't feel at all comfortably in that country. I know that in Bucharest we are only a hundred kilometres from our homeland, for you that would be nothing, but for me it was very far. We love our country so much, you see. I cannot understand a person you sometimes meet, an Englishman or American, who says he will retire to a warm country and things like that. I was very homesick in Romania.'

It was not a beautiful country like Bulgaria, the cafés of Bucharest were smart but not cheerful and friendly like those of Sofia. Since the American president's visit in 1971 the natives seemed to be contemptuous of the socialist ideal. 'When a Polish motor-car went by, our Romanian guide said sneeringly : "There goes the Gomulka Mercedes." It was rather shockingly for me.'

A red light downstream turned into a tug pushing a barge, making heavy work of it upstream. It had the mile-wide river all to itself. The two ports on either side of the bridge showed glimmers of light like two mountain villages; yet they are quite large towns. I would have liked to show Radka the Rhine at a comparable point, two hundred miles from the sea, where you cannot see the water for fast-moving, deep-laden shipping.

'After the visit,' she went on, 'it was excitingly that we came to the bridge again. We crowded to the front of the bus. When I saw the red and white houses of the Bulgarian towns along the shore I began to cry like a baby. Crossing the bridge we all sang *Bulgaria*

My Homeland. Believe me, we sang it all the way to Sofia.'

The Danube hotel in Roussé was crowded with Romanians. They are considered big spenders, but are not much admired. Few of those black-suited, thick-lipped diners were subsisting, I imagined, on the statutory foreign-travel rate of under a pound a day. Our Russian friends were conspicuous among them : they were homeward bound.

'*Mostar na Drouzhbida*, you have seen?'

'Very impressive.'

'In socialist land we build iron bridge, not iron curtain.'

South from Roussé the pavé runs straight for the hills, a historic Balkan route. Turnovo, the original capital of the Bulgarian tsars, perches on limestone cliffs above a serpentine river. Look, Radka said, how the houses run over the hills, are they not like a flock of frightened sheep? They are. They are making for the tower where Baldwin of Flanders languished and died, and you could almost come down to the murky ribbon of the Yantra by leaping on their backs, over blackened eaves and rusty ironwork.

Turnovo after dark is an eerie place. "One has the feeling," Stanislav Sivriev writes, "that the actors, their purple cloaks floating behind them, left this stage centuries ago, but the setting remains. At this hour the door of the church of the Forty Martyrs creaks softly, the light of the electric torch creeps along the column of the Great Khan, and defaced letters show faintly on the stone which, translated into modern Bulgarian, would read :

" 'Even if he lives well, man dies and another is born.' "

Turnovo does not suit our mood, and we shall sleep at a jollier town, the jolliest in Bulgaria, also on the Yantra a few miles upstream. To get into Gabrovo you cross a bridge and note, in midstream, a statue on a pinnacle of rock : Racho the Smith, alleged founder of the city.

It is the Manchester of Bulgaria, a cotton town, though as usual in the manufacturing centres of Bulgaria the industrial section is hidden away like a secret-weapons establishment.

A cotton merchant's son from Gabrovo went to learn the business in Manchester in 1876. Coming home for the holidays, he found a revolution going on : the disastrous April Uprising against the Turks. He joined in and commanded a pocket of resistance in the Dryanovo monastery, under the cliffs where the Yantra comes down off the Shipka summit . . . a three-cornered citadel of a monastery, which had withstood sieges before.

The rebels held out for three weeks and it would make a satis-factory end to the tale if the young man had returned to Manchester in time for the next session at his technical college; but matters went according to the customary Bulgarian-Turkish plan – the defenders were offered terms, they accepted and were slaughtered as soon as they laid down their arms.

Gabrovo is now a kind of Manchester, also – having a leather industry – a kind of Northampton, and also a kind of Aberdeen. 'However hard we work,' a town councillor says, 'we can't hope to clothe and shoe all mankind. But a Gabrovo joke goes round the world.'

He refers to the Aberdeen-type jokes Gabrovo specialises in. Every little iron curtain anecdote about thrift carried to excess has Gabrovo for its setting and a *gabrovets* for its hero. 'The fashion of narrow trousers,' the councillor goes on, 'and short skirts, the one-*stotinka* coin, the art of gliding . . . they were all invented here.' He signed a motion some years ago to send a smiles-across-the-sea offer to Aberdeen, proposing a twinning arrangement and a pooling of joke resources. Gabrovo congratulated the Scottish city on having achieved, like itself, "the dialectical unity of great opposites" – by which it meant a sense of proportion matched with a sense of humour. Communities like Aberdeen and Gabrovo, the missive went on, will never wage war, for war is no joke and it costs a mint of money. Aberdeen was lukewarm.

Gabrovo jokes are corny in print, but redeemed to some extent when Gabrovo people, dead-pan raconteurs, tell them. On the bal-cony of our hotel a black cat is draped – a cat without a tail, the civic symbol. Black cats are all over the main street, where posters of Lenin would normally be. The idea is that the *gabrovtsi* clip their cats' tails in order to shut the door on them more quickly on winter nights, thus conserving heat.

When fans were in fashion, the councillor says, Gabrovo ladies didn't wear them out by waving them from side to side – they wagged their heads instead. Men stop their watches and clocks at night, to save the machinery. Citizens offering houses for rent mention as an advantage that there is a street lamp outside the window. On days of celebration, when Gabrovo dances the *horo*, it does so in soft shoes in order to hear the music from Sevlievo down the valley – avoiding the expense of hiring a band.

The town actually did choose that midstream pinnacle for the statue to honour the founder because no one could find a use for the clump of rock.

Some of these jokes, transferred from their Bulgarian setting, have a familiar ring, some are ancient chestnuts and some are newly made, for the joke industry applies the formula to contemporary events. Our town councillor friend speaks of an Old Comrades association which made up a party to go to Munich for the World Cup in 1974. For economy's sake, it was agreed that every member should bring something with him. The man from Plovdiv brought a box of peaches, the man from Berkovitsa a crate of strawberry wine, the man from Varna some fish . . . the man from Gabrovo brought his brother.

20

The Oracle Speaks

All Bulgaria, most of eastern Europe, psychic societies the world over know her story. How she was a delicate child, subject to fits. How the doctors could do nothing, how her funeral was several times prepared. How, at sixteen, visiting her grandmother's grave to place on it the ritual offerings of wine and bread, she saw an angel in the wine bottle.

The angel spoke and offered her the choice between sight and second sight. She chose the latter and, a few weeks later, was caught up in a dust storm and whirled against some palings; which left her blind. Since then she has prophesied with such accuracy that she is considered the world's foremost fortune-teller.

She lives at Petric, a town of Bulgarian Macedonia, a land of superstition. But she is recognised by the government in Sofia, and when the Politburo is deadlocked over some thorny issue they appeal to Vanga; so Radka says. 'Last year she announced that she had seen the port of Varna disappearing under the waves. Now engineers have discovered that Varna stands on an underground lake, and they are to build no more high-rise flats.'

We came out of the mountains and turned for Petric. The road was on its long descent from Sofia's plateau to the Greek frontier and the Struma river, dark, destructive, opaque with mud, accompanied it. By tea time we had reached Macedonia. The café was a Turkish shack overhanging the river, tea was lime-tea in a black wooden bowl. From the clientèle you gathered that this was a good pull-up for carmen on the great south road, Bucharest-Sofia-Athens.

I walked out as far as I dared on a rope-and-plank bridge and peered through the slats at the Struma, which rolled branches and dead sheep down from the highland forests. It is an inescapable part of sightseeing in the People's Republic, this looking through planks at turbulent water.

The proprietor came after me. He lives only thirty miles from Petric, he must know Vanga. What is she like? 'I met her once. We had some troubles with our wives, my brother and I. We went to consult Vanga about them. She came out and saw us waiting in the queue. At Vanga's door there is always a queue, you know. She beckoned us to come in ahead of the others. She said, your problem is such-and-such. We agreed. She said, you will do so-and-so. We did it, and have had no more troubles.'

But what sort of person . . .? I have a vision of a cunning old serpent embedded in the stony desert. Capricious, no doubt, like that Dostoevsky monk who stripped the poor of their substance and heaped it on the rich.

'Not at all. She's humble. Small house, modest furniture. The town council has given her a companion, when Vanga is not seeing clients this girl reads the Bible to her.' The town council collects fees from Bulgarian clients and a special tax from foreigners, about two pounds a head. Vanga waives this in deserving cases.

'She's always in black, she's worn black since the death of her husband.'

Did she foretell that tragedy? 'On her wedding day she gave her husband the date of his death, and on that day he died.'

One day, they say, Vanga will lose her powers. The mantle of prophecy will fall on another's shoulders. When, and whose, Vanga does not know. It will be a French child. The candidate must be some young French girl, not yet sixteen, subject to fits.

We stopped again at the café on the way home. The proprietor was anxious to know how we had got on. For Radka, the journey had been worth while. 'I had written to Vanga previously, sending sugar and asking three questions. Vanga returned the sugar and said I must come and see her and bring honey. I did it. She received me at five o'clock this morning and gave me answers. I think they are very good answers. But she was in a bad mood against foreigners, and would not receive the Englishman.'

At lunch, Radka said the innkeeper was greatly concerned that I had had the long journey for nothing. 'They have a very good fortune-teller at the Old Tavern down the road. Not like Vanga, but good in spite of everything. He is sending for her.'

An inner door opened and a copper-coloured woman in shawls and jewellery made for our table. I rose, but she passed without a glance. Just another foreigner. The door swung open again. Radka came in, leading a young girl in the bombazine-and-mob-cap outfit some Macedonian places still go in for.

'Be gentle with her, she is very shy.'

Radka stroked her hand and said soothing words, and after a while the girl sat down. 'She is too modest, she is frightened of you.' We let her take her time and after some minutes more she began darting uneasy glances at me. Radka helped to undo her mob-cap and two smooth black curtains of hair fell down her face. The broad country features looked oddly refined, framed in that glossy hair. She took my tea bowl and looked into it. Radka translated. 'She sees scars.'

'Stars?'

'Scars. You have had some troubles. And here are two rocks . . .'

The fortune-tellers use an allegorical language, expounding the future in terms of camels, rocks, fountains and so forth. Without the key, you are as wise as before.

'There is a wedding.'

'Nonsense, Radka. This is fairground stuff.'

'This young girl, this waitress, insists on a wedding. She sees you drinking with the bride. It is quite soon.'

The girl fell silent, wept a little, rose and shook hands, declined payment and departed. 'How old is she?'

'Fifteen.'

'Of French extraction? Subject to fits?'

'You are joking, but this is serious. She has told fortunes since she was eight. She is famous, but of course not as famous as Vanga.'

Going north, Radka recommends a detour to Koprivshtitsa. It means a trek into the Sredna Gora, up to the source of a cascading torrent. Koprivshtitsa is the town of the Bulgarian revival (architectural) and consists of half-timbered stucco houses with deep eaves and oaken balconies. It spreads over an Alpine valley and from a distance its colour-washed cottages, red and blue, traditionally reflections of the sky and the earth, perched on the brink of streams, each with a footbridge to the door, are pretty as a picture.

Here was given the signal for that April Uprising, theme of balladeers for a century, though it did nothing to help Bulgarian independence from the Turk and in fact probably set it back a year or two.

Koprivshtitsa lives in that era. One of the famous cherrywood cannon of Balkan legend actually points its yellow trunk through a window of the House of the Conspiracy and draws a bead on the Street of the Affray . . . stumbling through back streets which are potholed, unlit, not fit to walk down in decent shoes, you trace the rebellion's brief sputter and extinction, for their names are drawn from the gazetteer of romance.

The following morning the wedding came true. From my bedroom window I saw bride and groom, the first arrivals, waiting at an office in the square, and I met them later in their car beside the Bridge of the First Rifle Shot. She sat beside the chauffeur, he was alone in the back. The radiator was adorned with paper flowers and a white lace handkerchief was pinned to the bride's door.

Radka said they would shortly be off to the Black Sea for their honeymoon, but later we came across the whole party in a field. They were dancing the *horo*, sixty or seventy guests circling hand in hand, and a shirt-sleeved youth coaxing a tune from a flute in the middle.

The reception was held in the back room of a shop. I peered through a window and saw guests sprawled on the floor or sitting on divans, one woman to about ten men. I saw the bride mount her three-legged stool to smear honey on the ceiling – a promise of sweetness to her husband, who carefully held her skirts round her ankles as she did it. An old man saw me peering, and waved me away.

Either Koprivshtitsa was one of those highland towns which resent the presence of strangers, or they had some superstition that strangers on wedding days brought bad luck. Everyone scowled at us, starting with the wedding car chauffeur, who chain-smoked throughout his day-long wait at the Place of the Scimitar Charge. Round the corner, in the Street of the Counter Attack, we tripped over four musicians, dirty as sweeps, snoozing in the potholes. Their cornets and trombones, equally grubby, were slumped with them. They drew their feet in and muttered something uncomplimentary.

Beside a stream I met some farm-workers loading cabbage-leaves into a painted cart. I stopped for a closer look. The oldest, a whiskery peasant, looked daggers and snarled curses. His language, from the sound of it, was atrocious. The slatternly female with him said nothing, but made objectionable gestures. Three bare-legged, sunburned girls, haggard beyond their years, looked as though they could barely restrain themselves from scratching my eyes out.

I did not move off fast enough for the old man's liking. He

fumbled in his coat for a weapon, hauled out a bottle and prepared
to knock its neck off . . . on to the Field of the Unprovoked Assault
came Radka, who had stopped behind to buy cigarettes.

'He wants you to drink with him,' she said. 'It is green brandy,
home-made.' I drank. Radka drank. The bottle went round and
returned to me and I finished it off. It was ghastly. The old man
thrust his face against mine and loosed off another stream of insults.
'He would like to invite you to his house,' Radka said.

Afterwards he led us to the shop and settled us down on a divan,
under a ceiling well smeared with honey. In a corner, apparently
not on speaking terms, sat bride and groom, side by side. Guests
came and went, everyone talking, no one listening. Their dialect
was harsh and aggressive, but their hearts were warm.

The green brandy flowed. The chauffeur appeared at the door
and was dragged in despite protests. The musicians mooched past
on their way to the Rivulet of Tears, the bride's father waved them
goodbye and so they came in : I realised my mistake, the mistake I
had made when I first came to Bulgaria, several years earlier. 'Why
didn't you come in before?' the bride's father said. 'When I waved
to you? Aren't we good enough for strangers?'

The musicians struck up : "If you have nice girls, send them to
us." The guests told Gabrovo jokes, risqué ones – 'Do you want a
little chocolate girl or a little chocolate boy?' asks the confectioner.
'A boy, of course,' says the smart young *gabrovets*. The father of
the bride, in a phenomenally deep bass, sang of Koprivshtitsa men
who love golden wheat in summer and a bowl of red wine in winter.
When the green brandy ran out, several guests crowded into the
kitchen to make punch out of Pliska brandy and water-melon.

The town was in darkness when we said goodnight. We saluted
bride and groom. They remained calm, with fixed expressions. In
wedding finery which they had worn, to my knowledge, for eleven
hours, they resembled two dolls.

I left with the feeling that the wedding had dissolved another
fold or two in the iron curtain. Under its influence, crossing the
Bridge of the Patriotic Resistance, I nibbled Radka's ear and she
said her heart was beating very fast. I knew how Conrad felt –
Conrad the Third, who crossed these hills with the crusaders and
sent back the first report on Bulgaria to the west : "We travelled
over a fertile valley in an exceedingly happy mood."

Where the torrent passed through pine trees before starting its
precipitous descent, the wedding guests were lighting a bonfire and

from the balcony of my hotel bedroom I smelled the wood smoke and heard the chorus, ever fresh, of *Bulgaria My Homeland* . . . looking over that quiet valley, in the starlight, I almost wished it was my homeland too.

Index

Aberdeen 193
Academy of Sciences (Bulgaria) 123, 177, 180
Aeneas 57
Aeneid, The 57
'Affie' see Alfred, Prince (Duke of Edinburgh)
Agnew, Spiro 189
Albena 164
Alexander the Great 150
Alexander II of Russia, Tsar 83, 84, 179–80, 185
Alexander of Yugoslavia, King 118–19, 123, 132
Alexandra of Russia, Tsarina 106–8, 178
Alexei of Russia, Tsarevitch 107, 178
Alfred, Prince (Duke of Edinburgh) 89, 90
Ali Pasha of Tepëlenë 13, 51–2, 56, 99–100
Anton of Austria, Archduke 132
Antonescu, General 120
Aphrodite 167, 169
Apollonia *see* Pojan
April Uprising 192–3, 197–8
Archangel 182
Arnota 73
Astor, Pauline 124
Astor, Waldorf 124–5
Athens 40, 195
Atlantic City 167
Azerbaijan 180

Babylon 164
Bachkovo 173
Balchik 90, 117, 123–8, 129, 131, 134, 164
Baldwin of Flanders 192
Balkan Range (mountains) 135–6, 142, 144, 159, 187
Balmoral 87, 90
Banat 74, 120

Bankhead, Tallulah 77
Bari 10
Bashkimi 58, 61, 64
Battenburg, Alexander of 76
Belgrade 79, 99, 112, 118, 168, 187
Berat 39, 47–51, 54, 58
Berkovitsa 189–90, 194
Bermuda 131
Bessarabia 74, 84, 112, 116, 120
Bibescu, Prince 108
Bohême, La see *La Bohême*
Boris of Bulgaria, King 119, 127, 162
Borodi, Gheorghe 74
Borsh 57, 64
Bosporus 183
Botev, Hristo 160, 182
Bourke, Captain Maurice 90–1
Boyle, Colonel Joe 124–5
Bran, Castle 88–9, 95, 131
Brancusi, Constantin 76–8, 81, 85
Brasov 88
Bratianu, Ion 80, 85
Bratianu, Ion (younger) 122
Bregdeti 57
Breslau 129
Brezhnev, Leonid 21
Bridge of Friendship 79–80, 190–2
Brindisi 17, 59
Broun, Heywood 122
Brown, John Mason 122
Budapest 80, 99, 112
Bucharest 71, 73, 74, 75, 79, 80, 81, 83, 86, 91, 92, 93, 94, 95, 97, 103, 116, 119, 120, 121, 122, 125, 127, 130, 134, 191, 195
Buenos Aires 132
Bukovina 74, 98, 120
Bülow, Prince Bernhard von 85, 88
Bulstrad 136
Burgas 135, 136, 159, 162, 164, 167
Buthrotum *see* Butrinto
Butrinto 57

Butterfly (opera) 149
Byron, Lord 13, 51-2
Byzantium 7, 73

Camperdown, HMS 91
Cannes 132
Capone, Alphonse 121
Caracal 71
Carmen 30, 149
'Carmen Sylva' 86-8, 90, 91, 92, 94, 105-7, 110, 118
Carmen Sylva (resort) *see* Eforie
Carol I of Romania, King 72, 76, 80-2, 83-9, 91, 92-3, 94-5, 96, 103, 106-8, 118
Carol II of Romania, King 83, 93, 107, 118, 122-3, 125-7, 130, 131, 132, 133
Carpathian mountains 70, 71-2, 73, 85, 86, 88, 100, 119, 129, 130
Cavalleria Rusticana 149
Ceausescu, Nicolae 73, 96, 103, 104, 132
Cernovitz 129-30
Cerrik 68
Chernovtsi *see* Cernovitz
Childe Harold 51-2
Churchill, Sir Winston 19, 20, 186
Ciano, Countess 57
Clemenceau, Georges 120
Cliveden 124
Cluj 130
Colchis 100
Conrad III (Hohenstaufen) 199
Constantinople 73, 169
Constanza 71, 98-110, 112, 117, 118
Corfu 39, 57
Così Fan Tutte 30
Cotroceni palace 94
Couza, John 75-6, 80
Cruikshank, George 186
Cunard, Nancy 77
Curtea de Arges 130, 131

Dajti (mountain) 61
Damascus (rose) 141-2, 156
Danube 70, 71, 72, 75, 78-80, 84, 86, 93, 99, 103, 111-16, 119, 126, 155, 182, 190-2
Decatur 188
Dempsey, Jack 121
Derevenko, Seaman 106
Dhërmi 57, 63, 64

Dickens, Charles 186
Diesbach, Ghislain de 87, 92
Dimitrov, Georgi 145, 160, 188
Dix, Dorothy 121
Dobrudja 74, 84, 111, 115, 117, 127, 131
Don (river) 178, 179
Dospat 177
Dostoevsky, Fyodor 196
Dracula 72-3
Dresden 129
Drin (North Drin river) 45, 59, 67
Drin (South Drin river) 52
Droitwich Spa 86
Dropull (valley) 40-3
Drouzhba 162, 164
Dryanovo (monastery) 192-3
Duca, Georges 122
Durazzo *see* Durrës
Durham, Edith 13
Durrës 17, 24-30, 42, 46, 59, 65, 68
Dyrrachium *see* Durrës

Eastwell 90
Edinburgh, Admiral the Duke of *see* Alfred, Prince (Duke of Edinburgh)
Edinburgh, Princess Marie of *see* Marie of Romania, Queen
Edison, Thomas 171, 173
Edward VII, King 87, 90
Eforie 105
Ekaterinburg 177, 178
Elbasan 50, 68
Elisabeta (cruiser) 103, 105
Elisabeth of Romania, Princess *see* Elisabeth of the Hellenes, Queen
Elisabeth of the Hellenes, Queen 107, 118, 130, 132
Elizabeth of Romania, Queen *see* 'Carmen Sylva'
Elizabeth of Wied, Princess *see* 'Carmen Sylva'
Enesco, Georges 77
Engels, Friedrich 34, 56
Epstein, Jacob 77
Estoril 131
Eugene Onegin 142
Eurydice 174
Euxinograd palace 124, 162

Fabrice, Auguste 124
Feodosia 103

Ferdinand of Romania, King 87, 89, 90, 91–2, 94, 95, 107, 118–19, 122, 124, 133
Ferdinand of Romania, Prince *see* Ferdinand of Romania, King
Fiesole 133
Foch, Marshal Ferdinand 120
Forty Martyrs 57, 192
Franz Josef of Austria-Hungary, Emperor 66, 80, 89, 105–6
Frederick 'The Great' of Prussia, King 123

Gabrovo 192–4, 199
Galati 112
Gdansk 100
Geneva 133
Genoa 70, 100
George V, King 89, 90, 121, 126, 178
George, Prince *see* George V, King
Gheorghiu-Dej, Gheorghe 96, 97, 119
Ghiaurov, Nicolai, 149
Giacometti, General 11
Giurgiu 79, 190
Gjirokastër 40, 42, 55–6
Godard (balloonist) 171
Goebbels, Frau 126
Golden Sands 135, 162, 163–4
Golescu, General 81–2
Gramos (mountains) 39
Grykë 63
Guinness Book of Records 180
Gulbenkian, Nubar 131n
Gulliver's Travels 188

Hammurabi 163
Hays, Shaban 29
Helen (of Troy) 167
Helen of Greece, Princess *see* Helen of Romania, Queen
Helen of Romania, Queen 118, 133
Heme 174
Hemingway, Ernest 122
'Hettingen, Karl' 80
Himarë 51, 52, 53, 63–4
Hitler, Adolf 20, 66
Hobhouse, John Cam 52
Hobitsa 77
Hohenzollern, Great Book of 119
Hohenzollern, Prince of *see* Nicholas of Romania, Prince
Hoven, Baroness von der 92

Hoxha, Enver 15, 20, 21, 27, 32, 55, 59, 60
Hristov, Boris 142
Hunedoara 71
Hurezu 73

Iasi 85, 120
Ignatiev, General 84
Ileana of Romania, Princess 107, 119, 121, 124, 126, 127, 130, 131, 132–3
Ionesco 77
Iron Gates 79–80
Isaj, Lazar 65–69
Iskender of Albania (king in exile) 11
Issarescu, Doctor 132
Istanbul 121, 145, 154, 187. See also Byzantium, Constantinople

Jane Eyre 159
Jason 100, 110
Jasnapoljana 165
Jassy *see* Iasi
Jiu (river) 76–7
John the Terrible 72
Joyce, James 77
Jundola 178

Kabaivanska, Raina 149
Kalofer 135, 142, 144, 145
Karaburun (cape) 64
Karlovo 135
Kazanluk 135, 136, 139, 140, 142, 143, 145
Khrushchev, Nikita 21, 28, 66
Kiev 169
Klissura 135
Kolarov, Vasil 175
Kom (mountain) 189, 190
Konitsa 136
Koplik 22
Koprivshtitsa 197–9
Kosygin, Aleksei 21
Kurbnesh 34–8

La Bohême 27–30
Laci, Vasil 69
Laferté, Victor 84
Lambrino, Zizi 118
Las Vegas 103
Lausanne 132
La Vallée 72
Lear Edward 13, 63, 64
Leeds 148

Lenin, V. I. 115, 193
Leningrad 66, 94, 124, 171, 185
Lipoveni *see* Raskolniki
Lisbon 131
Llangollen 121
Llogora 57
Loch Ness 158
Lom 190
London 70, 78, 105, 120, 148, 161, 186
Lucullus 65
Lupescu, Elena 118, 123, 125, 127, 131-2
Lurë 32
Lvov 129

Madrid 132, 147
Mali Gjerë 55, 56
Malko Turnovo 166
Malta 90, 118
Mamaia 112
Manchester 171, 192-3
Mangalia 112
Mao Ce-Dun 68
Mao Tse-Tung 10, 59, 96
Marie of Romania, Queen 88-95, 106-8, 111-12, 117-33, 142
Marie ('Mignon') of Romania, Princess *see* Marie of Yugoslavia, Queen
Marie of Yugoslavia, Queen 107, 118-19, 130, 132
Marie Alexandrovna of Russia, Grand Duchess 89, 90
Maritsa (river) 170
Marseille 119
Marx, Karl 34, 61
Mary, Queen 90n, 121
Mati (river) 61
McKenzie, Vernon 127
Melnik 175-7
Merlera 64
Michael the Brave 72
Michael of Romania, King 118, 125, 130, 133
'Mignon' *see* Marie of Yugoslavia, Queen
Mihailov, Ivancho 188
Millais, Sir John 90
Miller, Marylin 121
Mircea of Romania, Prince 123
Mirdita 31
Moisu, Aleksander 27, 30
Montparnasse 77
Moore, Bobby 186

Morand, Paul 77
Morning Star 186
Moscow 21, 65, 66, 171, 184, 185, 186, 187, 190
Mostar na Drouzhbida see Bridge of Friendship
Moussala 150, 152
Mrika 30
Munich 168, 194
Mussolini, Benito 20, 57, 66, 81

Naples 63, 66
Napoleon 66
Narishkin-Kurakin, Elizabeth 108n
Narta 65
Naso, Publius Ovidius *see* Ovid
Nastase, Ilie 78
Nessebur 164
New York 73, 77, 134
New York Herald Tribune 167
Nicholas of Romania, Prince 107, 118, 121, 127, 130, 132
Nicholas of Russia, Grand Duke 84
Nicholas I of Russia, Tsar 93
Nicholas II of Russia, Tsar 103, 106-8, 110, 118, 132, 177-8
Nijni Novgorod 170
Nile 71
Nixon, Richard 96, 97, 103, 104, 191
Northampton 193

Obrenovitch, Marie 75
Odessa 80, 99, 103, 116, 171
Old Believers *see* Raskolniki
Olga of Russia, Grand Duchess 107-8, 178
Oltul 72
Onchesmos *see* Sarandë
Orient Express 7, 155, 159
Orpheus 174, 176, 177, 178
Osman Pasha 84
Otranto 66
Ovid 100, 106, 110

Paget, Lady 105-6
Pamporovo 174
Paris 9, 26, 73, 74, 77, 84n, 87, 99, 120, 121, 171
Paris (of Troy) 167
Parker, Dorothy 121
Pasternak, Boris 160
Peking, 26, 57, 65, 68
Peles castle 86, 88, 93, 130
Përmeti 11
Peshkopi 32

Peter the Great 116
Petric 195–6
Petrokhan 187
Phanariots 73
Phthia 169
Piraeus, The 59, 172
Pirin 175, 176
Plevna 83–4, 94, 106
Pliska 182, 199
Ploesti 105
Plovdiv 158, 170–3, 178, 194
Poiana Brasov 85
Pojan 46
Polar Star 106, 108
Pope-Hennessy, James 90
Porto Edda *see* Sarandë
Porto Palermo 57
Post, Emily 121
Potemkin 103, 106, 110
Pravda 102, 110, 186
Predeal 85, 134
Prussia, Crown Prince of 124
Puccini, Giacomo 27
Pyrrhus 39

Qemal, Ismail 66
Queen's Husband, The 121
Quiet Nest, The 123–8, 129, 131, 164
Qukapec 39
Qukës 18

Racho the Smith 192
Ramadan 10, 12, 13
Raskolniki 112, 115–16
Red Hussars *see* Rosciori Regiment
Red Village 148
Regele Carol 111
Rhine 191
Rila 151
Rila (monastery) 150–1, 159, 173
Rila (mountains) 150, 159
Rodin, Auguste 77
Rodonit, Cape 59, 61
Rodop (mountains) 174–8, 180
Romania, Marie of *see* Marie of Romania, Queen
Romania, Prince Karl of *see* Carol I of Romania, King
Rome 26
Rommel, Lieutenant Erwin 119
Ropotamo (river) 164–6
Rosalie 121
Rosciori Regiment 95, 119, 124
Roses Valley 141–5, 155–6, 159, 160

Rostov-on-Don 84
Roussé 190, 192
Rozanov 81
Rozavec 135
Rozino 135, 141
Rozovo 135
Rreshen 33
Rubik 33
Ruth, Babe 121

Saint Mary the Virgin 46
Saint Petersburg *see* Leningrad
Saint Petka of the Saddlers 146, 147
Saint Sunday 147
Samarkand 170
Sans Souci 123
Santi Quaranta *see* Sarandë
Sappho 87–8
Sarandë 40, 56, 57–61, 63
Sasseno *see* Sazan
Sazan 66, 69
Sea Cossacks 111, 112, 113, 116
Seine 100
Selenice 66
Semani (river) 59
Serdica *see* Sofia
Sevastopol 99, 103
Severus, Septimus 71
Sevlievo 193
Seyko, Teme 59
Shakespeare, William 26, 188
Shekergevi 189
Sherwood, Robert 121, 122n
Shipka 159, 160, 193
Shkodër 12, 30, 44–5, 59, 60, 65, 67, 68
Shpiragrit 39
Shqipëria 39
Sigmaringen 119
Sigmaringen-Hohenzollern, Karl von *see* Carol I of Romania, King
Simeon, 'Bai' 126–8
Sinai, Mount 93
Sinaia 85–6, 88, 93, 94, 118, 130
Siroka Laka 177
Sivriev, Stanislav 192
Skanderbeg 9, 13, 14, 20, 21, 39, 67
Skobolev, General 84
Smolyan 174
Sofia 135, 136, 137, 138, 139, 145, 146–50, 153, 154, 155, 156, 159, 160, 177, 182–6, 187, 188, 189, 190, 191, 192, 195
Sredna Gora (mountains) 135, 197
Stafa, Qemal 9

Stalin, J. V. 20, 21, 51, 58, 102
Stalin City 66, 67
Standart 106, 107, 108
Stara Planina *see* Balkan Range
Stefan cel Mare (boat) 108
Stephen the Great 83, 108
Stirbey, Prince Barbu 124–5
Stone, Miss 175
Strandja 166
Struma (river) 195
Sulina 111, 112
Sunny Beach 153, 163–4, 165, 167–9
Surprise, HMS 90
Sydney 155

Tatiana of Russia, Grand Duchess 107–8, 178
Teapot Dome 121
Tenka Yuva *see* Quiet Nest, The
Tepëlenë 13, 51–4, 56
Tiflis 182
Times, The 121, 129, 186
Tirana 9, 10, 11, 12, 13–14, 15, 19, 21, 24, 38, 40, 47, 53, 60, 61, 65, 68, 69
Tirana Radio 18, 67
Tirgu Jiu 72, 76–9, 81, 85
Tito, J. B. 21
Toci, Vangjel 25–8
Todleben, General 84
Tolbuhin 127
Tomorrit 39
Toronto Star 122
Tosca 149
'Town of a Thousand Windows' *see* Berat
Tree, Beerbohm 105
Treska, Misto 10, 11–23
'Tsourtsill' *see* Churchill, Sir Winston
Tsushima 63
Tulcea 112
Tundja (river) 141
Tunney, Gene 121
Turandot 30
Turnovo 192
Turnu Severin 71, 80, 99

Uji Ftotë 66
Ulysses 176

Under the Yoke 189

Vacarescu, Hélène 73, 75, 87, 92, 100–1
Valcov 113–16
Valentino, Rudolf 121
Valletta 118
Valona *see* Vlorë
Vanga 195–6
Varna 117, 162, 164, 168–9, 178, 194, 195
Vazov, Ivan 150, 189
Venice 87, 115
'Venice on the Danube' *see* Valcov
Versailles 120
Vesuvius 66
Victoria, Queen 87, 89, 90, 129
Victoria, HMS 91
Vicu 56
Vidin 190
Vienna 26, 99, 105, 112, 145, 168, 170
Vijosë (river) 51, 52, 59
Vilkov *see* Valcov
Vit (river) 84
Vitosha 136, 156
Vittore Emmanuele 69
Vlad the Impaler 72
Vlorë 55, 62, 63, 64–9
Volga 178
Vuno 63

Walker, Mrs M. A. 72n
Warsaw 86
Warsaw Pact 22
Weisser Hirsch clinic 129
White Friars of Scutari (Shkodër) 44
Wied, Prince of 76
Wight, Isle of 90
Wilhelm II of Germany, Kaiser 83, 90
Woods, H. Charles 120

Yangtse 59, 71
Yantra (river) 192

Zëri i Popullit 38
Zeus 39
Zog, King 11–12, 14, 20, 32, 33, 55
Zwiedeneck, Colonel Eugen 124, 126